THE COMPETENT MANAGER

THE COMPETENT MANAGER

A Model for Effective Performance

RICHARD E. BOYATZIS
McBer and Company

A Wiley-Interscience Publication
JOHN WILEY & SONS
New York   Chichester   Brisbane   Toronto   Singapore

This publication is designed to provide accurate and
authoritative information in regard to the subject
matter covered. It is sold with the understanding that
the publisher is not engaged in rendering legal, accounting,
or other professional service. If legal advice or other
expert assistance is required, the services of a competent
professional person should be sought. *From a Declaration
of Principles jointly adopted by a Committee of the
American Bar Association and a Committee of Publishers.*

Library of Congress Cataloging in Publication Data:

Boyatzis, Richard E.
    The competent manager.

    "A Wiley-Interscience publication."
    Includes index.
    1. Management. I. Title.

HD31.B717   658   81-13113
ISBN 0-471-09031-X   AACR2

Printed in the United States of America

21 20 19

*To the Memory of
My Father*

Acknowledgments

The work reported in this book was the result of the collective efforts of many professionals. Not only were a number of people involved in the analysis reported here, but many others were involved in the original studies which became part of this aggregate study. The separate studies were only possible with the direction, leadership, and insight of David C. McClelland and George O. Klemp, Jr., and numerous professionals within the staff of McBer and Company and its clients over eight years. The development of the Job Competence Assessment method, which began with David C. McClelland in 1958, has emerged from the work of the innovative professionals of McBer and Company over the past 12 years. The particular analyses reported here were conducted with the unique contributions and perseverance of Bernard Cullen. Other professionals who significantly contributed to this effort were: Murray Dalziel, Patricia Flannery, Robert Oresick, Bettyanne Proctor, William Rogers, Mary Lou Schaalman, Nell Slawson, Gerard Smits, Leigh Sobetzer, Lyle M. Spencer, Jr., Stephen A. Williamson, David G. Winter, and Helen Vandkjaer.

Although the research involved in the separate studies was funded by various organizations, the aggregate analysis reported here was, in large part, funded by the American Management Associations with the remainder of the funding contributed by McBer and Company. James L. Hayes, the President of the AMA, had the insight and initiative to introduce the concept of their proposed Masters degree program which resulted in the funding of this aggregate research. Harry Evarts, Vice-President and the Director of Educational Services for the AMA, and Paul Grambsch, a consultant to the AMA, were responsible for efforts to begin the development of the program. It has been with the tremendous support, insight, and critical eye of Harry Evarts that this study has been completed and has contributed to the development and design of their innovative Masters in Management program.

A special acknowledgment of the contributions of David C. McClelland to this study is needed. It is from his leadership and continued guidance in the search for understanding human behavior that this study and its many revisions grew.

The unconditional and self-sacrificing support of my wife, Sandra, and son, Mark, has made the several years of analysis, writing, and rewriting of this study a humane and possible effort.

RICHARD E. BOYATZIS

Boston, Massachusetts
September 1981

Contents

Figures

Tables

THE COMPETENT MANAGER

CHAPTER ONE

Introduction

Organizations need managers to be able to reach their objectives. They need *competent managers* to be able to reach these objectives both efficiently and effectively. There is also an economic reason why organizations need competent managers. Noting the increased dominance of the service sector in the economy of the United States (e.g., in 1977 it employed 68 percent of the work force and in 1978 it accounted for 66 percent of the gross national product), and the increased importance of people in generating a return on the use of physical and technological resources, Ginzberg & Vojta (1981) have pointed out that ". . . human capital, defined as the 'skill, dexterity, and knowledge' of the population, has become the critical input that determines the rate of growth of the economy and the well-being of the population." It is the competence of managers that determines, in large part, the return that organizations realize from their human capital, or human resources. To acquire and retain competent managers, to let them know what they are expected to do, and to effectively utilize the organization's human and other resources, people in organizations use models of management.

A model of management is an answer to the question: What kind of a person will be effective in our organization in specific management jobs? It is a template which is used for decisions such as selection, promotion, firing, and design of and assignment to management developmental activities. It is used to interpret responsibility for success or failure with respect to accomplishment of performance objectives. It is used as the basis for communicating to managers how they should act and what they should be doing. It is also used as a basis for the design of management jobs and the organization's systems, policies, procedures, and programs.

McGregor (1960) claimed that

> Every managerial act rests on assumptions, generalizations, and hypo-
> theses— that is to say, on theory. Our assumptions are frequently implicit,
> sometimes quite unconscious, often conflicting   . .   .

Every manager has a model or a theory of management. It is used to make many different types of decisions and is critical to organizational functioning. Approaches to a model of management in this century have ranged from Frederick Winslow Taylor's "scientific management," which attempted to discover how to operate the human machine efficiently, to "humanistic management," in which attempts were made to stimulate human potential and self-actualization.

The search for a model of management is complicated by a person's confusion between his or her "espoused theory" of management versus his or her "theory in use" (Argyris & Schon, 1974). That is, even if a person can describe a personal model, or theory, of management, it is not clear that this is the model that he or she uses day-to-day in functioning as a manager, or day-to-day in designing and conducting management development activities.

Before the reader concludes that the search for a model of management is merely an intellectual exercise of questionable usefulness, several examples may help to illustrate the cost of inadequate models of management to organizations.

> Daryl Anderson, an entrepreneur who started his own company, brought
> it to $75 million per year in revenues. He decided that he would move up
> to Chairman of the Board and Chief Executive Officer and promote some-
> one to the position of President and Chief Operating Officer. He wanted
> someone to manage the operations of the company. Internal problems
> were evidence that he was having trouble managing operations. He pro-
> moted one of the vice presidents he felt showed the most promise. One
> year later, he fired the president and took over the COO job in addition to
> being CEO.

The internal problems had not diminished because Daryl had, unknowingly, promoted the vice president who was most like himself. The use of inappropriate criteria for such decisions is a problem to which many managers are vulnerable. Characteristics such as loyalty to the organization, seniority with the firm, or consistent agreement with the boss can easily outweigh characteristics related to job performance in the rush to make promotion decisions. Biological inbreeding may result in perpetuation of genetic mutations and the emergence of undesirable, recessive traits. Organizational inbreeding can have the same impact if the criteria for promotion decisions have not been thoroughly examined and tested as to their accuracy.

> Jason Ferent, regional sales manager of a consumer products company, was having difficulty reaching the regional sales goals. He had been an outstanding salesman and an excellent field sales director. The vice president of marketing decided that Jason's talent was too valuable to the company and that the current job was not working out. He promoted him to director of sales training. After several years of acceptable performance in this job, the vice president of marketing was surprised when Jason requested that he become a salesman again. Eight years later, Jason was doing exceedingly well as a salesman. He was generating new business for the company and was excited about his work.

Both Jason and the vice president of marketing had been mistaken in assuming that promotion "up the ladder" would present him with appropriate challenges and would respond to company needs. The Peter Principle was in operation but with a twist. Jason was not incompetent. He had merely been promoted into a job that did not use his specific competencies. He was a victim of the myth that "the best salesperson will make the best sales manager." This myth has been shown to be false in research as well as in many organizations (McClelland, 1961; McClelland & Burnham, 1976). The characteristics that made Jason an excellent salesman were not the characteristics needed to be an effective sales manager in his company.

> USI, Inc. had decided to develop its middle level managers through training. They invested a great deal of money in developing a training program. The early classes were receiving good reviews from participants; they were enjoying the program. The corporate director of manufacturing met Michael Simmonds, a manufacturing manager from one of the plants, at a cocktail party. The director of manufacturing knew that Michael had shown promise but had been having some difficulty lately. The plant manager, Steve Robins, had been encouraged to send Michael to the training program. The director of manufacturing asked him if he had learned anything interesting in the course. "Yes," replied Michael, "I learned that Steve is a Theory X manager." To which the director of manufacturing responded, "Well, what does that mean for you?" Michael looked at his drink for a moment, then said, "I don't know. All I know is that he's a Theory X manager."

Michael was exactly the type of middle level manager the training program was designed to help. USI was not getting an acceptable return for its investment in the course. They might have been causing some potentially effective managers to become increasingly dissatisfied. Too often training programs attempt to "teach the fundamentals" using lectures, readings, case discussions, films, and dynamic speakers to transmit knowledge to course participants. Unfortunately, it is usually not the lack of knowledge, but the inability to *use* knowledge that limits effective managerial behavior. USI's training program had been designed with inappropriate objectives which had been based on someone's view of what managers should know.

> Foldin Corporation had established that the most important criteria for the selection of product design managers was that they be creative. After several years of using this criteria for promotion and hiring decisions, they asked a consultant to help address the problem of the company having fewer new products than their two major competitors. The consultant discovered that the product design managers were generating the majority of the new product ideas. Once they began work on these ideas, they were reluctant to "let go," even in the face of production engineering problems. This reluctance was costing the company money and time, in terms of lost opporturnities for new product development.

The Foldin Corporation had used incorrect criteria in selecting product design managers. They needed people who could *manage* creative product designers, not necessarily people who were highly creative themselves. Companies may be making similar mistakes when they use selection criteria for entry level managers such as grades in college or business school. It has been pointed out that grades in school and performance on standardized aptitude tests correlate with each other but do not predict successful performance in a number of professions (McClelland, 1973). In Foldin's case, and if a company uses grades in college as a criteria, there is the possibility that someone or a group's values and myths are determining the selection criteria.

> The Broadway Manufacturing Company decided to empirically determine their model of management. They designed a study in which people who had entered the company as supervisory managers 20 years earlier would be examined. After matching the sample for age and education at point of entry, they analyzed their data on each of these managers against the criterion of promotion within the company. They found that the people who were promoted the most within the company were different than their less effective counterparts on only one dimension; they were taller.

The results of the study raised a serious question as to whether

Broadway Manufacturing had been promoting the most competent managers. In all of the companies and situations discussed, there was a model of management used. The particular models of management resulted in actions that were costly to the respective companies. The results included inadequate performance, lost opportunities, poor investments, and inappropriately used, if not lost, managerial talent.

IS YOUR MODEL ACCURATE AND USEFUL?

To determine how accurate and useful a model of management is, two questions must be answered: (1) what is the model of management that is being used? and (2) how was it developed?

What is the Model?

The model of management used in organizations is sometimes explicitly stated. It may have been described and discussed in management staff meetings. It may be described in a report or as part of the position descriptions written for various management jobs. Often it is assumed. Before the accuracy and utility of the model of management can be determined, the elements of the model must be stated explicitly.

A brief quiz may help you determine how well you understand your model of management, and how explicit you have made it.

1. Have you ever described your model of management to others? Have you ever described it in writing?

2. What are the sources of ideas, concepts, and assumptions in your model of management? What individuals have had the most impact on your model of management?

3. Have you or others tested the elements of your model against performance information? What are your measures of effective managerial performance?

4. How does your model of management differ from models held by various managers in your organization?

5. How is your model different from or similar to the model of management held by your largest competitor?

If you could answer these questions with some detail, the model of management you have may or may not be the model of management that you use. To generate a quick, but simplistic, picture of the model of management that you use, you may wish to complete the following exercise. If you could not answer these questions with some detail, you should complete the following exercise to develop a picture of your model of management.

1. Think of the last time you hired or promoted someone into a management job. Describe how the person selected differed from candidates whom you did not select. Describe the person in terms of his or her characteristics which you valued. If you made the decision based on the experience of the person in a prior job, describe the characteristics you think the person had based on his or her past experience.

2. Think of the last time you conducted a performance review of someone in a management job. Describe the behavior and accomplishments of the person which you felt deserved a positive comment or recognition. Describe the behavior and accomplishments of the person which you felt deserved a negative comment, even if you did not make these comments to the person. Describe the recommendations you made for the person's future development as a manager.

3. Think of the last meeting that you conducted. Describe the style you used in conducting the meeting. Describe why you felt that this style was appropriate and/or effective, or inappropriate and/or ineffective.

4. Think of the last time you, or someone you know in a management position, effectively resolved a conflict among individuals or departments in which you were involved. Describe the style that the manager used. Describe the steps he or she took in resolving the conflict.

5. If you are in a management position, think of the last time you reassigned priorities to objectives or activities in which you were engaged. Describe the reasons for these changes in priorities.

These descriptive statements, if made in sufficient detail, begin to provide you with a picture of the model of management which you use. Be cautious: this exercise merely touches lightly on the breadth, scope, and complexity of the model of management which you use. As these exercises have indicated, a model of management should include an image of the effective, ideal, or competent manager.

The Source of the Model

The models of management which individuals and organizations use come from a variety of sources. Sometimes the model comes from a theory. The theory may emerge from someone's thoughts about the desired characteristics of a manager, or about the characteristics of competent managers. Sometimes the model comes from a panel. A group of people, possibly in the job or at levels above the job within the organization, generates a model through discussion of what is needed to perform a management job competently. Models emerging from either of these sources tend to be vague, incorporating such characteristics as dedication, thoroughness, and creativity. Frequently such models are implicit and reside in the mind of one or more individuals. Because of the way the characteristics in these models are identified, they are often difficult to measure or assess. People attempting to use such a model often revert to personal interpretations of the "supporting evidence" which is used to generate or substantiate the model. This degree of subjectivity makes these models highly vulnerable to the prejudices, values, personal experiences, and ideas of particular individuals. Because most of the qualities are vague and difficult to measure, these models are seldom systematically tested against performance information.

Models of management also come from the acceptance and perpetuation of tradition. The tradition may emerge from the personal experiences of the individual making the decisions about who to hire, promote, train, or fire. The tradition may emerge from the organization's history, represented by statements such as, "We at General Products Company have always looked for managers with such and such," or "That's the way it's done here at The Plastics Company." Whether the tradition started with the notions of managerial competence as perceived by the founder of the organization, the impact of a management coalition which made the organization profitable, or the nature of the work force from which the organization selected its managers, models of management emerging from tradition seldom have been systematically tested to see if they actually differentiate competent from incompetent managers. Despite protestations that such models have stood the test of time, updating the accuracy of the models challenging exactly *what* has stood the test of time is rare (i.e., it may be the products of the organization and not the relative competence of its managers).

Models of management sometimes come from task and function analyses of management jobs. Someone studies what managers do, or what duties and responsibilities they are expected to perform, and then develops a model or image of what competent management is (Mintzberg, 1973). Typically, task and function analyses result in detailed descriptions of what activities must be performed in the job. Often these are not arrayed in any order of importance or relevance to the particular job or to the desired output from someone performing the job. Such models have been tested, in that systematic research is conducted to determine if the identified activities are part of the job. Unfortunately, models based on task or function analysis focus on the job and do not address the person in the job. In doing so, the models include many specific and detailed descriptions of activities, but no mention is made of the characteristics that enable or increase the likelihood of a person's performing those activities. These models do not establish a causal link between characteristics of people and performance in a job.

Models of management also come from systematic observation of and research into the types of people in management jobs (see Campbell et al., 1970, for a comprehensive review of research on managerial behavior). Such studies vary in both the methods used and the types of results, but they represent an attempt to systematically discover what competent management is. Some of these models come from observation and studies of people in management jobs over a number of years (Barnard, 1938; Drucker, 1954; McGregor, 1960; Levinson, 1980) or from research studies specifically designed to determine the characteristics of competent managers (Bray et al., 1974; Bass et al., 1979; Blake & Mouton, 1964; Stogdill, 1974; Argyris, 1962; Kotter, 1982). Some of these models have been tested against managerial performance. Some are based on a theoretical model of causality. Some identify characteristics which are the basis for the specific behaviors demonstrated by competent managers (Campbell et al., 1970).

To summarize, the model of management used within an organization should be explicit. It should be developed and performance-tested with the same care and precision as are models that managers use for other types of decisions, such as product design, marketing strategy, business planning, and capital investment decisions. By using an accurate model of competent management an organization can increase its return on managerial assets.

THE PURPOSE OF THIS STUDY

The purpose of this study was to determine which characteristics of managers are related to effective performance in a variety of management jobs in a variety of organizations. It was not an objective of this study to predict managerial performance to a high degree (i.e., explain a majority of the variance in performance). Specifically, the objective was to explain some of the differences in general qualitative distinctions of performance (e.g., poor versus average versus superior managers) which may occur across specific jobs and organizations as a result of certain competencies which managers share. This will be accomplished by presenting research evidence regarding the elements of a performance-tested competency model of management.

An additional purpose of this study was to investigate how these competencies may affect each other (i.e., a competency model of management) and to propose a framework of how they relate to other aspects of management jobs. In addition to the competency model of managers, this will result in a broader theoretical model of management.

The model developed in this study should be viewed as preliminary and not conclusive. It is offered as a vehicle to provoke careful thought about aspects of managerial competence which may or may not have been previously examined. Nonetheless, it should provide a basis for people to compare and assess their models of competent management, and to provide some guidance as to the aspects of their model that need further revision to be most useful to them and to the organizations that they serve.

This is not a "how-to-do-it" book for managers, rather a research and theory book for people interested in management development. For the reader interested primarily in potential applications or stimulating ideas, I recommend that he or she read Chapters 2, 11, and 12 in that order, and then return to the introduction, interpretation, and summary sections regarding the competencies in Chapters 4 – 10. For the reader interested primarily in theory and research, I recommend that he or she read the chapters in their order of appearance in the text.

CHAPTER TWO

Competence and Job Performance

Before launching into the specifics of this study, it is important to review and explain the concepts that are the foundation for the model developed from the study. One reason is to provide the reader with a logical map with which to interpret the findings. Another, and possibly more important reason, is to introduce the reader to a new paradigm (Kuhn, 1962) for understanding managerial behavior. For some, the paradigm may be merely a refinement on concepts that they already hold. For others, the paradigm may be a new way of looking at managerial behavior and performance. Definitions of certain words and concepts must be clarified to aid in the understanding of the model.*

This chapter begins with an introduction of the basic model, or theory, of action as it applies to a management job. Two of the three elements of the model are addressed in this section: (1) the functions and demands of the management job; and (2) the organizational environment in which the job exists. The third element in the model, an individual's competencies, are developed in great detail in a later section. Understanding the concept of competency is a prerequisite to understanding the remainder of the study and the integrated model of management which is discussed in the later chapters.

*The language in this study may appear to be full of jargon. The words have been carefully chosen to help members of various disciplines understand the concepts that they represent. The words have also been chosen with an emphasis on accurately describing or reflecting the concepts that they represent. This may, at times, appear to violate or conflict with vernacular interpretations.

EFFECTIVE JOB PERFORMANCE
A Model

Effective performance of a job may be assessed by looking at the attainment of output objectives (i.e., results) or at the appropriate execution of procedures and processes. Some jobs allow for easy assessment of performance because performance measures and goals are available, such as sales per month for a salesperson, completion of an income statement by the tenth of the month by a controller, or the redesign of a production machine to reduce waste by 20 percent for a manufacturing engineer. Effectiveness in management or administrative jobs requires the assessment of performance of an organizational unit. Some of these jobs allow for easy measurement of a unit's performance. Output per month of a particular product may be a measure that assesses the performance of a plant manager through evaluating the performance of the entire plant operation.

Other jobs do not provide easy access to nor interpretation of measures of performance, such as a research and development manager, an employee relations specialist, a product design engineer, or a scientist. Often in these types of jobs it is more relevant to assess whether or not the person in the job is following certain procedures or processes that are thought to be important to the organization. Unfortunately, it is often easier with such jobs to identify when a person's performance is not accomplishing its purpose or not facilitating desired processes or results. For example, a product manager may be responsible for managing the interactions among the manufacturing, research and development, and marketing divisions within a company with regard to his or her product. Corporate executives will be more likely to notice when conflicts emerge between the various divisions regarding the product than to recognize effective performance when things are going smoothly.

The problem in assessing the performance of a person in a job and determining what constitutes effective and ineffective job performance is that it requires understanding and measuring a number of factors at the same time. Programs have been developed that attempt to simplify this assessment by stating that a person's effective performance in a job is reflected in the degree to which he or she attains specific objectives. Unfortunately, these objectives are often stated in ways that are myopic (Levinson, 1970) and do not incorporate a full appreciation of what performance of the particular job means. For example, a sales manager may have an objective of generating $10 million in sales in a particular quarter. If his or her sales unit produces that amount of sales but experiences 50 percent turnover of staff in the same quarter, has the sales manager performed his or her job effectively? It is not clear.

Although a bit wordy, the following definition of effective job performance is comprehensive. *Effective performance of a job is the attainment of specific results (i.e., outcomes) required by the job through specific actions while maintaining or being consistent with policies, procedures, and conditions of the organizational environment.*

The "specific results required by the job" must contribute to the results from other jobs in such a way as to yield the organization's product or service (i.e., the organization's output). This contribution may come in two forms. Either the results from a job may contribute directly to the creation and production of the product or service, or the results from a job support or maintain systems to facilitate others making their contribution to the organization's product or service.

The definition of effective job performance also includes the statement that the specific results required by the job occur because "specific actions" have been taken. Technically, these actions may be demonstrated by a person, a droid (i.e., a robot), or a machine. Since the objectives of this book do not include analysis of job and organization designs, it will be assumed that a person holds the job for the remainder of the book. The important point is that the specific actions cause, or lead to, the specified results. Results obtained through random events or divine intervention cannot be considered evidence of effective performance of a job. Even in those situations in which the spiritual intervention is invited, such as during an exorcism or a miraculous healing someone is doing something to set the stage for spiritual intervention. The question can be asked: What enables a person to demonstrate the "specific actions" that lead to the "specific results?"

Certain characteristics or abilities of the person enable him or her to demonstrate the appropriate specific actions. These characteristics or abilities can be called competencies, which will be defined and discussed at length later in this chapter. At this point, it is sufficient to say that the individual's competencies represent the capability that he or she brings to the job situation. When the responsibilities of the job to produce the desired results require the demonstration of specific actions, the individual draws from his or her inner resources for the capability to respond. These requirements of the job can be considered the job's demands on the person.

All of this occurs in the context of an organization. The organization has policies and procedures, which are usually reflected in the internal structure and systems of the organization. It also has a direction. This may take the form of a mission, purpose, or corporate strategy. The organization has physical, financial, and technical resources, which include its assets and its products. It also has a tradition and a culture. All of these factors contribute to the internal organizational environment. The organization exists in the context of a larger environment, consisting of the social and political community, an industry or industries, and economic conditions. The internal organizational environment transmits and translates the external environment to its members.

For the performance of a job to be effective, the definition states that specific results and actions taken to obtain them must "maintain or be consistent with policies, procedures, and conditions of the organizational environment." The factors mentioned as part of the organizational environment affect the specific results that are expected from a job and the actions that are "appropriate" in the attempt to generate those results. The value (i.e., benefits versus costs) of the results and the actions are, in large part, determined by the organizational environment.

The model is illustrated in Figure 2-1. The graphic representation of the model suggests that effective action, and therefore performance, will occur when all three of the critical components of the model are consistent, or "fit." If any one or two of these components are inconsistent and do not correspond with each other, then it is expected that ineffective behavior or inaction will result.

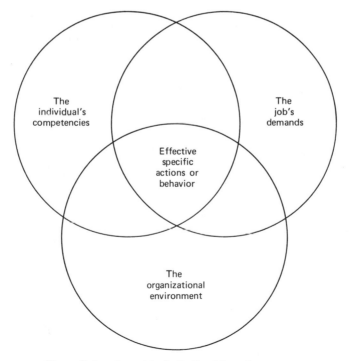

Figure 2–1. A model of effective job performance.

The model also suggests that if any two of the components are consistent, or congruent, then there is an increased likelihood that effective performance will occur. A plant manager responsible for production of a chemical solution with medical applications must be concerned about quality control to a great extent. It could be said that one of the job demands, or responsibilities, of this plant manager is to *ensure* that quality specifications are met on *all* of the products that leave the plant. This would represent a congruence between his or her job demands and an important aspect of the organizational environment, which is that a recall of such a product would severely damage the public image of the firm. The purchasers of the product will be reluctant to take a chance that the problem may have only occurred in one batch of the chemical solution. If the user is a hospital, public confidence in the hospital is at at stake. If, in addition, the procedures supported by corporate management emphasize continual rechecking of quality standards through appropriate allocation of resources (i.e., people to do the job) and reasonable delivery deadlines for the product being negotiated by the marketing and sales groups, a further congruence is established between the plant manager's job demands and the organizational environment.

In contrast, suppose that the organizational environment does not provide such support. Corporate management may emphasize reducing delivery times for the product and support the marketing and sales groups in making commitments that put increasing pressure on the plant manager to reduce delivery time. Corporate manufacturing management may not approve requests for additional personnel to conduct frequent quality checking of the product and tell the plant manager to do a more efficient job with the resources at his or her disposal. In such an organizational environment, the job demand on the plant manager for ensuring high-quality products with *no* mistakes may suffer. At best, this conflict between the organizational environment and the manager's job demands places additional pressure on the plant manager. At some point, this pressure may result in compromises that increase the risk of shipping a product with inadequate quality.

The popular feature film, *The China Syndrome*, portrayed a situation in which a construction manager "cut corners" on quality inspections of welds in the nuclear power plant being built. The viewer is presented with the impression that it was corporately induced pressure to meet deadlines in construction and reduce costs that implicitly or explicitly encouraged the construction manager to look for cost- and time-saving steps.

If the job demands conflict with aspects of the organizational environment, effective performance will either not be forthcoming or it will be costly and highly inefficient. For example, the research and development division of a $150 million a year industrial products company changed to a matrix structure in an attempt to increase the number of new products designed. A senior scientist or engineer was appointed as project leader for each project. The project leader was given a budget by the vice president of the division and a statement of objectives. When five of the seven project teams failed to meet their first-half-year objectives and most were over budget, the vice president concluded that he had placed the wrong people in the jobs as project leaders. Several questions asked of the project leaders quickly revealed that the company, and in particular the research and development division, had failed to change two critical procedures. First, the company's procedure regarding development of objectives had not been modified to include the newly appointed project leaders and/or the designated project staff in developing the objectives and ascertaining their feasibility. Second, the management information system had not been converted to allow for the various scientists, engineers, and technicians to charge their time to more than one project when in fact many were asked to work on several projects. Project leaders were given budgets determined on the basis of number of person days needed to perform various phases of the work, but their quarterly statements of labor and other costs reflected the full labor cost of staff who were primarily, but not exclusively, assigned to their projects.

In this case, either the demands on the project leader had to be changed, or aspects of the division's procedures (i.e., organizational environment) had to be changed. They were clearly in conflict, or at the minimum inconsistent. Without these changes, the vice president of the research and development division could not determine accurately whether or not he or she had made correct selection decisions in assigning particular senior scientists or engineers as project leaders. He or she may have had that problem as well as the confusion of job demands and organizational procedures.

Although it is possible that effective performance may result when only two of the components are congruent, or fit, it is less likely that *consistent* effective performance will occur. If the job demands and organizational environment are congruent (i.e., support each other) but the individual in the job does not have the appropriate competencies, effective performance may occur early in the individual's job tenure as a result of residual effects of the prior manager. Similarly, organizational procedures and processes may structure the job and performance in such a manner to provide minimum opportunities for someone without the needed competencies to interfere with effective organizational performance. In the latter type of situation, a change in the job demands or environment that required initiative on the part of the manager would probably result in ineffective performance. The manager could no longer rely on the structure of the job and environment to dictate appropriate behavior. In attempting to respond to the changes, a manager without the needed competencies would not have the capability to independently perform effectively.

The model can be considered an adaptation of the classical psychological model of behavior. That is, behavior is a function of the person and the environment (McClelland, 1971). The refinement of splitting the environment into a job demand component and an organizational environment component has been advanced by many authors in the management field (Campbell et al., 1970). The distinctions of the model from prior research and theory will emerge from the discussion of what constitutes the "individual" component of the model.

The model can be summarized with the following set of statements. The job demands component reveals primarily *what* a person in the job is expected to do. The organizational environment component reveals some aspects of what a person in a management job is expected to do, but primarily reveals *how* a person is expected to respond to the job demands. The individual's competencies component reveals what a person is capable of doing; it reveals *why* he or she may act in certain ways.

Functions and Demands of Management Jobs

A job is usually described in terms of a title and list of responsibilities that the job occupant is expected to perform, decisions that he or she is expected to make, and outcomes that he or she is expected to produce. Every job can be said to have a set of functional requirements, that is, requirements that a person in the job should fulfill in terms of the functions and tasks to be performed. These functional requirements and the associated output are, ideally, designed to contribute to the output of people in other jobs. Taken as a whole, the output of the integrated performance of the jobs by all members of an organization yields the performance of the organization with respect to its mission and objectives.

All employees of organizations can be classified as either managers or individual contributors on the basis of the functions and outputs demanded of their jobs. The title of the job that they hold is not related to this distinction. Titles are often granted on the basis of prestige value to the job occupant, others in the organization, or the environment external to the organization. Having the word "manager" in one's job title does not necessarily mean that the person is a manager.

A person in a management job contributes to the achievement of organizational goals through planning, coordination, supervision, and decision making regarding the investment and use of corporate human resources. A manager is someone who "gets things done through other people" (Appley, 1969). The results of the manager's actions can be linked to performance of an organizational unit. Production supervisors are managers. Actions they take have an impact on and contribute directly to the performance of the entire production line, or at least of their section of a larger production line. A vice president of a marketing division is a manager. Actions he or she takes have an impact on and contribute directly to the performance of the marketing division.

Management job demands may be stated in terms of output. For example, a plant manager is supposed to produce 250,000 units of product A and 75,000 units of product B during the quarter. This may be further qualified by the addition of conditions regarding the quality of the products, seasonality of production, and so forth.

Management job demands can be described in terms of general functional requirements. A synthesis of the work of Appley (1969) and Drucker (1973) with some additional clarity would result in a description of a management job in terms of five basic functions: planning, organizing, controlling, motivating, and coordinating. The functions may be described in specific terms, such as selecting staff, delegating responsibility, establishing goals, making decisions, reviewing performance, rewarding subordinates, or disciplining subordinates.

Management job demands may be described in terms of tasks that the manager is to perform. For example, a marketing manager is expected to plan, design, and coordinate a new marketing campaign for one of the company's major products at least once a year. This marketing manager is expected to identify, in conjunction with the corporate strategic planning staff and financial analysts, which product is most in need of the new campaign. The campaign should be designed on the basis of market research which his or her staff have conducted. The marketing manager is expected to present the budget for the campaign to the vice president of marketing by August of the calendar year preceding the campaign.

Management job demands can also be described in terms of various roles. The role describes a set of activities and responsibilities expected of a person in the management job. Managers may be expected to perform an administrative role (Mintzberg, 1973). Managers may be expected to perform an instrumental role with responsibility for "line" functions with specific output objectives for the unit that they manage. Managers may be expected to perform an integrative role with responsibility for "staff" functions with specific working process objectives for the activity that they manage. Managers may be expected to perform a representational role with responsibility for an "interface" among organizations or organizational units with specific objectives regarding the interactions that they manage. This interaction may be between the organization and aspects of the external environment (Morrison, 1980;

Stogdill, 1974). Although a manager may have a job that calls for one of these roles, a management job usually calls for a constellation, or integration, of various roles (McGregor, 1960; Hodgson et al., 1965; Schoenfeldt, 1979; Brush & Manners, 1979).

In contrast, a person in an individual contributor job contributes to the achievement of organizational goals through individual thought and actions. The result of the person's actions can be linked directly to these actions. For example, a salesperson's actions result in sales. When the organization receives a sale from a particular customer, this outcome can be linked to the salesperson's specific actions in obtaining that sale. Similarly, product design results from the actions of a designer, production results from action of a production line worker, a status report of accounts receivable results from actions of an accountant or bookkeeper, the number of new employees hired results from actions of a personnel interviewer or recruiter, and a new product results from actions of a scientist or engineer. The specific functions and responsibilities required in their jobs will vary according to the particular job that they occupy.

Organizational Environment

Every organization creates and exists in an environment. As to whether the internal environment is appropriate for its mission and to accomplish its organizational objectives is an issue. The question of whether all aspects of the environment are understood by members of the organization, or whether these aspects of the environment are explicitly stated or not, are also issues. All of these issues determine how the organizational environment contributes to effective performance of individuals in jobs.

The organizational environment can be described in terms of a number of different factors. Organizational climate or culture has been used as a concept to describe the impact of the organization's structure, policies, and procedures on its members (Litwin & Stringer, 1968; Taguiri & Litwin, 1968; Klemp, 1975; Spencer, Klemp & Cullen, 1978). Whether organizational climate is used as an indicator variable or whether the actual policies, procedures, and structure of an organization are used directly, the atmosphere or environment that the organization creates and transmits to its members affects their performance. For example, McClelland and Burnham (1976) reported that sales divisions within a consumer products company that had higher degrees of clarity and team spirit achieved higher sales volume than did other divisions with relatively less of these variables in their "climate." Dalziel (1979) showed that manufacturing plants within an industrial products company that had higher degrees of concern about performance standards and clarity showed greater cost savings due to waste reduction than did other plants with less of these variables in their climate. Kincaid and Becklean (1968), Lawrence and Lorsch (1967), and many others similarly have demonstrated the importance of climate, structure, policies, and procedures in regard to organizational performance and individuals' contribution to that performance.

For example, organizations with promotion and compensation policies that reward managers who demonstrate their effectiveness by meeting or surpassing clearly identified performance goals communicate to their employees values of taking risks, setting clearly measurable goals, and achieving or surpassing a standard of excellence. Managers in this type of organizational environment know that they are expected to perform effectively in terms of specified goals and that if they reach these goals they will be rewarded appropriately. Often, an organization with these types of values will also have a norm (i.e., rule of acceptable or appropriate behavior) that allows a manager to miss a goal occasionally, which results in the manager not receiving certain rewards.

Organizations with promotion, compensation, and recognition procedures that punish managers who fail to reach identified performance goals, or with those in which the performance goals are unclear or confusing, communicate values of taking few risks, self-protection, and "keeping a clean record" to their employees. Managers in this type of organizational environment attempt fewer innovations for fear of negative consequences, often overlooking or underestimating the beneficial consequences to the organization. They may, in addition, avoid conflict or in-depth and candid assessment of their own or their unit's performance to minimize the threat of punishment. Managers in this type of organizational environment may establish a norm of setting achievable goals and avoiding challenging goals as a way of ensuring success.

The strategic position of a company in its industry and the condition of its industry also will affect the internal organizational environment, which in turn will affect managers' behavior. A manager in a company that is part of a low-growth, mature industry, whose products are in the declining years of their product life cycle, will be encouraged to minimize capital investment, control expenses, and inhibit potentially costly innovations. The same manager in a company that is part of a high-growth and dynamic industry, whose products represent an innovation in technology or packaging, will be encouraged to make capital investments and attempt innovations to maximize growth of volume or market share.

In the public sector, the strategic position of a federal organization, in terms of its relationship to segments of the executive, legislative, and judicial branches of government, will affect the organizational environment, which in turn will affect managers' behavior. The policies of the current political administration, the partisan composition of the legislature, and other similar factors at state, county, and municipal levels of government will similarly affect the organizational environment and, therefore, managers' behavior.

Whether in the public or private sector, the mission, goals, and objectives of the organization will also affect the value and normative messages given to managers. The degree of clarity, the degree of understanding of the rationale behind their development, and the procedure utilized in establishing the mission, goals, and objectives of the organization will also affect managers' behavior.

In a larger context, the economic, political, social, and religious conditions of the culture in which the organization exists will affect its climate and managers' behavior. Cultural values that determine the degree of status and respect given to people in management jobs will have an impact. The cultural values regarding the particular products and reputation of the organization will affect managers' behavior.

All of these aspects of the cultural and organizational environment in which managers function will affect their behavior by communicating what kind of behavior is viewed as appropriate and acceptable and what kind of behavior is not appropriate. Even if a manager has a competency that includes planning, for example, but neither the organization nor the cultural environment support or encourage looking ahead, assessing risks, and methodically developing a plan of action, this aspect of the manager's competence will not be aroused, stimulated, or called upon in his or her job. If the manager decided to use the competency despite organizational and/or cultural demands against it, he or she would be viewed as demonstrating inappropriate behavior and possibly punished.

With respect to the model of effective job performance, the job demands and organizational environment components have been described. The third component, an individual's competencies, will be examined in detail for several reasons. One reason is that of all of the components in the model, it has received the least systematic attention within the fields of management and organization studies. Another reason is that the concept of individual abilities has received a lot of pop-psych attention. Although this serves the purpose of introducing people to psychological ideas, it limits all but the most naive reader and misleads people with simplistic conclusions.

AN INDIVIDUAL'S COMPETENCIES

What is a Competency?

As illustrated in Figure 2-1, an individual's competencies are necessary but not sufficient for effective performance in a job. *A job competency* is *"an underlying characteristic of a person which results in effective and/or superior performance in a job"* (Klemp, 1980). A job competency is *an underlying characteristic of a person* in that it may be a motive, trait, skill, aspect of one's self-image or social role, or a body of knowledge which he or she uses. The existence and possession of these characteristics may or may not be known to the person. In this sense, the characteristics may be unconscious aspects of the person (i.e., he or she is not aware of them or is unable to articulate or describe them).

Because job competencies are *underlying characteristics*, they can be said to be generic. A generic characteristic may be apparent in many forms of behavior, or a wide variety of different actions. Baldwin (1958) explained that when a person performs an act (i.e., demonstrates a specific behavior) which has a result or several results (i.e., outcomes), it is also expression of a characteristic or of several characteristics. Actions, their results, and the characteristics being expressed do not necessarily have a one-to-one correspondence. The reason for the lack of direct correspondence is evident in Figure 2-1. The action, or specific behavior, is the manifestation of a competency in the context of the demands and requirements of a specific job and particular organizational environment. Given a different job or different organizational environment, the competency may be evident through other specific actions. In the same manner, the result of the action (i.e., the effect it has) is related to the requirements and setting in which it occurs.

For example, someone could describe you in terms of the clothes you were wearing last Tuesday afternoon. Would this be an accurate description of your style of dress, your variations in dress, or your wardrobe? It would probably not be an accurate description of how you dress on Saturday mornings. Is it an accurate description of how you are dressed for a dinner party, an afternoon of boating, a softball game, or mowing the lawn? Furthermore, would inferences, or attributions, as to your values, skills, or style be accurate if they were based on the knowledge of what you were wearing last Tuesday afternoon?

Making these kinds of inferences about your style of dress or other aspects of your behavioral style would be assuming that a specific action (i.e., what you wore on Tuesday afternoon) had a direct relationship to an underlying characteristic (i.e., what you might wear at any time, in any place, for any activity). Similarly, if you were able to create a favorable impression on others on Tuesday afternoon because your clothes conveyed an image of a conservative, careful person who pays attention to detail, it does not mean that you would create the same impression (i.e., effect or result) on others if you wore the same clothes to a volleyball game.

A great deal of the inaccuracy in models and frameworks as to what constitutes "competence" in various jobs emerges from this confusion.

It has been complicated by methodological problems of what is actually being assessed or measured. It has been further complicated by the use of the term "competency" by many professionals who are referring to different concepts.

Let us take the example of a manager, Helen, giving a subordinate, George, information as to the effectiveness of something George did. Helen's actions in this interpersonal interaction can be described in terms such as "communicating with subordinates" or "providing subordinates with feedback with respect to a performance goal." In either case, we are describing an interaction in which Helen is telling George how well he did according to Helen's view. The result, or effect, of this interaction can vary. George may walk away feeling rewarded, recognized, helped, punished, disciplined, or criticized.

Aspects of the interaction may contribute to which effect occurs. If Helen asks George for his assessment of the performance before providing her view, George may feel that he is being given a chance to explain what happened. If the performance was not "up to par" and George knows this, this action by Helen allows George to demonstrate his ability to know when something has not gone well. If Helen provides this information along with a discussion of the performance goal, how the goal was established, and why the goal is important to the job and to the organization, George may not feel condemned as a person but may recognize how an aspect of his performance was ineffective. With this behavior, Helen is allowing George to feel that only this one incident is in question, not his entire performance of the job.

If you attempt to define Helen's competency in this incident in terms of her actions alone, you are back to the problem of "what were you wearing Tuesday afternoon." If you define Helen's competency in terms of the results alone, you may have committed a serious error. Suppose George walked away from the interaction feeling that he had not done a part of the job adequately. This could be an accurate description. It could merely be another example in a long history of inadequate performance suggesting that George's job is in danger. It could mean that Helen or George was having a "bad day" and one was particularly cryptic with the other. It could mean that Helen's performance is inadequate and to cover herself Helen is looking for ways to blame others.

Even if you define Helen's competency, expressed in this situation, in terms of her actions *and* the results, you may not know *why* she acted in this manner, nor would you know whether she could act in the same manner and produce the same result if the situation were somewhat different. Therefore, *to define a competency, we must determine what the actions were and their place in a system and sequence of behavior and what the results or effects were and what the intent or meaning of the actions and results were.*

It is through such a definition that the concept of a job competency represents an ability. A person's set of competencies reflect his or her capability. They are describing what he or she *can do*, not necessarily what he or she does, nor does all the time regardless of the situation and setting. Referring to Figure 2-1, to understand the individual's specific behavior that was effective, we should know what capability the individual has brought to the situation (i.e., the job in the organizational environment). Without knowing this about the person, it would be difficult to predict, describe, or interpret his or her specific actions and why they were effective.

Competencies are characteristics that are causally related to effective and/or superior performance in a job. This means that there is evidence that indicates that possession of the characteristic precedes and leads to effective and/or superior performance in that job. In addition to a theoretical prediction as to the causal relationship between a characteristic and job performance, an empirical relationship between the characteristic as an independent variable and job performance as a dependent variable should exist.

A threshold competency is a person's generic knowledge, motive, trait, self-image, social role, or skill which is essential to performing a job, but is not causally related to superior job performance. For example, speaking the native language of one's subordinates would be considered a threshold competency. On the other hand, those characteristics that differentiate superior performance from average and poor performance are competencies.

Different Types and Levels of Competencies

Earlier it was mentioned that a competency may be a motive, trait, aspect of the person's self-image or social role, skill, or a body of knowledge which he or she uses. This is an important distinction with implications not only for the full understanding of competence, but also for methodological issues in measuring and assessing competence.

To explore this issue, let us examine the competencies of two people. One person is a neurosurgeon who specializes in brain surgery, and the other is a computer technician who specializes in repair and maintenance of computer hardware (i.e., circuitry). Let us further assume that each is effective in his or her job. They both work on brains which are essential to the functioning of the "system" of which they are a part. For the sake of the illustration, let us assume that their jobs differ in that the computer technician works primarily alone and the neurosurgeon works in conjunction with other surgeons, nurses, an anesthesiologist, and attendants.

There are a number of competencies both must have. Each must have an ability to diagnose a problem in the functioning of the system they are treating. Each must think logically and have a "systems" orientation to conduct such diagnosis. Each must have fine muscle control to operate with precise movements in small spaces. Each must be able to take initiative to find additional information needed to solve problems to repair or maintain the system on which they are working. Each must have an accurate understanding of his or her abilities (i.e., strengths and limitations) to know when to call on others to help or transfer the "client" to another practitioner. Therefore, the neurosurgeon and the computer technician each must have several traits (i.e., fine muscle control and a disposition to take initiative) and skills (i.e., thinking in terms of systems, diagnostic ability, and accurate self-assessment).

On the other hand, to be effective in carrying out their respective responsibilities, each must have some competencies that differ from the other's. While both want to have positive results from their actions, the computer technician must have an efficiency orientation. He or she must be concerned with how to solve the problem and "fix" the computer as quickly as possible. The repairs should involve a minimum of lost computer functioning time, a minimum of time spent (i.e., cost of labor), and a minimum of replacement parts (i.e., cost of materials) to satisfy the needs of the computer user and the computer manufacturer or service agency which he or she represents. To do this, he or she can take moderate risks in attempting solutions, maximizing effort at the repair and the result to the user and his or her organization.

The neurosurgeon must take a minimum amount of time during the surgery, but cannot take moderate risks and seek shortcuts that *might work* as a means to the desired results. Such action would conflict with a key element in the neurosurgeon's job, namely, keeping the patient alive. Neither the neurosurgeon nor the patient can afford experimentation. The results may preclude further attempts at repair of the problem. Although the neurosurgeon must be concerned about efficiency, it does not emerge from a similar disposition, nor can it involve a level of risk similar to that of the computer technician.

In addition, each uses a different body of knowledge to perform his or her functions. Given one of our assumptions, we can also add that the neurosurgeon must have skills of effectively working with a team to orchestrate all of their efforts during an operation. These are skills that are not necessary for the computer technician who works alone, beyond the interpersonal skills needed to communicate with the users of the computer.

In examining those competencies that differ for the effective neurosurgeon and the effective computer technician, we find a variety of competencies. They should differ in certain traits (e.g., risk orientation), skills (e.g., interpersonal ability to manage or orchestrate the work of others), and in specialized knowledge (e.g., facts and understanding of the systems on which they are operating).

In this example, different levels of competencies have been described. That is, traits and skills are considered different *levels* of competencies. For example, the trait mentioned of a disposition to take initiative was considered relevant to effectiveness for both the neurosurgeon and the computer technician. There is probably a skill associated with this trait that involves an ability to search for information, something like a research or fact-finding skill which is equally relevant for both people. The distinctions as to levels of competencies will be explained in detail in later sections of this chapter. At this point, it is sufficient to note that different levels of competency can exist. These levels of competencies are different than various *types* of competencies. Various types of competencies involve different domains of human functioning. For example, fine muscle control, an interpersonal skill in orchestrating the work of a team, and the specialized knowledge of transistor circuitry are various types of competencies. Each pertains to a different domain, or arena, of human functioning.

To have a full understanding of the capability that a person brings to a work situation, we must be able to conceptually distinguish among these types and levels of competencies. These distinctions have implications for application of this understanding to selection systems and training programs. They also have implications for how each type of competency is measured or assessed. This latter point helps to explain findings from various investigators which appear, on the surface, to disagree. With proper definition and measurement they may, in fact, support each other.

Dimensions of the Management Competency Model

A competency model of managers should have two dimensions. One dimension should describe the types of competencies. Different types of management competencies are associated with various aspects of human behavior and a person's capability to demonstrate such behavior. For example, a planning competency would be associated with specific actions such as setting goals, assessing risks, and developing a sequence of actions to reach the goal. An influence competency, on the other hand, would be associated with specific actions such as having an impact on others, convincing them to perform certain activities, or inspiring them to work toward organizational objectives. These two characteristics would be called different types of management competencies in that they involve somewhat different aspects of human behavior.

Usually the types of characteristics examined in a competency assessment study emerge from the data collected on managers (see the section in Chapter 3 on The Job Competence Assessment Method for clarification). In this study, the sample size was too large to follow typical procedures. Instead, the previous competence assessment studies of specific management jobs conducted by the staff of McBer and Company and their colleagues were examined. The objective was to generate a list of every competency that had been shown to relate to effectiveness as a manager, regardless of the specific job and the organization. In addition, competency assessment studies that had been conducted on numerous other types of jobs such as salespeople, product designers, consultants, and so forth, were examined. Again, a list was developed of competencies that had been shown to relate to effective performance in various jobs. These lists were integrated with two criteria in mind: (1) the characteristic had distinguished effective performance in a job with statistical significance; and (2) the characteristic was not unique to the specific product or service that the organization provided.

The resulting list included 21 types of characteristics which are defined and discussed in detail in Chapters 4–9 (see Chapter 3 for detail on the methods used). They were (in alphabetical order): (1) accurate self-assessment; (2) conceptualization; (3) concern with close relationships; (4) concern with impact; (5) developing others; (6) diagnostic use of concepts; (7) efficiency orientation; (8) logical thought; (9) managing group process; (10) memory; (11) perceptual objectivity; (12) positive regard; (13) proactivity; (14) self-confidence; (15) self-control; (16) specialized knowledge; (17) spontaneity; (18) stamina and adaptability; (19) use or oral presentations; (20) use of socialized power; and (21) use of unilateral power.

Specialized knowlege is listed as a type of competency and yet it appeared in the definition of a job competency. Clarification of this is in order. Specialized knowledge is defined as a usable body of facts and concepts. Literally, knowledge refers to the retention of information, whether that information is technical or a method of communication (e.g., a language). The ability to utilize knowledge effectively is the result of other competencies that involve ways of thinking or reasoning. The notion of "specialized" knowledge assumes that some factual information may be irrelevant to performance in a particular job. For example, it could be argued that the Second Law of Thermodynamics is relevant information for everyone. On the other hand, there are many management jobs that can be performed effectively even though the manager is unable to recite the Second Law of Thermodynamics. This type of characteristic has been called specialized knowledge to define what facts and concepts are relevant for the particular job or jobs being examined. This aspect of knowledge was further emphasized by the inclusion of "usable" in the definition of the characteristic. The utility of the factual information is an important test of its relevance for the job being examined.

Specialized knowledge can be considered a type of competency for two reasons. First, there are different levels of knowlege. For example, to determine whether a company has achieved a satisfactory return on equity during the past year, a person must know the formula for calculating return on equity. He or she must know where to look on a financial statement for the specific numbers needed as input to the formula. The person must also know how to multiply or divide (or at least know how to work a calculator). Second, any particular set of facts and concepts may be used in the demonstration of a number of different competencies. If it were merely another level of competencies, specialized knowledge relevant to each type of competency would be distinguishable.

The other dimension of the management competency model should describe the levels of each competency. Each competency may exist within the individual at various levels, with motives existing at the unconscious level, self-image at the conscious level, and skills at the behavioral level. Each level may vary in its impact on the disposition of the person to use the competency. This would be reflected in the frequency with which the person applies the competencies in his or her job, as well as in the degree to which the competency is applied in any situation. For example, a planning competency probably exists at multiple levels. At the motive level, the competency may appear as a desire to achieve goals as a reflection of improving one's performance. At the skill level, the competency may appear as the ability to state a goal, list the action sequence that would result in achieving the goal, and determine the costs and benefits of using this plan of action. A person possessing the motive level of the planning competency will be more likely to think frequently about and perceive goals than someone who does not possess this level of the competency. A person possessing the skill level of the planning competency will be more likely to develop a plan of action and assess the risks involved once a goal is articulated or identified than someone who does not possess this level of the competency. In this manner, the different level of competencies will affect different aspects of the individual's application of a particular competency in a job, even though these aspects are related to the same type of human behavior.

This second dimension of the competency model was thought to have three basic levels: (1) the motive and trait level; (2) the self-image and social role level; and (3) the skill level. These categories reflect the components of a competency appearing in the definition of a competency. These levels are described in more detail in the following sections of this chapter.

Motives and Traits

A motive is a "recurrent concern for a goal state, or condition, appearing in fantasy, which drives, directs, and selects behavior of the individual" (McClelland, 1971). A trait is a dispositional or characteristic way in which the person responds to an equivalent set of stimuli (McClelland, 1951). Motives and traits exist at both the unconscious and conscious levels within people. Motives are different from traits, as shown in Table 2–1.

A motive includes thoughts related to a particular goal state or theme. For example, people who think (consciously or unconsciously) about improving and competing against a standard of excellence are said to have an achievement motive (McClelland, 1961; Atkinson, 1958; McClelland et al., 1953). When people with a high achievement motive encounter a situation in which their performance can be measured and a goal can be stated, their achievement motive is aroused. Once aroused, the motivated thought directs and selects their behavior. That is, they will choose to do things that help them get feedback on their performance and engage in activities that may result in improved performance.

A trait, on the other hand, includes thoughts and psychomotor activity related to a general category of events. For example, people who believe themselves to be in control of their future and fate are said to have the trait of efficacy (deCharms, 1968; White, 1963; Rotter, 1966; Boyatzis, 1969; Stewart & Winter, 1974). When people with this trait encounter a problem or issue in any aspect of life, they take initiative to resolve the problem or understand the issue. They do not wait for someone else to do it, nor expect that luck or fate will take care of it. The thought pattern and resultant behavior occur in response to any general set of events which allow the trait to be expressed. Traits are relatively easier to arouse than are motives.

In our example, the computer technician would probably perform his

TABLE 2-1   Comparison of Motives and Traits

	Motives	Traits
Orientation of thoughts	Concern for a theme, or goal state	Generalized response to events
Stimulus (i.e., what arouses the thoughts)	Perception of situational cues as related to the particular theme or goal state (i.e., the person perceives an opportunity for attainment of the goal state)	Any of a number of related situational cues
Observed resultant behavior	Varied behavior related to attainment of the goal state	Stylized behavior (i.e., behavior typical of the person) in a variety of related situations which have no apparent theme
Overall probability that any event will arouse the thought pattern	Moderate	High
Examples	n Achievement, n Power	Taking initiative, walking fast

or her job more effectively if he or she had a high n Achievement (i.e., need for Achievement) than with a lower degree of this motive. Although the neurosurgeon would be expected to have a moderate degree of n Achievement, we would not expect it to be as strong as the computer technician's motive. If it were, an undesirable level of risk taking (i.e., moderate risk taking) might occur. As mentioned, both would be exepcted to have traits of fine muscle control and an orientation to take initiative in collecting information and solving problems.

Self-Image and Social Roles

Self-image refers to a person's perception of himself or herself and the evaluation of that image. This definition of self-image incorporates the constructs of both self-concept and self-esteem. People's evaluation of the self-concept results from a comparison of themselves to others in their environment (Pettigrew, 1967), and an assessment of where they stand in terms of values held by themselves and others in their environment. Self-image is therefore not only a concept of the self but an interpretation and labeling of the image in the context of values. These values and the resulting judgments may have roots in the individual's past beliefs, current beliefs, or beliefs held and espoused by people in the environment within which those individuals live and work.

For example, Edward Farnsworth had a concept of himself which included such statements as: "I am creative and innovative, I am expressive, and I care about others." If Edward were in a job that required routine performance of tasks in an organization that expected him to be highly self-disciplined, his evaluation of this self-concept would alter the self-image. In such a situation, imagine Edward waking up on a Friday morning and saying to himself, as he looked in the mirror to shave: "I am creative and innovative, I am *too* expressive, I care about others, and I lack a degree of self-discipline." Edward changed his evaluation of his self-concept as a result of reactions and comments he was receiving from others with whom he worked. Of course, such a change would not occur quickly, but it would occur, especially if most of Edward's friends and colleagues were the people at work who were making the comments that led to his reevaluation of his self-concept. If Edward were in this situation, he would probably add, "Thank God it's Friday!"

Social role refers to a person's perception of a set of social norms for behavior that are acceptable and appropriate in the social groups or organizations to which he or she belongs. The various social roles people adopt help them to determine how they should behave as members of an organization, business, social group, family, community, church, or nation. A social role, therefore, represents an individual's view of how he or she "fits in" with regard to the expectations of others. The particular social role adopted by an individual is a function of his or her view of both the characteristics he or she possesses and of how others expect the person to act.

The social role level of a competency differs from other uses of the concept of "role" in a number of ways. First, the social role level of a competency refers to a set of expectations that is more limited in range and scope (i.e., it involves expectations regarding fewer actions) than the concept of role referred to by Mintzberg (1973), Hodgson et al. (1965), and Stogdill (1974). Second, the social role levels of the competencies are linked to the competencies, not to management job demands (i.e., tasks and functions) as in the role concept used by Mintzberg (1973). Third, it is less situationally determined than the concept of role as described by Bales (1970). In his framework, Bales described the roles that a person may take in a particular group. The role is determined by the interactions of the person with others in the group. The social role level of the competencies is a distinction based on the contention that individuals will demonstrate a degree of consistency in the roles that they take in various groups at work and in their lives. This consistency is linked to the competencies of the person.

For example, think of the last time some of your friends and you were sitting and trying to decide what to do with an evening. There was probably one person in the group who is referred to as the "wet blanket" by others. This is the person who will usually find something wrong with any idea about what to do. "It's too late, the movie started already." "They're playing the Yankees and that means that they'll lose. Why bother going? It'll be such a depressing event." "No, we shouldn't go over to Frank and Nancy's house, they're having some difficulties and seem to be embarrassed whenever people stop in to see them." This person inhibits the action of the group, or at least tries to inhibit it. He or she may not be trying to slow the group down intentionally. It seems that whenever an idea is suggested, he or she can find fault with it. If this same person has a similar inhibiting effect on groups at work, the "wet blanket" social role is probably linked to competencies that the person possesses. The consistency of the person demonstrating the role suggests that it is linked to his or her characteristics rather than specific aspects of a particular group. If he or she is a commercial loan officer at a bank who specializes in financing large equipment purchases, this inhibiting social role may reflect skill level competencies concerning assessing risk, influencing others to minimize their financial risks, and self-image level competencies of being a fiscal conservative. What was seen as a "wet blanket" social role in the evening setting may be a "protector of the bank's assets" social role during the day.

Two observations can be made about this example. One is that the person's actions in a group setting (i.e., what he or she can be expected by others to do) may be similar even though the groups are different. The person's social role travels with him or her; it is one of his or her capabilities. In this way, it is a level of his or her competencies. The second observation is that a social role that is appropriate and functional in one setting (i.e., slowing investment decisions of others during the day) may be inappropriate in other settings (i.e., slowing down decision making by the social group at night). The results from the person using this level of his or her competencies during the day would be a "safer" loan portfolio for the bank, but at night, the result would probably be several hungry friends.

Aspects of self-image and social role levels are further described in Table 2–2. Self-image and social role aspects of competencies are mediators of motives and traits in determining actual behavior. That is, where motive or trait levels of a competency exist, self-image and social role levels of the competency help in the selection of actions to be taken,

TABLE 2-2 Comparison of Self-Images and Social Roles

	Self-Images	Social Roles
Process involved in their formation	Intrapersonal process	Interpersonal process
Stimulus for a change	Change in personal values; or	Change in personal capability as viewed by others; or
	Change in personal characteristics	Change in expectations of others regarding appropriate behavior in person's job
If explained to others, what would they know about the person?	What the person thinks of himself or herself	How the person fits in and will work with others on tasks
Examples	I am efficient I am likable I am persuasive	Innovator Systems analyst Leader

by defining which actions are appropriate. They operate as translators and integrators of the person's other characteristics (i.e., motives, traits, and skills) and his or her environment's expectations and values regarding these characteristics and the appropriateness to the job that the person holds.

The example of the neurosurgeon might have a self-image that included that he or she was precise, careful, an expert in the field, and one of the few who could perform such operations. With such a self-image, he or she may adopt a social role of being the "star" or "prima donna" in the medical field and in the hospital. While this self-image and social role might not cause any problems at his or her country club, it could lead to conflicts in the operating room. Interactions with the other professionals assisting in an operation could be filled with undertones of resentment, arguments, or differences of opinion as to procedures, all of which decrease the neurosurgeon's ability to effectively orchestrate the team of professionals during the operation. A similar self-image and social role held by the computer technician would not necessarily lead to any problems. The technician, assuming that he or she works alone, would not run the risk of stimulating resentment from others.

As with any of the types of competencies, self-image and social role levels of the competencies must be appropriate to the job and organizational setting in which the work occurs for the individual to be most effective. Unlike other types of competencies, the appropriateness of self-image and social role competencies to effective performance in the job involves perceptions of others as to appropriateness. The views of others as to appropriate self-image and social roles become part of the organizational environment of the person.

There is a type of competency that is a notable exception to this dynamic. Competencies related to a person's ego development or maturity contribute to a person's self-image, but do not affect his or her social roles. Although some aspects of the individual's environment promote values regarding some of the specific behaviors that result from such characteristics, these values place a normative demand on how the person views himself or herself (i.e., self-image). They do not place a demand on the social role that a person may adopt. The result is that social role levels of competencies related to maturity do not exist.

Skills

Skill is the ability to demonstrate a system and sequence of behavior that are functionally related to attaining a performance goal. Using a skill is not a single action. The relationship among the specific actions is such that each contributes in some direct manner to the capability of people to function effectively or ineffectively in a situation. Since a skill is the ability to demonstrate a system and sequence of behavior, it must result in something observable, something that someone in the person's environment can "see." For example, planning ability is a skill. People who have this skill can identify a particular sequence of actions to be taken to accomplish a specific objective. They can identify potential obstacles to those actions. People with this skill can identify sources of help in avoiding obstacles or overcoming them when they interfere with the action sequence. None of these separate actions constitutes a skill, but the system of behavior does. Together these various behaviors, called skill in planning, aid individuals in reaching an objective or performing an aspect of a job. People who have this skill can apply it in any number of situations or contexts. Completing a weekly activity sheet for subordinates does not necessarily constitute demonstration of a planning skill: it may merely indicate the ability to complete that specific form.

It is also important to distinguish skills from tasks, or functions, which are required in the job. A function such as organizing resources requires a person to use multiple skills to perform it effectively. Performing an organizing function would involve analytic and planning skills. In communicating a particular organization of resources to others, additional interpersonal skills would be needed, such as influencing others. *Therefore, selecting staff, decision making, delegating responsibility, or repairing a machine are tasks or functions and are not skills.* They are aspects of the job and not aspects of the individual's capability or competencies.

Other models or theories often incorporate concepts termed attitudes and style. Comparison of this model to these concepts is useful. Attitudes consist of feelings or statements for or against certain issues. If a person is in favor of free enterprise, he or she has an attitude favoring the capitalist system. The reason behind the attitude is based on a value or values on which the issue is judged. It is more sensible to work with values directly than with the attitudes that result from them. In this model, values are part of self-image and social role. Thus, a value such as freedom of choice is seen as part of a manager's self-image and also as part of his or her and others' perception of his or her social role as a businessperson.

Style, or managerial style, is often described as a set of skills, attributes, or characteristics of a manager (Schoenfeldt, 1979; Brush & Manners, 1979). The concept refers to a pattern of behavior that the manager demonstrates and values that he or she holds. In terms of the model and concepts presented in this study, managerial style can be considered the result, or effect, of the manager using various competencies. While this "shorthand" may be useful in some settings (i.e., in training programs), it confuses understanding of managerial competence through oversimplification.

DYNAMIC INTERACTION

The dynamic aspects (i.e., the interaction) of the components of the conceptual model used as a basis for this study can be described in terms of a force-field representation, as shown in Figure 2–2. The interaction between the person (inside the dotted zone in Figure 2–2) and his or her environment (outside the dotted zone) results in action, or demonstrated behavior. Feedback occurs between the person's competencies and specific actions. A person's competencies have a direct impact on what specific actions are demonstrated. Each time an action is demonstrated, there is some impact on the person's competencies. Feedback occurs between the functional and situational demands of the job and specific actions. The demands of a job have a direct impact on what specific

Figure 2–2. Dynamic interaction of components of job performance and levels of competencies.

actions are demonstrated and how they are demonstrated, regardless of whether they are mental or physical actions. Each time an action is demonstrated, there is some impact on the functional or situational demands of the job. The organizational and cultural environment set the stage as to what "appropriate" action is, but exert their impact on individual action through affecting the functional and situational demands of the job.

Each of these components, which relate to performance in a job, have some impact on each other. The nature and strength of the impact varies. In some cases the impact will be a refinement, or fine tuning, of what specific action will be demonstrated. In other cases, the impact will be a stimulation, or arousal, of something in one of the other components.

Over time, each of these components should affect each other so as to increase consistency. That is, if certain tasks and functions are repeatedly required by the job, the person will either: (1) increase the frequency with which certain competencies are applied, or aroused, to address this function, thereby improving the quality of performance of that function; or (2) avoid that task or function of the job if he or she does not have any of the competencies which are applicable to performance of the function. In the latter case, the person may delegate the function to someone else, not perform that aspect of their job, or merely redefine the job as he or she sees it to exclude the need for competencies not possessed. Similar interactions will occur over time between each of the other components.

Within the competency component, Figure 2–2 shows how the level of competencies will probably interact with each other. Motive and trait levels of competencies will have the most direct impact on the self-image and social role levels of the competency. They will also have impact on the skill level of the competency through the impact on the self-image and social role levels. Similarly, specific demonstrated action or behavior will have the most impact on the skill level of a competency. Over time, the demonstrated actions may have impact on the social role, self-image, and motive and trait levels of the competency, but only following some degree of impact on the skill level of the competency.

An example of a person who received a promotion from being an individual contributor to a manager will help to illustrate. David Bertini was an outstanding salesman. He was promoted to branch manager of his sales branch when the former branch manager left the company. In terms of Figure 2–2, the functional and situational demands of David's job changed, but the organizational and cultural environment did not. As branch manager, David was responsible for planning, organizing, controlling, motivating, and coordinating his salespeople.

He was pleased with the promotion. Although he was not sure how a manager should behave, he decided that he would not try to mimic the former branch manager. He had left the company after a period of conflict with the regional sales manager, Bill Rinehart. David did not want to take the chance that the conflict concerned his old boss's behavior. He assumed that since he received the promotion for being such a good salesman, this was the key to being a good branch manager—be a model salesman.

He started officially as branch manager on Monday morning. Tuesday, one of his salespeople, Sally Chapin, told him that one of his old accounts was considering going to the competition. David told Sally not to worry. "I'll find out what's going on." He leaned over his desk and began dialing the customer's number before Sally had a chance to finish her explanation as to why she thought the customer was considering the competition. Within 15 minutes, David discovered that price was the problem and made a special deal with the customer. He confirmed the sale. After he finished the telephone call, David smiled at Sally and said, "Any time you need help, come right in and ask!"

Two months later, David was talking to Bill Rinehart and asked him, "How do I get my salespeople to come and ask me for help? They seem to stay away and I know that some of them are having problems." Bill offered to visit David's branch and help him find out what the problem was.

After spending several hours at the branch office, Bill sat down with David. Bill had been surprised to find out that David was making his salespeople feel incompetent because he always interfered with their sales efforts. At least, that is how they saw it. Bill knew that David had sound coaching skills; that was why David had received the promotion. The conversation was enlightening to David. He discovered that he got the promotion because of skills he had shown in helping some new salespeople from another branch a year earlier, not because of his own sales record. As he and Bill discussed the situation, David began to see that the branch manager is supposed to guide, coach, and help his salespeople. He should be helping each of them figure out why a customer was backing down, or why a customer ordered less than he had the month earlier.

David had many of the appropriate competencies to be branch manager. Bill had known that good sales managers have some different skills than good salespeople and had considered this in making the promotion. David's problem had been that his self-image and social role levels of the competencies had not changed when his job demands changed (i.e., when his job changed). Bill felt that the talk, reviewing his image of the branch manager's responsibilities with David, and giving David several books on sales management would take care of the problem. David called Bill several weeks later and said, "Being a manager is tough, but I like it. Thanks for the talk, Bill."

Bill thought the problem had been solved until eight months later when he noted that sales at David's branch had dropped continuously for three months. Bill was concerned because this represented the first quarter that the branch had been operating under sales goals and plans that were developed while David was branch manager. Bill called David and said, "I notice that sales are down. What's going on?"

"Well, Bill, this damn recession has people cautious. They're afraid of getting caught with too much inventory," replied David.

Bill was not satisfied with that answer. "But you have been down each of the past three months. Are you sure that's all due to inventory concerns?"

David added, "Actually, it's a combination of things. One of them I could use your help with. Some of my salespeople don't seem to be working as hard as they have before. It's like they never came back from vacation." Bill decided it was time for another trip to David's branch. What Bill discovered was complicated. At first it seemed that several of David's key salespeople were still angry at David for having fired Sally Chapin a number of months previously. He asked David if he had considered discussing why he had fired Sally at one of his staff meetings. David did not like the idea because it meant that he would have to hold a staff meeting. Bill was again surprised that David did not have regular staff meetings. He asked David, "How do you know what's going on with your people?" David told him that he met with each person individually and discussed various issues at least once a month. David tried to explain to Bill that it allowed him to develop a more personal relationship with each one. The story unfolded like an onion. Soon Bill learned that David had never met with his staff to discuss the branch's sales goal and plan of action. Some of the salespeople did not even know what the branch's overall goal was.

"David, how can you get people to pull together if they don't even know their shared sales goal?" Bill was feeling frustrated with David and began pushing his questions at David faster. David attempted to explain. "I have always felt that individual sales goals are important. The branch goal is only meaningful for me."

Bill learned that David did not have several competencies that Bill knew were important in branch managers. One of them was the ability to build a sense of team spirit among the branch staff. Although meetings are not the only way to accomplish this spirit, David's lack of understanding the need for them worried him. David did not have the set of competencies related to this aspect of branch management at any of the levels of competencies. If Bill had been able to articulate and assess these competencies, he might not have promoted David. If Bill had understood what help David needed, he might have been able to send him to a training program, or apprentice David to an experienced and effective branch manager at another branch for several months. Bill had not done these things. His frustration and disappointment with David increased. Before the year had ended, David resigned and went to work as a national account representative for a competing firm. David was never sure what had gone wrong. He blamed his salespeople, Bill, and the economy for his difficulties as branch manager. Bill summarized the story about David by saying, "He never learned to think like a manager."

The interactions between the various components in Figure 2–2 do not always result in ineffective performance. With adequate understanding and resources, a person like David can be helped to develop the needed competencies before he is asked to use them in a job. He can be helped to integrate the competencies that he has at all levels. Unfortunately, none of these changes occur naturally or automatically in response to changes in the job demands or the organizational environment.

A change in any aspect of the system illustrated in Figure 2–2 requires changes in other aspects of the system. This not only affects people entering new jobs but also people who have been in jobs for a certain amount of time. Many founders of organizations and chief executive officers who had saved their organizations have found themselves wondering what was going wrong recently, especially since they had been doing so well in running the company in earlier years. For executives in this situation, the organizational environment and the demands of their specific jobs have changed in the past several years even though their titles have not. To appropriately respond to such changes, they would have to change aspects of their competencies and the way in which they use them. In Chapter 12, various applications of the concept of job competency and the implications of the models presented in Figures 2–1 and 2–2 are discussed.

CHAPTER THREE

The Research Design And Methods[*]

The research design was chosen to reflect the purpose of this study and the nature of available raw data. At the time of this study, the author and his colleagues at McBer and Company had completed a number of competence assessment studies on various management jobs. The author decided to reanalyze all of the available information in its raw form rather than to merely conduct a metaanalysis or secondary analysis. The information reported here comes from 12 organizations and more than 2,000 people in 41 management jobs within those organizations.

Twenty-one of the management jobs were in four organizations from the public sector. These organizations were federal departments or agencies within the United States government. One organization was a branch of the military; one was involved in foreign relations; one was involved in international trade; and one was primarily involved in aspects of domestic trade. Managers in this study were at various levels and in various functions within these organizations.

Twenty of the management jobs were in eight organizations from the private sector. These organizations were on the Fortune 500 list. One organization was a major retail conglomerate. One organization was in the industrial-products business; one was in a high-technology, industrial-products business; one was in the consumer-goods business; one was in the high-technology industrial and consumer-products business; one was in the communications business; one was in a variety of indus-

[*]It is recommended that the reader who is not technically or research oriented skip this chapter.

trial and consumer products businesses; and one was in the medical, health-care, and drug business. Managers in this study were at various levels and in various functions within these organizations.

THE JOB COMPETENCE ASSESSMENT METHOD

The Job Competence Assessment method was developed by the staff of McBer and Company and uses five steps to generate a validated model for a job (Klemp, 1979; Klemp & Spencer, in press), as shown in Table 3-1. The first step involves determining the appropriate measure of job performance and how it is to be assessed. Without an adequate measure of job performance, validation of a model is impossible.

The second step involves job element analysis, which was developed from concepts of job analysis (Primoff, 1973). The result of job element analysis is a weighted list of characteristics that managers perceive as important in distinguishing superior from average performers, and those characteristics required by anyone in the job.

The third step involves a form of critical-incident interviewing (Flanagan, 1954) called Behavioral Event Interviewing (McClelland, 1975). The result of the interviews is a detailed description of a number of critical incidents on the job in which the interviewee's behavior and his or her thoughts and feelings are documented. These events can be systematically coded for various characteristics, or "competencies." The coding of characteristics is then related to performance criteria.

The fourth step involves identification and administration of tests and measures that are chosen to assess various competencies. The specific competencies examined are empirically determined through the coding of the interviews. Responses to the tests and measures are related to job-performance criteria. The result of the third and fourth steps is a list of competencies that have been validated. That is, certain characteristics have been shown to relate to effective and superior performance while others have not.

The fifth step involves integration of the results of steps two through four. The result of this activity is a model of job competence based on various characteristics assessed through various methods of measurement.

In this study, the objective was to expand the fifth step into a generic model of the competence of managers. The data and competency models from a number of prior research projects were to be integrated to determine if a model could be generated and empirically supported across organizational and job-specific boundaries.

TABLE 3-1   The Job Competence Assessment Method

Steps	Activities	Results
Identification of criterion measure	Choose an appropriate measure of job performance Collect data on managers	Job performance data on managers
Job element analysis	Generate list of characteristics perceived to lead to effective and/or superior job performance Obtain item rating by managers Compute weighted list of characteristics Analyze clusters of characteristics	A weighted list of characteristics perceived by managers to relate to superior performance A list of the clusters into which these characteristics can be grouped
Behavioral Event Interviews	Conduct Behavioral Event Interviews Code interviews for characteristics or develop the code and then code the interviews Relate the coding to job performance data	A list of characteristics hypothesized to distinguish effective and/or superior from poor or less effective job performance A list of validated characteristics, or competencies
Tests and measures	Choose tests and measures to assess competencies identified in prior two steps as relevant to job performance Administer tests and measures and score them Relate scores to job performance data	A list of validated characteristics, or competencies, as assessed by these tests and measures
Competency model	Integrate results from prior three steps Statistically and theoretically determine and document causal relationships among the competencies and between the competencies and job performance	A validated competency model

The Job Competence Assessment method differs from other methods in a number of important ways (Klemp, 1978; Spencer, 1979). It differs from task and function analysis in three ways. One, it examines the person in the job, not only the job. Two, it results in a model of competence, not merely a laundry list of characteristics. Three, the model can be validated in terms of performance data. The Job Competence Assessment method overcomes three potential problems of theory or panel methods. First, a theory or panel approach determines what an individual or group of "experts" think is relevant; this may be an "espoused theory of action" and not a "theory in use" (Argyris & Schon, 1974). Second, theory and panel methods often result in identification of characteristics, such as courage or dedication, that are not behaviorally specific and are difficult to assess. Third, results from theory and panel methods are often assumed to be related to performance and not empirically tested against performance data. In addition, since coding systems are empirically derived and rigorously applied, with high intercoder reliability, in the Job Competence Assessment method, some of the methodological problems that plague assessment centers and other operant techniques (e.g., unstructured interviews) are adequately addressed (Williamson & Schaalman, 1980).

JOB PERFORMANCE AS A CRITERION MEASURE

Assessment of Performance

To generate a model that is performance-tested, one must examine these components in their relationship to some measures of performance. The use of any performance measures may suffer from a criticism concerning the use of a "current" measure of performance. A measure of performance that is currently in use by an organization or by the people in it only reflects effective performance as they see it. The use of such a measure does not confront the problem of potential shortsightedness of the entire organization, or of its possible lack of understanding of some larger significance that a different basis for determining effectiveness or a different set of goals may have. Of course, the problem with any other measure of performance or effectiveness is that it emerges from an individual's or a group's ideal image of an appropriate goal for the organization or the people in specific jobs within that organization. Such a measure, which may be theoretically or philosophically sound, is a relatively subjective judgment. Therefore, it is based on a particular theory or set of values.

To avoid embroilment in a philosophical argument, it can be said that the performance measures used in this study seemed to be the best available. Instead of imposing some arbitrary, theoretical or value-based assumption as to what constitutes effectiveness as a manager, each organization involved in these studies determined what effectiveness was, or who was demonstrating it, in the context of its goals and objectives.

Measures Used in This Study

Validation of a competency model and its constituent competencies requires the statistical use of a measure, or measures, of job performance. In competency studies, these are often called criterion measures (i.e., they are the standard against which other information will be compared). There are three types of performance or criterion measures: (1) supervisory nominations or ratings; (2) peer nominations or ratings; and (3) work-output measures. The degree of confidence one has in the validity and potential utility of research findings in competence assessment projects is a direct function of the degree of confidence one has that the criterion measure really is a measure of performance in the job being examined.

While a work-output measure is the most direct performance measure, supervisory and peer assessments are also valid performance measures. Supervisory ratings have been shown to be significantly related to work-output measures (McGrath & Altman, 1966; Hall, 1956; Hood et al., 1957; Williams & Leavitt, 1947). The utility of peer assessments has also been documented (Kane & Lawler, 1978). Lewin and Zwany (1976) reviewed studies that demonstrated the link between peer ratings and nominations and various work-output measures. They also reported that supervisory and peer ratings tend to be highly correlated.

There are three ways to establish confidence in the criterion measure. First, whenever possible, the criterion measure should be a direct reflection of the work performed in the job. For example, a criterion measure for a competency study of salespersons should include the individual's actual sales, possibly adjusted for region or season. Unfortunately, direct output measures often are not available or are difficult to identify. For many staff jobs and many management jobs, for example, identifying and accurately measuring work output is difficult.

Second, if direct output measures are not available, then supervisory and/or peer judgements must be used. If these judgments are used, nominations are more effective than ratings (Lewin & Zwany, 1976; Klemp, 1979). Ratings are a respondent measure in which a person is asked to use some form of scale to assess the performance of a number of persons. Issues of personal attraction, concern over someone's feelings or public image, and/or equity confound judgments made during a rating process. Nominations are an operant measure, in which a person is asked to identify, from his or her knowledge of the job incumbents, one or more individuals who have performed in an effective and/or superior manner the job being investigated. Since nominations are an operant measure, the people identified through them are more likely to have demonstrated excellence in performance. Third, to maximize confidence in the criterion data, several of these measures should be used whenever possible.

Although the original aggregate sample included over 2000 managers, performance measures considered adequate for this study were available on only 1009 managers. Of these managers, information from tests and measures was available on 756 managers. Information for Behavioral Event Interviews was available on an additional 253 managers. The performance measures of these managers included work-output measures, supervisory nominations, and supervisory ratings. Information on each of these types of performance measures was available on approximately one-third of the sample (see Appendix B for the specific distribution). Multiple measures were available on a segment of the sample.

Since the objectives varied for the separate studies that constituted the aggregate sample used in this study, tests and measures had been used on different samples from the samples that had been interviewed. Therefore, interview and test data were not available on the same managers. In addition, 345 of the 2000 managers in the total sample participated in the job element analysis aspect of the studies. Owing to the process of data collection and the objectives of the job element analysis, criterion-measure information was not available for persons included in the job element analysis sample.

The aggregate study of managers' competencies involved a problem that the separate (i.e., organization and job specific) competency studies did not. That was: How do you compare performance across organizations? There are no absolute measures of managerial performance, so there was no common standard against which all of the managers in the study could be compared. The quality of a manager's performance (i.e., the degree of his or her effectiveness) must be assessed in the context of each organization's values, norms, standards, objectives, and so forth.

Another consideration is the nature of the performance information originally collected in the separate studies. In those studies in which supervisory nominations were used, the information was, by definition, ordinal. That is, managers' performance was classified as "poor, average, or superior." In those studies in which supervisory ratings were used, the information had been classified into ordinal categories for methodological reasons. It seemed that to compare performance across organizations and jobs on the basis of interval information might overstate differences in performance and be difficult to justify. Therefore, it was determined that ordinal categories of performance would be more appropriate and potentially less biased than interval scales of performance.

Each of the separate organizational and job samples within the test and measure sample was trichotomized into poor, average, and superior performers. This was an appropriate technique because the sampling methods used in the separate studies that composed this sample included either all incumbents in a particular job or some other selection criteria such as location (e.g., East or West Coast), that did not have any systematic or empirical relationship to the criterion measure.

In the Behavioral Event Interview sample, the same procedure was followed for the separate samples from the public sector. The separate samples from the private sector were only categorized into average and superior performers. In the interview samples from the private sector, samples were chosen from among those who were the superior performers in a job and those who were performing "adequately." Private-sector organizations involved in the interview studies did not want marginal or poor performers examined, since their future with the organizations was, at best, questionable. The result is that none of the persons in the Behavioral Event Interview sample from the private sector was designated a "poor" performer.

It was concluded that a basis for comparability across organizations and specific jobs had been established. For example, suppose that we could construct an absolute scale of managerial performance ranging from 1–10. The average performance rating of middle-level manufacturing managers of The Plastics Company may be 6, while the average performance rating of middle-level manufacturing managers in Computer Wizards Incorporated may be 8. Through the use of ordinal classification of performance, we would probably find that the superior middle-level manufacturing managers of The Plastics Company varied in ratings from 6–10, with an average of 8. We might also find that the superior middle-level manufacturing managers of Computer Wizards Incorporated varied in ratings from 7–10, with an average of 9. A category of "superior" middle-level manufacturing managers across both organizations might be considered to include managers with ratings of

7–10. There might be a few managers from The Plastics Company who would be classified as superior performers who would not be so classified if they were working for Computer Wizards Incorporated, but they would be relatively few.

In this manner, an ordinal classification removes a good deal of the variation across organizations and specific jobs. From a methodological view, this is more desirable than comparisons of interval performance assessments, which would raise the question of whether the difference between an 8 and a 9 rating were the same in both organizations. It is also more desirable than a theoretical or philosophical attempt to devise an absolute scale of managerial effectiveness and to apply it to managers in various organizations.

It should be remembered that the purpose of the study was to determine differences in competencies of managers from various organizations and jobs that could be considered generic, or common, managerial competencies. This assumes that managers will be working for organizations that differ in their overall effectiveness and performance. The result of such an analysis does not, as stated numerous times throughout this study, ensure that a manager with such competencies will be effective in a particular management job in a specific organization. It does, however, provide clarificication as to what competencies we would expect to find in effective managers, regardless of the organization or specific management job.

SAMPLES IN THIS STUDY

The entire sample used in this study includes men and women, minorities, and people from various ethnoreligious and socioeconomic groups. Since the objective of the separate studies that constitute the aggregate sample in this study was to examine competencies related to job performance, information on demographic variables was not systematically collected. Greenberg and Greenberg (1980) reported that age, sex, and race differences did not significantly relate to performance in an aggregate sample of salespeople from many organizations. They did find that characteristics of the salespeople, which are called competencies in this study, did relate significantly to sales performance. Since such information would have been difficult to obtain retroactively, and job performance was considered the focus of this study, analyses of characteristics possessed by people of different demographic groups were not conducted.

For functional comparisons, managers in public-sector operation functions were incorporated into the manufacturing sample. Public-sector managers in budget and procurement functions were incorporated into the finance sample. Public-sector managers in public-relations functions were incorporated into the marketing sample. In each of the cases, it was concluded that the public- and private-sector function involved responsibilities and activities that were more comparable than any other type of classification.

Neither the sample of managers nor organizations in this study was random. They were selected on the basis of available information. Therefore, caution in generalizing from these findings and conclusions must be exercised. The findings and conclusions should be considered exploratory and not definitive.

ASSESSING THE SOCIAL-ROLE LEVEL: THE JOB ELEMENT ANALYSIS METHOD

A list of characteristics was generated in group sessions composed of job incumbents (i.e., managers). The participants were asked to "brainstorm" characteristics that they viewed as distinguishing effective or superior performers from others. For each job being examined, several group sessions were held. The lists were then compiled; the original wording that emerged in the group sessions was neither edited nor changed, but duplicate items were eliminated.

The list of items and the job element inventory form were then sent to all persons who participated in the group sessions. Occasionally the list and job element inventory were sent to other job incumbents who did not participate in the group sessions but who were informed as to the intent of the study.

The job element inventory asked the respondent to answer four questions on each item:

1. Does this element differentiate between *superior* and *average* performance in the job?
2. Do *marginal performers* in this job possess this element?
3. Is *trouble likely* if this element is not considered in selecting or training a person for this job?
4. If this element is demanded, could job openings be filled?

For some jobs, the fourth question was not included in the inventory if it did not seem appropriate. Respondents answered yes or no to each question on each item.

Although the specific items identified in the various samples varied considerably, the types of characteristics listed were, for example, "personal pride in doing a job well," "evaluating alternatives in decision making," "ability to inspire confidence," "knowledge of personnel policies," "ability to manage groups," "giving subordinates feedback on their job performance," "analytic ability," "getting information from subordinates and acting on it," "helping employees with personal problems," and "managing one's time." Each of the separate job element analysis studies included from 25–100 such items.

The ratings on each question were combined through a weighted formula to yield a score for each item for each respondent. One formula yielded a score indicating that the characteristic is related to superior performance. The other formula yielded a score indicating that the characteristic is related to marginal or merely adequate performance.

The weighted scores emerging from the formula distinguishing superior performance were factor-analyzed to determine clusters of characteristics that managers perceived to be related. Characteristics that loaded substantially on one factor and not on others (i.e., factor loading above .500 on one factor and no less than .200 greater than the loading on any other factor) were listed.

Each characteristic's scores on the two formulas were examined. Each characteristic that appeared in the factor analysis that had a particularly high loading on the formula distinguishing superior performance and a particularly low loading on the formula distinguishing marginal performance was labeled as discriminating superior from marginal performance. It was concluded that such a characteristic would probably be found only in superior performers.

Other characteristics that appeared in the factor analysis could be considered characteristics that were found in managers performing their jobs adequately. In other words, these were characteristics that managers perceived to be related to performing a management job, with no particular distinction as to degree of effectiveness. Information from the job element analysis was available from seven separate studies (see Appendix B for details).

Since the results from the job element analysis provided information on managers' perceptions of what characteristics an effective manager should have and how he or she should act, they constitute a substantial aspect of the expectations that managers have and express about one another's behavior. In this way, these results provide information on the social-role level of competencies.

ASSESSING THE SKILL LEVEL:
THE BEHAVIORAL EVENT INTERVIEW METHOD

The Behavioral Event Interview

The Behavioral Event Interview (BEI) is a form of critical-incident interview in which the respondent is asked to describe three incidents in which he or she felt effective in the job and three incidents in which he or she felt ineffective in the job. The format for the interview is similar to a journalistic inquiry. The interviewer attempts to obtain as accurate an account of the incident as possible by asking probing yet nondirective questions and requesting specificity, clarification, and examples whenever possible. The interviewer writes a running documentation of the responses. The write-up is often accompanied by a typed transcript or audiotape of the interview.

Identifying Characteristics

In most competency assessment projects, the interview responses of average and superior performers, or poor, average, and superior performers, are compared. Through a compare-and-contrast thematic analysis, characteristics are identified that differentiate the managers in various criterion groups. Any characteristics that appear to distinguish members of one criterion group from another become a hypothesis for future investigation. The hypothesis is that superior performers demonstrate more of the characteristic than do average performers and/or that average performers demonstrate more of the characteristic than do poor performers.

The interview method has certain limitations, which should be noted. First, since the interview method relies on the recall of the respondent, only information that the respondent happens or chooses to remember is presented in the interview. This can result in self-serving, biased information. The method of thematic analysis can overcome this limitation through searching for and identifying patterns in the persons's detailed recollections. These patterns, or themes, may reflect a disposition or an underlying characteristic of which even the respondent is unaware. A second limitation arises from the fact that the interviewer asks for decisions, actions, thoughts, and feelings, but not for knowledge or specific information that was the basis for decisions, thoughts, or actions. Therefore, the interviews are not considered adequate sources for determining the specialized knowledge needed by managers to perform their functions.

The Behavioral Event Interview can be considered a content-valid assessment method. That is, the interview obtains a sample of the person's actual behavior in the job. It is more cost-effective than following a person for a number of days to actually observe his or her behavior. It also provides information on aspects of managerial behavior that would not be directly observable. Campbell et al. (1970) claimed that the critical-incident method is one of the most effective techniques for assessing managerial behavior. For example, through the interview format a person's sequence of thoughts and feelings can be obtained that may directly relate to effective performance but not be directly observable to someone else in that person's presence. The Behavioral Event Interview represents a sampling of a person's behavior in that it results in information about six critical incidents in the person's recent job activity. This allows for documentation of a pattern of demonstrating specific competencies. If such a sampling were not obtained, a single demonstration of an action could be evidence of a unique event rather than of a competency that the person possesses.

This method of assessment appears to be most useful in determining skill-level competencies. As mentioned, it does not tend to generate information about specialized knowledge used in job-performance situations. To determine other levels of competencies (i.e., motives, traits, self-image, or social roles), the analyst of these interviews would have to infer the competencies from the events described. To obtain a valid assessment of these other levels of competencies, a substantial distribution of events in the person's life would be necessary, to allow the inference that one of these intrapsychic competencies was determining the person's behavior. Therefore, the distribution of critical incidents collected through the Behavioral Event Interview does not necessarily provide enough information to infer motive, trait, self-image, or social-role levels of competencies.

A Coding System

The hypotheses identified during the analysis of the interviews become the basis for a coding system. A coding system is a standardized guide for analysis of interviews. The coding system attempts to explain how an interview should be assessed to determine the presence or absence, or degree of presence, of any particular characteristic (as reflected in the hypotheses). It is essential that the coding system be explicitly defined, so that its application results in highly reliable data and so that two judges applying it to the same interview agree to a great extent on how it is to be coded.

For this study, coding manuals from prior research studies were combined, with minor editing and revision, to incorporate characteristics not adequately addressed in prior studies but hypothesized to be of critical importance. The result was a list of 19 characteristics to be examined in the BEI aspect of this study. The operational hypotheses for this study were that superior and/or average managers would demonstrate more of each of the 19 characteristics than would poor managers.

Although the coding manual did emerge from prior studies in which various elements were applied, prior coding of the interviews was done by various coders. To standardize the coding for this research, all interviews were recoded. Two coders independently coded 24 interviews for each of the characteristics, or competencies, examined in this study. Reliability was computed as a percent-agreement score.* The two coders demonstrated reliability scores of between 67 percent and 97 percent on 18 of the characteristics, and 44 percent on 1 characteristic. The average reliability was 80 percent, and the median was 81 percent. When all scores were combined (i.e., for all 19 characteristics), the reliability was 84 percent.

All 253 interview write-ups or transcripts were coded by one of these two persons. In addition, if either of the coders felt that a segment of an interview or the entire interview was particularly difficult to code, the two coders discussed the interview and coded it jointly. The coders did not know the performance rating or classification of the interviewed persons during the coding.

The interviews were coded for frequency of occurrence of each of the 19 characteristics. Although the average length of the interviews was 2 hours, the interviews did vary somewhat in length of time. To test whether or not this variation could possibly contaminate the results, an examination of distributions was conducted. First, the distribution of each characteristic was found to be almost identical for the entire set of interviews. Second, the frequency coding of each characteristic for each person interviewed was converted into a presence or absence code; that is, if the characteristic was coded at any point in the interview, the person received a code of "present," regardless of the number of times it appeared. The major source of possible contamination of length of interviews was considered to be the possibility that a characteristic that was coded frequently in a long interview would not appear as frequently in a

---

* Percent agreement is computed by dividing the numeral 2 times the number of times both coders agreed that a characteristic was present in an interview by the number of times one coder scored the characteristic as present plus the number of times the other coder scored the characteristic as present.

short interview. The reduction of the coding to a presence or absence classification would help to test this possibility. The correlations of the criterion measure and the frequency coding and of the criterion measure and the presence or absence coding were compared. The correlations did not vary by more than 10 percent, and in no case did the variation affect statistical-significance levels. It was concluded that the variation in length of the interviews would not confound the results.

The available data allowed comparisons to be made on managers in each of the performance groups: poor, average, and superior. Managers in the public sector were compared with managers in the private sector. This comparison was based on average and superior performance groups only, owing to the nature of the private-sector sample. Within each sector, managers in each performance group were compared with managers in the other performance groups. Managers in entry, middle, and executive level jobs were compared. Within each managerial level, managers in each performance group were compared with managers in the other performance groups. Managers in marketing, manufacturing, and personnel functions were compared. Sample sizes permitted performance-group comparisons among the manufacturing function managers only. The sample for the Behavioral Event Interview analysis included 10 separate subsamples (see Appendix B for detail).

ASSESSING THE MOTIVE, TRAIT, OR SELF-IMAGE LEVELS: TESTS AND MEASURES

Although many tests and measures were used in the research studies incorporated in this project, only tests or measures on which data were available from two or more separate studies were included. Two tests satisfied this condition: the Picture Story Exercise and the Learning Style Inventory. Eight separate subsamples were used for this analysis (see Appendix B for detail).

The Picture Story Exercise

The Picture Story Exercise (PSE), developed by McBer and Company, is a form of the Thematic Apperception Test (Murray, 1938). The response to the test was coded for a number of variables by professional coders, who were tested periodically against expert coding of each of the scoring systems (at least 85-percent agreement with expert coding) to ensure their reliability. Each variable was coded by a system developed specifically for that variable. The variables were:

1. *n* Achievement (Atkinson, 1958; McClelland, 1961).

2. *n* Affiliation (Atkinson, 1958).

3. *n* Power (Winter, 1973).

4. *n* Activity Inhibition (McClelland et al., 1972; McClelland, 1975).

5. *n* Self-Definition (Stewart & Winter, 1974).

6. Stages of Adaptation (Stewart, 1977).

The *n* Achievement is a measure of a person's motive to do better. The *n* Affiliation is a measure of a person's motive to be a part of warm, close relationships. The *n* Power is a measure of a person's motive to have impact, or to be strong and influential. Activity Inhibition is a measure of a person's disposition (i.e., trait) to control his or her impulses. Self-Definition is a measure of a person's disposition to discover opportunities in the environment and to see himself or herself as an initiator in acting on the environment. The Stages of Adaptation score reflects the four developmental stages of maturity, or ego development, originally described by Freud (1933) and later expanded and described by Erikson (1963).

Since protocols varied in length and the number of words in a protocol appeared to correlate with certain of the above variables, some of the scores were adjusted for length of protocol. The *n* Achievement, *n* Affiliation, *n* Power, and Self-Definition scores were adjusted via the regression coefficient of number of words on each of the variables, respectively (Winter, 1979). The adjusted standardized scores were not found to correlate with the length of protocol.

Although the test-retest reliability of this type of projective test has shown to vary considerably in various research studies (Kagan & Lesser, 1961; Murstein, 1963; Tomkins, 1947), it has been shown that high test-retest reliabilities to a level considered methodologically acceptable can be obtained if this type of projective test is appropriately readministered (Winter & Stewart, 1977).

In addition to having evidence regarding the criterion validity of each of these measures (see the references cited), these scoring systems applied to the PSE are content-valid assessment techniques. That is, the test obtains samples of thought patterns that a person utilizes in his or her life and during on-the-job situations. The PSE presents the individual with relatively ambiguous stimuli and calls for open-ended, or free, responses (termed operant responses). In this manner, it obtains a sample of thought patterns that represent the individual's cognitive processes in numerous life situations (McClelland, 1979). While satisfying the methodological criteria for reliability, validity, sensitivity, and uniqueness (McClelland, 1958; McClelland, 1971), these scoring systems applied to responses on the PSE provide information on motive and trait level competencies (Winter et al., in press).

The Learning Style Inventory

The Learning Style Inventory was developed by Kolb (1971, 1976). Reliability and validity of the instrument have been shown (Kolb, 1976). It is a self-descriptive inventory, which assesses a person's orientation to the environment in terms of a preferred learning style; that is, it distinguishes the way in which a person interprets aspects of the environment and recodes and encodes information for future use in other situations and events. Owing to the form of the Learning Style Inventory (a self-descriptive, adjective checklist), results from it can be considered assessment of aspects of a person's self-image.

A person's style is assessed on four dimensions: concrete experience; reflective observation; abstract conceptualization; and active experimentation. Concrete experience is an orientation to current events in which the person is an active participant. Reflective observation is an orientation to reviewing the events of the recent or distant past. Abstract conceptualization is an orientation to theoretical, written, or abstract material. Active experimentation is an orientation to a trial-and-error method of learning. A person scoring high on the concrete experience and reflective observation dimensions appears to learn through an iconic-imaging process, referred to as a divergent style (Kolb, 1971). A person scoring high in the abstract conceptualization and active experimentation dimensions appears to learn through a deductive-reasoning process, referred to as a convergent style (Kolb, 1971).

Levels of Competencies Assessed

Each of these test variables assessed the motive, trait, or self-image level of particular competencies. The operational hypotheses were that superior and/or average managers would demonstrate higher scores on these variables than poor managers.

The available data offered comparisons of managers in each of the performance groups: poor, average, and superior. Managers in the public sector were compared with managers in the private sector. Managers in entry level, middle level, and executive level jobs were compared. In the case of the public sector, private sector, entry level, middle level, and executive level managers, managers in each performance group were compared with managers in other performance groups. Managers in marketing, manufacturing, and finance functions were compared. Sample sizes permitted performance-group comparisons within marketing and manufacturing functions only.

A NOTE ON STATISTICAL METHODS

Statistical methods are an aid to understanding and interpreting data. The methods utilized should be appropriate to the type of data and the objectives of the research. There were two specific objectives of this study, as mentioned in Chapter 1. To address each of these objectives, certain statistical methods were considered appropriate and others were considered inappropriate.

The Relationship Between Competency and Performance

The first objective of the study was to explain differences in general qualitative distinctions of performance (i.e., poor, average, and superior performance) of managers in a variety of jobs and organizations. The first statistical method applied was a one-way analysis of variance with a trend analysis. This method was applied to the overall performance groupings for each competency. If a significant relationship was found at this level, then it was important to discover the relative impact of performance-group differences for managers within various sectors, managerial levels, and, if possible, functions. In addition, occasionally an overall relationship between a competency and performance was not significant but a significant relationsip was discovered in a sector or at a particular managerial level. Such findings are reported with appropriate caution in the text.

It was important to obtain refined distinctions as to which performance groups were differentiated for each competency. As a result of this conceptual need and the unequal cell sizes within some of the comparisons, it was decided to use t-tests for the detail analyses. When possible, t-tests were applied to poor versus average, poor versus superior, and average versus superior performance-group comparisons. Correction factors were included in these analyses to adjust for unequal cell sizes. Since hypotheses predicted a specific direction of such results, one-tailed tests of statistical significance were utilized on these t-tests. In addition, t-tests, with the correction for unequal cell sizes, were computed for comparisons of sector, managerial level, and managerial function. Since no hypotheses were made concerning the direction of these results, two-tailed tests of statistical significance were utilized on these t-tests.

Other statistical methods, such as correlations, were not used for the analyses on each competency, for two basic reasons. First, the objective was to examine performance-group distinctions as to each competency, not to predict, or account for, a maximum amount of the variance in the performance measure. If the latter were the objective, it has been explained (in Chapter 2) that a study of managerial competence across various management jobs and organizations would not be conducted. Since job-specific and organization-specific characteristics are critical with respect to the utility and effectiveness of competencies, it was expected that competencies in common to managers in general would not account for a great deal of the variance in performance measures. Second, there was a desire to determine specific relationships, such as: Does the competency distinguish superior from average and/or poor performers? Does the competency distinguish superior and average performers from poor performers? Each of these distinctions has different meanings and implications for understanding managerial competence. Many statistical methods, such as correlations, would not allow for such comparisons and distinctions.

The Impact of Competencies on Other Competencies

A second objective of this study was to examine the impact of competencies on other competencies. This calls for a multivariate statistical method. The objective of this portion of the study was not to determine the joint impact of the competencies on the performance measure. Therefore, certain multivariate methods—such as multivariate analysis of variance, discriminant function analysis, and multiple regression—were not appropriate. In addition, multiple regression is most useful when the independent variables are assumed to have unique or separate impact on the dependent variable. This is clearly not the case with this study. It is assumed that the competencies affect one another and operate in context with one another so as to result in performance as a manager.

Factor analysis was determined to be inappropriate for several reasons. First, the factor-analysis method utilizes the fewest number of underlying grouping principles (Anderberg, 1973). In this study it was likely that relationship to the performance measure was a basic underlying principle in the data. Groups emerging from such analysis would be too broad for precise interpretation. Second, choosing a method for rotation of the factors would presuppose a structure of the grouping of competencies. Although a variety of rotation methods are available, an orthogonal rotation would certainly not be appropriate, because such a relationship among the competencies was neither predicted nor expected.

Cluster analysis was chosen as most appropriate for the information in this study and the objectives. Cluster analysis provided the opportunity for successively splitting the characteristics into sets of components within which characteristics relate more to one another than to characteristics in other components. To obtain the cluster, a maximum-split algorithm called CONCOR was used (Breiger et al., 1975). Once the cluster analysis yielded the most elemental components, or grouping (which occurred after three iterations), raw scores for each of the competencies were converted separately into standard scores for each competency. The sum of the standard scores for the competencies within each cluster was computed as a cluster score. With this conversion, the relationships among the clusters could be examined. Five distinct clusters resulted from the analysis and are reported in Chapters 4–10.

Although predicting or accounting for the maximum variance in the performance measure was not an objective of this study, it would be difficult to interpret several aspects of the data without examination of the joint impact of the competencies on managerial performance. Two such analyses are reported in Chapters 10 and 11. Since the performance measure was ordinal, it was decided that discriminant function analysis was the most appropriate method for these analyses. These analyses are supplementary to the objectives of the study and therefore have utility distinct from the cluster analysis.

A Note on Statistical Significance

There are various sections in this study in which a test of statistical significance is relevant. In particular, it is relevant in the examination of each competency and its relationship to managerial performance overall, within each sector, within each managerial level, and within each function, when available data permitted such analyses. It is also relevant in examining how the competency may be differentially evident in managers from each sector, each managerial level, and each function. The former relationships have been predicted in terms of the operational hypotheses; the latter have not.

Throughout the text, when a test of statistical significance is used, a finding labeled significant is one that satisfied the commonly accepted level of .05. In addition, when findings satisfied the commonly accepted degree of near significance, which is .055–.10, it has been so indicated. "Near significant" findings should be considered suggestive and not as substantial as "significant" findings. Given the nature of the aggregate sample and the somewhat arbitrary nature of these cutoffs in determining significance and near significance, it was decided to report both types of findings.

Many tests of statistical significance are reported in this study. Although the nonresearch-oriented reader will find these cumbersome, the research-oriented reader may feel that some "significant" findings are bound to emerge when so many relationships are tested. For this reader it should be pointed out that of all possible relationships tested and reported in Chapters 4–8, 40 percent were statistically significant or near significant. Examination of the overall relationships to managerial effectiveness (see Appendix A) indicated that 58 percent of the relationships tested were significant or near significant in the predicted direction, and only 5 percent were significant or near significant in a direction opposite to that predicted.

CHAPTER FOUR

The Goal and Action Management Cluster

At the core of every manager's job is the requirement to make things happen toward a goal or consistent with a plan. Whether in terms of making profits, staying within budget, or producing to deadline, there are many forms of the "bottom line" to which managers attempt to move their organizations. Although the demands may vary among specific management jobs and their organizational context, most managers are required to establish goals and plans of action, determine what and how people and other resources should be used, and solve problems to keep the organization functioning. To do this they must assume certain risks, have a clear image of the desired outcome, and understand when and how to take initiative. What is it about certain managers that enables them to respond effectively to these demands?

The first image that often comes to mind about such a person is the entrepreneur, the "shaker and mover" who can start with a hamburger stand and build it into a worldwide network of fast food shops whose corporate symbol is more easily identified than the Seven Wonders of the World. This image of a person who starts with few resources, struggles to the top, and is a success is one type of entrepreneur. Another type starts with an idea, gets new things going, and breathes new life into a sleeping giant conglomerate. Whichever of these or the many other types of images of effective managers you may have, he or she must be able to make things happen toward a goal or consistent with a plan. This entrepreneurial requirement of management jobs must be addressed by any person hoping or attempting to be a competent manager.

Four underlying characteristics that enable a manager to respond to the entrepreneurial requirement described above were identified through the cluster analysis of the managers in this study. They were labeled the *goal and action management cluster*. The four competencies are: (1) efficiency orientation; (2) proactivity; (3) diagnostic use of concepts; and (4) concern with impact. Managers with these competencies will view themselves as players in a game (Maccoby, 1976) and see the organization as a player in a larger game. The present and future will be seen as a series of challenges and problems to be solved. Events in life are viewed as opportunities to test themselves, accomplish something, or take risks. Such managers have a sense of where they and the organization are heading. They assume certain risks and look for evidence of their progress. Concern for the "bottom line" (i.e., a concern for outcomes or results and return on investment) is a focus. Possession of these competencies is similar to: a manager's emphasis on production as described by Stogdill (1974); a manager's bias toward action (*Business Week*, 1980); and behavior demonstrated by managers with organization and planning skills and decision-making skills as described by Bray et al. (1974).

Managers in a manufacturing operation, when presented with a product modification idea from a subordinate, may react in different ways, depending on their outlook. Managers with these competencies will begin to think about how this product modification may result in the product's being "better"; that is, serving the customer's needs more effectively. They may begin to think about a new product being developed and the potential marketing opportunities this will provide. Additional sales that could be generated will come to mind. If the product is not new, managers may begin to think about cost savings or increased profitability, which can result from the product modification.

In contrast, manufacturing managers without these competencies may initially react with concern about interrupting the production process. They may think about the time lost in exploring the feasibility of the product modification, or in attempting to explain it to the manufacturing engineers, marketing personnel, or upper management. If the current product design and manufacturing processes are functioning smoothly and efficiently, these managers may see the modification as a potential threat to operations and not worth the risk of exploring.

To explore the evidence linking the goal and action management cluster of competencies to effective management, an explanation, examples, empirical results, and interpretation will be presented on each of the four competencies in the cluster separately. A summary of the findings for the competencies in this cluster concludes the chapter.

EFFICIENCY ORIENTATION

Efficiency orientation represents a concern with doing something better. This may mean someone is doing it better than he or she did it previously; better than it has been done before by anyone else; or better in terms of increased performance according to a standard of excellence. At the motive level, efficiency orientation is the *n* Achievement (McClelland et al., 1953; McClelland, 1961). The motive occurs in conscious or unconscious thought as images of performing against a standard of excellence or accomplishing something uniquely (i.e., as it has never been done previously). The person sees himself or herself as someone who can do things better and who is efficient. In social or organizational contexts, the person adopts a role of being an innovator. The person demonstrates skills in goal setting, planning, and organizing resources efficiently.

People who possess efficiency orientation tend to think and act in particular ways. They set goals or deadlines that are challenging but realistic; that is, the goals are within the range of feasible accomplishment but require effort. These goals would be considered moderate risk goals or outcome statements. They may take the form of precise agendas for meetings (Kotter, 1982). In either case, the goal is a bench mark or evidence of accomplishment.

These people express concerns about doing something better than it has been done previously. They may state this in terms of progress on an explicit standard of excellence, or a unique accomplishment. Such people are able to describe clearly their personal standard of excellence for a particular activity or performance on a task. They have "inner work standards" and a "need for advancement" (Bray et al., 1974).

People who possess efficiency orientation write or describe plans for accomplishing tasks or achieving goals. The plans include identification of specific actions to be taken, resources needed, and potential obstacles which may be encountered. They organize resources (e.g., time, personnel, or finances) in such a manner as to accomplish the task or reach the goal efficiently and effectively. These people emphasize efficiency in the use of resources. They speak of relative returns on investments or relative results from allocation of resources.

Marketing managers who possess efficiency orientation think of market penetration in terms of a specific desired increase of market share. Sales managers with efficiency orientation identify a specific sales target. Neither merely thinks of an increase in market share or sales without stating it in terms of a specific, measurable standard. Manufacturing managers with this characteristic think of a specific increase in waste reduction or a specific decrease in the production time per unit produced.

The following examples from managers in the sample illustrate the demonstration of efficiency orientation in their jobs.

> Our letter of credit was close to running out. So if it had expired before we had shipped our goods, we'd have to wait for another letter of credit before we could make our shipment. So I sat down with the production manager in operations and went through the requirement and emphasized the criticality of the order. He set aside some of his work in order to be able to handle my request in a more timely fashion. And I said the same to engineering. We actually made it the day that the letter of credit ran out, by the skin of our teeth.

> One of our competitors was making a short, half-inch component and probably making $30,000–$40,000 a year on it. I looked at our line: we have the same product and we can probably make it better and cheaper. I told our marketing managers: "Let's go after that business." I made the decision that we would look at it as a marketplace rather than looking at it as individual customers wanting individual quantities. I said, here's a market that has 30,000 pieces of these things, and we don't give a damn where we get the orders. Let's just go out and get them. We decided we were going to charge a specific price and get the business. Right now we make $30,000–$40,000 on these things and our competitor makes zero.

> I was asked by the vice president to help him replace the general manager of one of our product lines. I told the VP that he, the VP of Personnel, and myself should sit down and determine what kind of person we wanted. They asked me to prepare questions to ask. All of us then interviewed each of the six candidates. After the interviews, the three of us sat down with our notes. I was pleased at three outcomes: (1) the questions did seem to surface the data that the VP wanted; (2) both VP's used the questions that I wrote as guidelines; and (3) I was pleased with the final decision. It was the first general manager that the VP had ever selected. My boss, the VP of Personnel, said that this was the first really professional selection he had ever seen.

Results at the Skill Level

At the skill level, efficiency orientation (referred to as EO) as coded in the interviews is significantly related to effective managerial performance ($F = 4.48$, $df = 2$, $p < .01$), with a significant linear trend ($F = 8.125$, $df = 1$, $p < .005$) favoring those considered superior. Comparison of the groups, shown in Figures 4-1 and 4-2 (see Appendix A for means, sample sizes, and specific levels of significance), with t-tests indicated that:

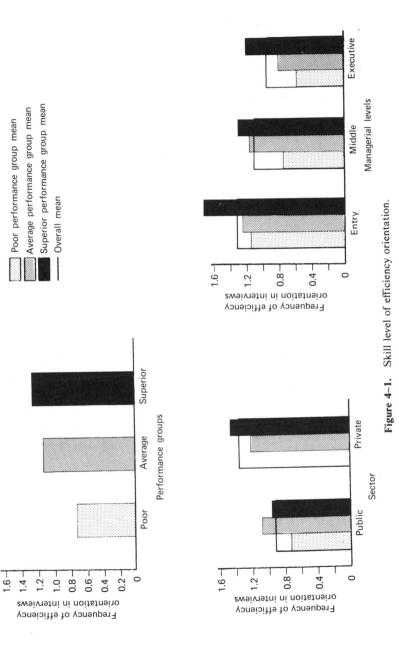

Figure 4-1. Skill level of efficiency orientation.

64

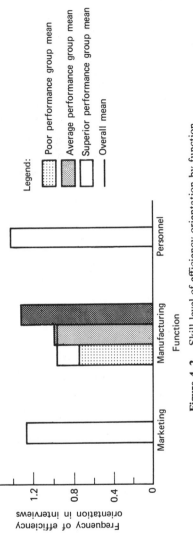

Figure 4-2. Skill level of efficiency orientation by function.

1. Superior and average managers demonstrated significantly more EO than did poor managers.

2. Private sector managers demonstrated significantly more EO than did public sector managers.

3. Among public sector managers, average performers demonstrated more EO than did poor performers at a near significant level.

4. Entry level managers demonstrated more EO than did executive level managers at a near significant level.

5. Among middle level managers, superior and average performers demonstrated significantly more EO than did poor performers.

6. Among executive level managers, superior performers demonstrated significantly more EO than did poor performers, and more EO than did average performers at a near significant level.

7. Managers in manufacturing functions demonstrated significantly less EO than did managers in personnel, and less EO than did marketing managers at a near significant level.

8. Among manufacturing managers, superior performers demonstrated significantly more EO than did poor performers.

Results at the Motive Level

At the motive level, efficiency orientation was assessed by the achievement motive score (referred to as n Ach or Achievement) from the Picture Story Exercise. Comparison of the groups, shown in Figures 4-3 and 4-4 (see Appendix A for means, sample sizes, and specific significance levels), with t-tests indicated that:

1. Superior managers had significantly higher n Ach than did average managers.

2. Public sector managers had significantly higher n Ach than did private sector managers.

3. Among public sector managers, superior performers had higher n Ach than did poor performers at a near significant level, and superior and poor performers had significantly higher n Ach than did average performers.

4. Among private sector managers, superior performers had significantly higher n Ach than did average performers.

5. Executive level managers had significantly higher n Ach than did

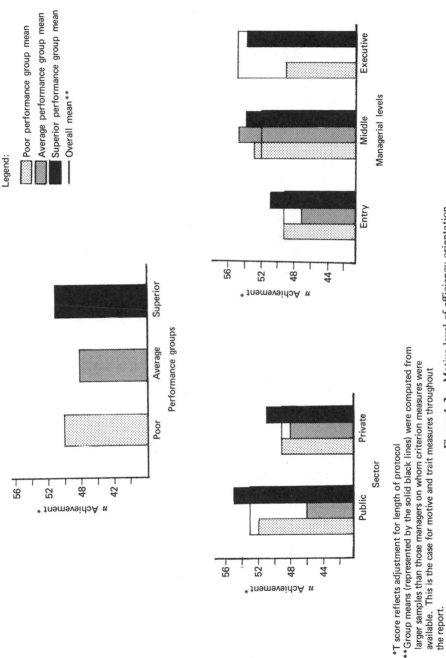

Legend:

Poor performance group mean
Average performance group mean
Superior performance group mean
Overall mean**

*T score reflects adjustment for length of protocol
**Group means (represented by the solid black lines) were computed from larger samples than those managers on whom criterion measures were available. This is the case for motive and trait measures throughout the report.

Figure 4–3. Motive level of efficiency orientation.

67

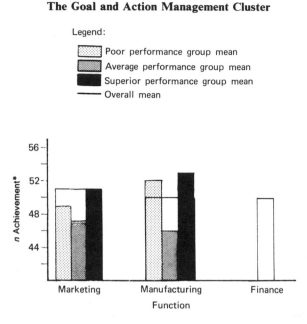

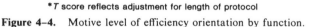

*T score reflects adjustment for length of protocol

Figure 4–4. Motive level of efficiency orientation by function.

middle and entry level managers, and middle level managers had significantly higher *n* Ach than did entry level managers.

6. Among entry level managers, superior performers had significantly higher *n* Ach than did average performers.

7. Among executive level managers, superior performers had significantly higher *n* Ach than did poor performers.

8. Among marketing managers, superior performers had significantly higher *n* Ach than did poor performers, poor performers had significantly higher *n* Ach than did average performers.

9. Among manufacturing managers, superior and poor performers had significantly higher *n* Ach than did average performers.

Results at the Social-Role Level

In all of the seven studies of managers' perceptions, items relating to efficiency orientation were listed as required for performance as a manager. In five of the studies, managers perceived these items as characteristics that distinguished superior performance as a manager. This included items such as: "ability to set realistic goals," "ability to effectively organize one's time," "ability to think in terms of results," and "ability to prioritize."

Interpretation

At the skill level, at the motive level, and in terms of managers' perceptions of their role, efficiency orientation appears related to superior performance as a manager. Managers in the private sector appear to demonstrate more efficiency orientation at the skill level than do managers in the public sector. This is understandable in that private sector managers have access to and usually are provided with information on various specific measures of performance. They can obtain information about personal performance as well as organizational performance on specific outcomes more easily than can managers in the public sector. This may be not only a function of different types of work performed by public and private sector organizations, but also a result of a self-selection by managers as to the type of organization in which they would like to work. Whether self-selection is a dominant factor or not, measures of productivity and efficiency are substantially easier to obtain in private sector organizations than in public sector organizations. People with efficiency orientation are frustrated working in an organization in which they cannot assess performance against an explicit standard of excellence. They also need identifiable outcomes from organizational or individual action to be able to establish goals, assess efficiency and return on investment, and document whether or not they are doing better than previously.

In the private sector, measures of performance are available in every aspect of organizational functioning. Marketing managers can assess market share; manufacturing managers can assess productivity as a function of costs and waste; personnel managers can assess effectiveness in terms of personnel turnover, number of days lost to strikes, and so forth. In the public sector, analogous measures are difficult and sometimes impossible to obtain. For example, how can a manager of an agency in the executive branch assess his or her effectiveness? If he or she is in a group that contracts out research, program design, or program implementation projects, acceptability of the projects by constituents in the public may be a measure of effectiveness. Is it a measure of the effectiveness of the manager or the quality of the project developed by the contractor? One performance measure might be the passage of legislation related to new government regulations. Would this be a measure of a manager's performance, a measure of the partisan composition of Congress at the time, or the potency of a special interest lobby? In any case, even if the information were a performance measure for the manager of a branch of a government agency, it would take a year and often several years before the performance could be assessed. Although any government operation has organizational units that can assess the organizational unit's performance, and therefore managers can assess their own performance against some easily measurable standard, such units are relatively few. For example, the Government Printing Office can measure the efficiency with which it produces a pamphlet or report.

The reverse of this relationship was found at the motive level; public sector managers had higher motive levels of efficiency orientation than did private sector managers. This suggests that if a self-selection process occurs based on their efficiency orientation competency, possessing a high degree of the motive level of the competency favors the public sector. A likely interpretation of this dynamic is that the public sector offers a person a relatively stable and secure career path. This is particularly relevant to people who are upwardly mobile and are concerned with moving into a socioeconomic status that is greater than that of their parents. Long-term career orientation is characteristic of people with a high motive level of efficiency orientation (i.e., high n Ach). Once in public sector managerial jobs, they may find the opportunities for demonstrating efficiency orientation and reaping the rewards of such behavior are not prominent. If this occurred, it would be expected that they would develop a number of activities outside the job to satisfy their motive level of efficiency orientation.

Results at the skill and motive level indicated that superior performers at entry, middle, and executive levels of management had more efficiency orientation than did either average or poor performers at these managerial levels. Although executive managers had higher levels of the motive level of efficiency orientation than did middle or entry level managers, almost the opposite seems to be the case regarding the skill level of efficiency orientation. This difference may be a result of varying job demands. As managers move from entry to middle management to executive management, they usually have decreasing access to measures of individual performance and increasingly must rely on measures of organizational performance, such as profitability of a division or an entire company. These measures of organizational performance do not yield comparisons against a standard of excellence or goals as rapidly as do comparable measures at lower levels of management.

Production supervisors receive daily, if not hourly, information on the performance of their organizational unit. Middle level sales or marketing managers may get weekly information on performance, while branch or retail-store sales managers have access to daily performance information. The time frame of performance information and the ease of associating measures of performance with specific individual actions both contribute to executives' ability to spend less of their time and focus on assessing individual performance to goals, and more of their time and focus on many other aspects of organizational functioning. Therefore, while executives may have a higher motive level of efficiency orientation, they cannot demonstrate the skills as frequently each day or each week as do middle or entry level managers.

With regard to functional differences in efficiency orientation, the most important observation appears to be that superior performers within manufacturing functions have higher motive levels of efficiency orientation and demonstrate more frequently the skill level in efficiency orientation than do poor performers. The indication that managers in manufacturing functions demonstrate less efficiency orientation at the skill level than do managers of marketing or personnel functions may be less relevant than the difference among performance groups of manufacturing managers. This difference among functions may be a reflection of the fact that some manufacturing managers may have less control over performance standards and goals than do managers of other functions. Managers at higher levels in the organization may determine these goals or standards of performance.

PROACTIVITY

Proactivity is a new word originally used to describe the opposite to someone who is reactive or who guards the status quo (Zaleznick, 1966). Proactivity represents a disposition toward taking action to accomplish something. This usually means that proactive people instigate an activity for some purpose. At the trait level, proactivity is people's sense of efficacy (Stewart & Winter, 1974; White, 1963; deCharms, 1968; Rotter, 1966; Boyatzis, 1969). A sense of efficacy is the disposition to see oneself as the originator of actions in one's life. People with a sense of efficacy view events in life as opportunities for taking action and see themselves as the agents who must precipitate such action. Rotter (1966) labeled this trait "internal control of reinforcement." DeCharms (1968) defined the disposition as people's orientation toward seeing themselves as "origins," or masters of their life, in contrast to people who view themselves as "pawns," at the mercy of luck or fate. The various concepts and labels appear to describe a characteristic that White (1963) termed people's sense of efficacy (Boyatzis, 1969). These people perceive themselves to be in control of their lives, and therefore responsible for taking action if there is a desire for events to unfold in a certain direction or manner. In social or organizational contexts, such people adopt a role of being an initiator. They demonstrate skills in problem solving and information seeking.

Proactive people tend to behave and speak in particular ways. They initiate action, communication, proposals, meetings, or directives to accomplish a task (Maccoby, 1976; Zaleznick, 1966). They take the first step in what is seen as a sequence of activities rather than wait for something to happen or for a situation to develop. If an obstacle to task accomplishment is encountered or even anticipated, they take multiple steps to circumvent the obstacle. Whether solving a problem or merely investigating an issue, such people seek information from a wide variety of sources. Identifying these sources and gaining access to them is usually the result of actions taken by such people. This can be contrasted with people who obtain needed or useful information, but only when other people provide it. Proactive individuals accept and readily admit their personal responsibility for successes or failures in task accomplishment or problem solving.

Proactive marketing managers do not wait for the research and development unit to present a product idea. They actively search the environment and marketplace for "needs" that can be translated into product ideas. Proactive personnel managers periodically interview or survey employees to ascertain the employees' perspective on certain issues and solicit recommendations for program or policy improvements. They may wait for someone else to identify a solution to an interpersonal conflict that emerges among staff members, but inquire about the conflict and instigate actions that could begin a conflict resolution process. Proactive financial managers who discover an increase in an expense item, as compared to budget expectations, contact managers in the organizational unit involved to find out what might be causing the increase in expenses. Financial managers with low proactivity may complete their financial reports and only address the issue of the increased expense item if their supervisor or an operating manager raises the issue and asks for an interpretation.

The following examples from managers in the sample illustrate the demonstration of proactivity in their jobs.

When I began my job, I interviewed about 80 people, asking them how they could use the training and development function. I talked to one supervisor who mentioned an employee that she would soon be giving a performance review. The employee was a Level 2 and wanted to be a Level

4. The supervisor felt that they were not communicating and that the employee wasn't showing initiative. My part in the conversation was to get the supervisor to see the problem. I asked a few questions and waited for her responses. She finally said, "Maybe you or one of your staff can help me. Can you or someone in your group talk with me?" I assigned one of my staff to the problem, and it worked out well in both the supervisor's and the employee's eyes.

I called the Chief, and he said he couldn't commit the resources, so I called the budget and finance people, who gave me a negative response. But then I called a guy in another work group who said he was willing to make a trade for the parts I needed. I got the parts and my group was able to complete the repairs.

Signal Corp. was in a jam two weeks ago. The purchasing manager of Signal called me and indicated that they had $1 million worth of electronic components sitting on their production line but no strips of an alloy that we produce. When we went through it, we both discovered to our mutual surprise that they had forgotten to order the alloy strips. On their side it had looked like they had ordered them, but they hadn't and somebody on my sales force must be sleeping. So I went scrambling around. I got my production people together to get a readout on what material was available. There was everything but this alloy. It also turned out there would be between an eight- and ten-week delivery. So I walked over to Building 2 and talked to the engineering manager. We went through all the cabinets. We were able to find enough bits and pieces of the stuff to deliver 100 pieces to Signal within three days.

Results at the Skill Level

Provactivity (referred to as P) at the skill level, as coded in the interviews, was significantly related to effective managerial performance ($F = 5.287$, df = 2, $p < .005$), with a significant linear trend ($F = 9.764$, df = 1, $p < .002$) favoring those considered superior. Comparison of the groups, shown in Figures 4-5 and 4-6 (see Appendix A for detail), with t-tests indicated that:

1. Superior managers demonstrated significantly more P than did average and poor managers.
2. Private sector managers demonstrated significantly more P than did public sector managers.
3. Among public sector managers, superior performers demonstrated more P than did average and poor performers.
4. Among entry level managers, average performers demonstrated significantly more P than did superior and poor performers.

Legend:

Poor performance group mean
Average performance group mean
Superior performance group mean
Overall mean

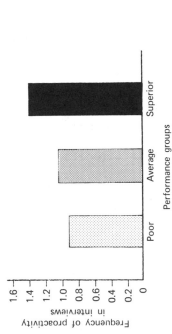

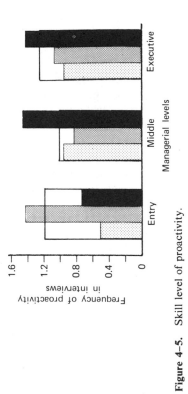

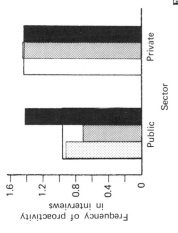

Figure 4–5. Skill level of proactivity.

74

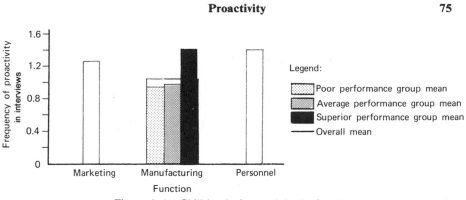

Figure 4–6. Skill level of proactivity by function.

5. Among middle level managers, superior performers demonstrated significantly more P than did average and poor performers.

6. Among executive level managers, superior performers demonstrated significantly more P than did poor performers.

7. Personnel managers demonstrated significantly more P than did manufacturing managers.

8. Among manufacturing managers, superior performers demonstrated significantly more P than did average and poor performers.

Results at the Trait Level

At the trait level, proactivity was assessed by the Self-Definition score (referred to as SDEF) from the Picture Story Exercise. It was significantly related to managerial performance, but in a curvilinear manner. Comparison of the groups, shown in Figures 4-7 and 4-8 (see Appendix A for detail), with *t*-tests indicated that:

1. Superior and poor managers had significantly higher SDEF than did average managers.

2. Public sector managers had significantly higher SDEF than did private sector managers.

3. Among public sector managers, superior and poor performers had higher SDEF than did average performers at near significant levels.

4. Among private sector managers, superior and poor performers had significantly higher SDEF than did average performers.

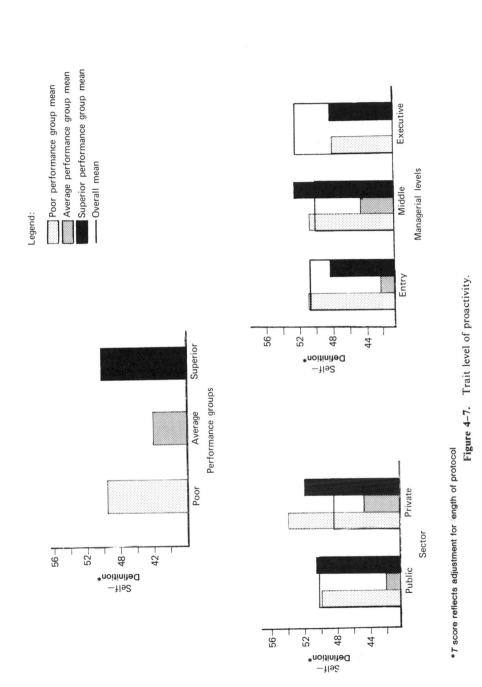

Figure 4–7. Trait level of proactivity.

*T score reflects adjustment for length of protocol

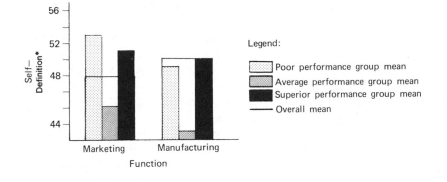

*T score reflects adjustment for length of protocol

Figure 4–8. Trait level of proactivity by function.

5. Among middle level managers, superior and poor performers had significantly higher SDEF than did average performers.
6. Manufacturing managers had significantly higher SDEF than did marketing managers.
7. Among marketing managers, superior and poor performers had significantly higher SDEF than did average performers.
8. Among manufacturing managers, superior and poor performers had higher SDEF than did average managers at near significant levels.

Results at the Social-Role Level

In six of the seven studies of managers' perceptions, items relating to proactivity were listed as required for performance as a manager. In all six, managers perceived these items as characteristics that distinguished superior performance as a manager. This included items such as: "ability to cut through bureaucratic red tape," "initiating action," "getting support and services from outside the unit," and "initiating change, acting as a catalyst."

Interpretation

At the skill level and in terms of managers' role perceptions, proactivity is related to superior performance as a manager. At the trait level, proactivity also is related to superior performance as a manager, but is complicated by a curvilinear relationship in which superior and poor performers appear to have similiar high levels of this trait. The finding at the trait level may suggest that certain poor managers with this trait take initiative and instigate activity so often that it may be inappropriate at times. They might be doing it in such a manner as to violate organizational norms and/or precipitate reduced organizational performance. In such cases, those managers have high Self-Definition, but are relatively poor performers as managers. It is also possible that these poorly performing managers are taking initiative and solving problems that they should be allowing their subordinates to solve. They may be so oriented to taking initiative that they interfere with their subordinates' being able to take initiative, and therefore doing their jobs effectively. Managers with a high degree of the trait level of proactivity may respond counterdependently to situations that are troublesome; that is, they may perceive a supervisor's actions as causing a problem for them. In such a situation, the managers may initiate actions to circumvent their boss. This also could result in relatively poor performance ratings.

For example, one of the managers in the sample was the vice president of marketing for a large consumer products organization. He discovered that one of the sales representatives was having difficulty closing a large national account. The vice president had a high degree of Self-Definition. He called and arranged a meeting with an executive he knew from past marketing presentations at the company that held the large national account. Then he called the sales representative with instructions to meet him at this executive's office. As a result of the meeting, the consumer products organization got the account. Another result was that the sales representative felt humiliated in front of his client. The day after this meeting, the regional sales manager and his boss, the national sales manager, wrote angry memos to the vice president. They claimed he had interfered with their jobs by passing two layers of management in his action. This type of event occurred periodically for two years until the president decided that the vice president's style of handling problems and not the economy was contributing to the company's lack of growth in sales volume. The vice president was to take a regional sales job or leave the company. He took the regional sales job and has been doing well. While proactivity is related to effective managerial performance, there can be situations in which having a high degree at the trait level can lead to actions that are dysfunctional for the organization.

Differences between managers in the public and private sectors are revealed. Managers in the private sector appear to demonstrate more proactivity at the skill level. The discussion regarding efficiency orientation and the private versus the public sector applies here as well. Private sector managers may have more opportunities to solve problems and take initiatives which lead to change. Similar to the case of efficiency orientation, managers in the public sector appear to have more of the trait level of proactivity than do managers in the private sector. When this is examined in the context of the significantly greater amount of demonstrated proactivity skills by superior managers in the public sector, a different conclusion is reached from the case of efficiency orientation. The public sector does provide opportunities for managers to take initiative and solve problems.

Functional differences in proactivity appear similiar to those found with efficiency orientation. Although personnel managers demonstrate more proactivity at the skill level, the superior manufacturing managers demonstrate more proactivity than do average or poor manufaturing managers. It also appears that manufacturing managers have somewhat higher trait levels of proactivity than do marketing managers. This may suggest that manufacturing managers, although having the trait level of proactivity, have relatively fewer requirements and opportunities for demonstrating proactivity at the skill level than do managers of other functions.

DIAGNOSTIC USE OF CONCEPTS

Diagnostic use of concepts is a way of thinking in which the person identifies or recognizes patterns from an assortment of information, by bringing a concept to the situation and attempting to interpret events through that concept; that is, the person has a framework or concept of how an event should transpire. In contrast to other ways of thinking, diagnostic use of concepts is a way of thinking in which people "test" the information by systematically applying it to the concept. This can be termed deductive thinking. The self-image of people with this characteristic is that of being deductive and analytic. In an organization or social group context, they adopt the role of scientist, and others see them as trying to "figure things out" or analyze various situations. Such people demonstrate the skill of pattern identification through concept application.

People who use diagnostic use of concepts tend to behave and speak in particular ways. As with certain competencies, the manifestations of diagnostic use of concepts are not obvious in terms of people's behavior, and the thought processes people use must be deduced from their various actions. People with this characteristic usually have a model, theory, or framework with which to interpret or explain events. They might use this competency in finding a job and organization that "fits" or is appropriate for them (Kotter, 1982). For example, they might identify an argument between a corporate personnel manager and a divisional personnel manager as evidence of a "line-staff conflict." These people can recognize patterns and interpret aspects of the situation by applying information from the specific event to an organizational model that they have. In this example, they have a concept of line and staff conflicts in organizations.

If these people do not have a concept that is relevant to a particular situation, they quickly will attempt to find one. They do not try to find a relevant concept by examining the information (which is the approach a person who uses a different competency would take); rather, they seek source material to provide the concept. In a learning or educational setting, such people often demand a "road map" at the beginning of the experience, claiming that they cannot adequately appreciate the elements of the experience without understanding the overall concept of what is being presented and why this particular material is being presented.

Frequently, people who can identify coalitions in an organization or group, recognize the informal influence network in an organization or community, or quickly identify a "leader," are demonstrating diagnostic use of concepts. They are applying a concept of interpersonal organizational influence and politics to the respective situation. Because people with this characteristic have a concept or framework for understanding how things occur, they can often distinguish relevant from irrelevant information in a particular situation, which may be evident as an ability to "perceive threshold cues" (Bray et al., 1974). For example, let us examine the personnel manager who has a model of the patterns of sick leave taken at various times of the year, which is a function of rapid changes in the climate. When there is an increase in sick leave during the month of October, he may not spend time bringing this to the attention of top management or surveying employees to identify sources of dissatisfaction; he would conclude that it represents an ordinary human response to the arrival of cold, damp, fall weather. On the other hand, if there is a dramatic increase in sick leave in August, or the high rate of sick leave observed in October continues throughout November, the personnel manager would hypothesize that some factor other than climate is the cause. It could be evidence of a decrease in morale, an organized attempt at work slowdown, or something that does deserve attention from and probably action by the organization's management.

The following examples from managers in the sample illustrate the demonstration of diagnostic use of concepts in their jobs.

> At the time it was first manufactured, it was made for about $200 a piece. At the time I had a couple of guys selling it for me and we decided that we wanted the price to come down to the thirties. If we could sell it for $30, the volume would go up. When I took over the division as manager, I said we need to go the next step—we need to come down to $20. We decided to get the cost down and not worry about orders. We lowered the cost and geared ourselves up to producing more. Now we're selling 2000 pieces a month.

> One of the managers was having trouble with a supervisor. I talked to each one of them. Then I asked the supervisor if he would be interested in a three-way meeting. He set up the meeting. I asked questions and restated things if I thought they weren't hearing what the other had said. In a situation that involves a boss and subordinate, I state the supervisor's issues more strongly because that's a lopsided set up. The supervisor was in the weaker position. They were able to work out a plan to cover each other's problems, and as far as I know the manager isn't having any more problems.

> I had a meeting this morning with Frank and his tube manufacturing manager about personnel replacements. We have a facility in New Hampshire that could be doing some of this work, with less expensive labor, so my job was to persuade them instead of replacing them, to send the work up to New Hampshire. So I said, "How do you think about increasing productivity? How do we meet our before-tax margin goal?" I suggested several ways to do this. You can increase the price of the product or decrease the cost of the payroll. Well, it made the point.

Results at the Skill Level

At the skill level, diagnostic use of concepts (referred to as DUC) as coded in the interviews was strongly related to effective managerial performance ($F = 11.472$, df $= 2$, $p < .0001$), with a highly significant linear trend toward superior performance ($F = 19.67$, df $= 1$, $p < .0001$). Comparison of the groups, shown in Figures 4-9 and 4-10 (see Appendix A for detail), with t-tests revealed that:

1. Superior and average managers demonstrated significantly more DUC than did poor managers

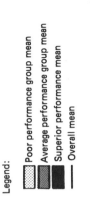

Legend:
Poor performance group mean
Average performance group mean
Superior performance mean
Overall mean

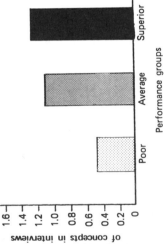

Frequency of diagnostic use
of concepts in interviews

Performance groups

Poor   Average   Superior

1.6 1.4 1.2 1.0 0.8 0.6 0.4 0.2 0

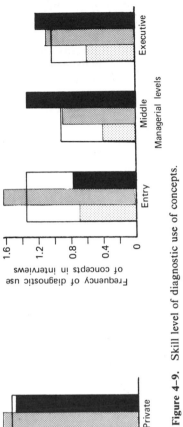

Frequency of diagnostic use
of concepts in interviews

Managerial levels

Entry   Middle   Executive

1.6 1.2 0.8 0.4 0

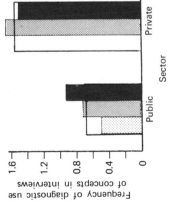

Frequency of diagnostic use
of concepts in interviews

Sector

Public   Private

1.6 1.2 0.8 0.4 0

Figure 4-9. Skill level of diagnostic use of concepts.

82

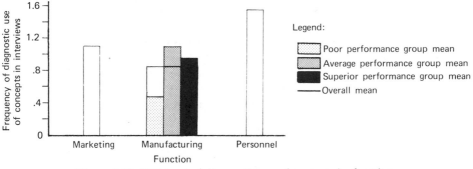

Figure 4-10. Skill level of diagnostic use of concepts by function.

2. Private sector managers demonstrated significantly more DUC than did public sector managers.

3. Among public sector managers, superior performers demonstrated significantly more DUC than did poor performers, and average performers demonstrated more DUC than did poor performers at a near significant level.

4. Entry level managers demonstrated significantly more DUC than did middle level managers and more than executive level managers did at a near significant level.

5. Among entry level managers, average performers demonstrated more DUC than did poor and superior performers at near significant levels.

6. Among middle level managers, superior performers demonstrated significantly more DUC than did average and poor performers, and average performers demonstrated significantly more DUC than did poor performers.

7. Among executive level managers, superior performers demonstrated significantly more DUC than did poor performers, and average performers demonstrated more DUC than did poor performers at a near significant level.

8. Personnel managers demonstrated significantly more DUC than did marketing and manufacturing managers, and marketing managers demonstrated more DUC than did manufacturing managers at a near significant level.

9. Among manufacturing managers, superior and average managers demonstrated significantly more DUC than did poor performers.

Results at the Self-Image Level

Diagnostic use of concepts was measured at the self-image level by the abstract conceptualization and active experimentation learning styles (Kolb, 1976). These styles involve people using models or frameworks to discover or explain events. The overall relationship between the abstract conceptualization and active experimentation learning styles and performance was not statistically significant (see Appendix A for detail). Since the sample on which these measures were obtained represented only middle level managers in the marketing function, no managerial level or function comparisons were possible. Differences between sectors on abstract conceptualization were not significant. Public sector managers showed significantly higher active experimentation than did managers in the private sector. Within the private sector, superior performers had higher active experimentation than did poor performers at a near significant level.

Results at the Social-Role Level

All seven studies of managers' perceptions listed items relating to diagnostic use of concepts as required for performance as a manager. Managers in six of the seven studies perceived these items as related to superior performance as a manager. This included items such as: "judgment as to when to act independently and when to refer situations to higher authority," "ability to separate the important from the unimportant aspects of a situation," and "ability to differentiate between real and apparent problems."

Interpretation

Diagnostic use of concepts appears related to effective performance in a management job. A number of different analyses showed that, at the skill level, it distinguishes superior managers from average managers, and superior and average managers from poor managers.

Although this characteristic appears relevant to effective management at all managerial levels, entry level managers demonstrate more of the skill than do middle or executive level managers. This could be a function of the relatively less diverse sources and types of information to which an entry level manager is exposed. With less diverse sources and types of information, the manager at the entry level can be more efficient and effective by having concepts, models, or frameworks in mind when approaching events. It also could be that whether the result of inexperience, youth, or less formal and specialized training in management, the entry level manager has not developed as broad a spectrum of experiences as have other levels of managers. Experienced middle and executive level managers often speak of the great difference between their past and present interpretations and understanding of events that occurred earlier in their careers, a difference resulting from what they have learned subsequently. The functional utility of certain concepts may diminish with time and experience—not because they are incorrect, but because they do not address the complex and variegated problems and issues faced in middle and executive level management positions. To the extent that diagnostic use of concepts is less functional at these levels, we would expect managers in middle and executive level jobs to demonstrate less of it.

A possible explanation for the greater demonstration of diagnostic use of concepts by private sector as compared with public sector managers may be an unintended consequence of policies, procedures, and structural arrangements within the public sector that were designed and implemented to serve other purposes, but which routinize what is to be thought and done. The observation that effective managers in the public sector utilize this competency more than do their less effective peers suggests that diagnostic use of concepts may be an important competency in effectively applying the standardized concepts that public sector managers are required to use.

The observation that manufacturing managers demonstrate less diagnostic use of concepts than do marketing or personnel managers could be a function of general job requirements. Manufacturing managers are exposed to less diverse types, and certainly to fewer sources, of information than are managers in the other functions examined. Nonetheless, in the context of maintaining manufacturing processes and procedures, superior performing manufacturing managers demonstrate more of the competency than do poor performers.

CONCERN WITH IMPACT

Concern with impact represents a concern with symbols of power to have impact on others. At the motive level, this is called the n Power (McClelland, 1975; Winter, 1973). People with this motive collect objects of prestige, become officers in organizations to which they belong, and act assertively (McClelland, 1975). These people see themselves as important. In social and organizational contexts, they adopt roles associated with a relatively high degree of status. They are interested in and good at influencing others.

People who have concern with impact behave in certain ways. Such people would dress in a fashion and style considered desirable and attractive in their surroundings. They are concerned about status and reputation, often to the point of worrying about having appropriate office furnishings and perquisites commensurate with their position in the organization. They often express concern about the prestige or reputation of the organization or products. Regardless of the issue, such people have a need to persuade or influence others.

An example of this was a marketing executive who had recently been promoted to vice president. It was his view that the consumer products company had for too many years defined itself in terms of manufacturing operations. He felt that marketing should be substantially more important to the company and act as a prime mover in corporate decision making as well as strategy. One of the first steps he took was to instruct several members of his staff to conduct audits of the research and development, manufacturing, personnel, and administrative groups in the company and compare their functioning to those of corresponding groups in their three main compeitors. He convinced the president that it would be valuable information for long-range planning.

It took several months and a considerable investment in consultants to obtain the needed information on the competitors and compare their functioning to that of their own company. The vice president first presented the information to the president, and then, with his support, to the other vice presidents. It was clear in his presentations that the operational involvement of a marketing perspective in R&D and manufacturing had helped two of their competitors increase market share and open up several new product lines. The presentation and information were convincing. Soon he was meeting regularly with the vice president of R&D to review various R&D projects and examine their potential impact on the business. This was now a monthly meeting, whercas previously it was at most an infrequent interaction. His bimonthly meeting with the vice president of manufacturing was focused on engineering modifications to existing products, modifications that could aid in promotional campaigns. The result was that the company's product line changed dramatically over two years and the company regained some of the market share it had lost.

Regardless of the effectiveness of these actions or the appropriateness of a marketing perspective having such importance in R&D and manufacturing, this manager moved himself into a more potent organizational position than had his predecessor. Not only the marketing perspective but his personal views were now an ongoing part of the functioning and direction of three of the components of the organization. The regularly scheduled meetings, with the particular agenda established, provided him with the symbolic power and opportunity to influence almost every aspect of the organization's functioning.

The following examples from managers in the sample also illustrate the demonstration of concern with impact in their jobs.

> We had submitted a bid on Thursday and knew that there was one other outfit in competition with us. The city manager, who was the client, had placed a call to me Monday morning when I was up north. I called him back and he said, "Herb, the contract was awarded to another company. As far as I'm concerned I had a deep appreciation of all the work you did but I am a one-man vote on a five-man board and I really think that there was some politics involved." At that point, I felt that I had begun a good relationship with the city manager so I said, "I gave you my best shot and I enjoyed working with you. If you ever have another job like this, I'll be glad to come back and work for you some more." I felt this was good PR work. He said that he appreciated that and hoped he could get back to me at some point. What do you know, the next day I get a call from him. Apparently the competition had bid on the basis of some specs that didn't conform to their need. He wanted to talk it over with me. The city manager wasn't sure that the proposed specs would do the job. It turned out that he was right, and we got the job.

> The present general manager, when he came in, gave me the quality control organization. This is relatively unique. They're usually either independent or part of another organization. I think it's very important that I have them under my wing. One of the things that I did was change the name from Quality Control to Quality Services. The image I wanted to create was that it's not just a policeman organization, but it provides technical input, too. But, only in an advisory capacity. So now we have an iron grip on tracking down quality complaints from customers and the production people don't get defensive right away.

Results at the Skill Level

At the skill level, concern with impact (referred to as CWI) as coded in the interviews was significantly related to effectiveness as a manager ($F = 4.983$, df $= 2$, $p = .008$), with a significant linear trend favoring superior managers ($F = 9.054$, df $= 1$, $p = .003$). Comparison of the groups with t-tests, shown in Figure 4-11 and 4-12 (see Appendix A for detail), indicated that:

Legend:

☐ Poor performance group mean
▨ Average performance group mean
■ Superior performance group mean
— Overall mean

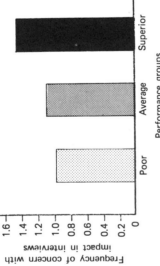

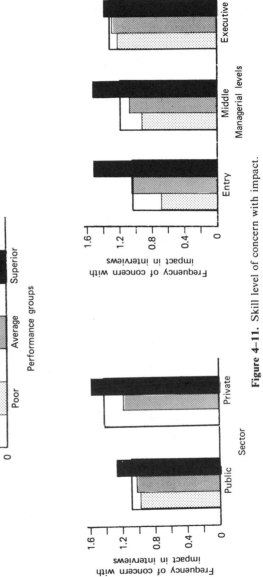

Figure 4-11. Skill level of concern with impact.

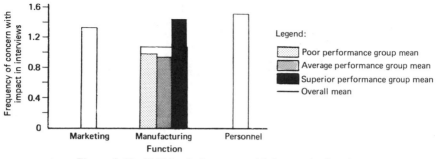

Figure 4–12. Skill level of concern with impact by function.

1. Superior managers demonstrated significantly more CWI than did average and poor managers.

2. Private sector managers demonstrated significantly more CWI than did public sector managers.

3. Among public sector managers, superior performers demonstrated more CWI than did poor performers at a near significant level.

4. Among private sector managers, superior performers demonstrated significantly more CWI than did average managers.

5. Executive level managers demonstrated more CWI than did entry level managers at a near significant level.

6. Among middle level managers, superior performers demonstrated significantly more CWI than did average and poor performers.

7. Personnel managers demonstrated significantly more CWI than did manufacturing managers, and marketing managers demonstrated more CWI than did manufacturing managers at a near significant level.

8. Among manufacturing managers, superior performers demonstrated significantly more CWI than did average and poor performers.

Results at the Motive Level

At the motive level, concern with impact was measured by the power motive (referred to as *n* Pow or *n* Power) from the Picture Story Exercise. Concern with impact was somewhat related to managerial effectiveness at the motive level. Comparison of the groups with *t*-tests, shown in Figures 4-13 and 4-14 (see Appendix A for detail), indicated that:

1. Superior and poor managers had significantly higher *n* Pow than did average managers.

2. Public sector managers had significantly higher *n* Pow than did private sector managers.

3. Among public sector managers, superior and poor performers had significantly higher *n* Pow than did average performers.

4. Among private sector managers, superior performers had higher *n* Pow than did average performers at a near significant level.

5. Executive and middle level managers had significantly higher *n* Pow than did entry level managers.

6. Among entry level managers, poor performers had significantly higher *n* Pow than did average performers, and superior performers had higher *n* Pow than did average performers at a near significant level.

7. Among executive level managers, superior performers had significantly higher *n* Pow than did average performers.

8. Manufacturing managers had significantly higher *n* Pow than did marketing and finance managers, and marketing managers had significantly higher *n* Pow than did finance managers.

9. Among marketing managers, average performers had significantly higher *n* Pow than did poor performers.

10. Among manufacturing managers, superior and poor performers had significantly higher *n* Pow than did average performers.

Results at the Social-Role Level

In one of the seven studies of managers' perceptions, items relating to concern for impact were listed as required for performance as a manager. In this one study, these items were perceived by managers as characteristics distinguishing superior performance as a manager. This included items such as: "persuasive," "ability to influence others," and "maintains the prestige of our products and the good name of the company."

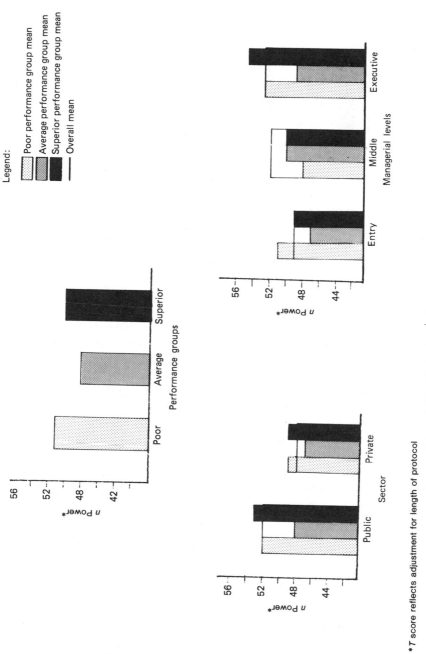

Figure 4–13. Motive level of concern with impact.

*T score reflects adjustment for length of protocol

91

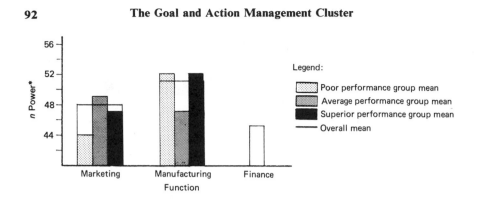

*T score reflects adjustment for length of protocol

Figure 4-14. Motive level of concern with impact by function.

Interpretation

Concern with impact appears related to effectiveness as a manager at both the skill and motive levels. Although poor managers appear to have this characteristic at the motive level, they do not express the skill level as frequently as do their more effective counterparts. This suggests that having both the motive (i.e., the disposition or orientation toward wanting to have impact) and the skills in symbolic influence behavior is needed to be effective as a manager. People might have the internal need for impact, but if they cannot translate this into behavior, it does not contribute to performance. If managers can translate the motive into behavior, or what is more likely, translate the need into appropriate behaviors, they can be effective.

Managers in the public sector have a higher motive level but demonstrate the skill less frequently than do managers in the private sector. This may be a function of the many checks and balances built into government organizations, and the fact that managers have less direct impact on direction and results of activities than do the legislature, judiciary, or appointed officials in the executive branch. Operating managers in such an organization must manage and lead their organizational units within the mandate and policy established by groups outside their immediate organization. Even though this was observed to happen, superior performers in both sectors express more of the skills and have higher levels of the motive as compared to their less effective counterparts.

In terms of managerial level, it appears that concern with impact is more relevant to executive and middle level managers than to entry level managers. Not only do managers at these higher levels have more of the "trappings" of power, but they are required to exercise power more frequently to perform their jobs than are entry level managers. As a manager moves up in the hierarchy, he or she must spend more time influencing others to do their jobs and less time performing the actual tasks that result in production or sales (Kotter, 1979).

Although superior manufacturing managers express more concern with impact at the skill level than do average or poor performers, manufacturing managers appear to demonstrate less of the skill level and have more of the motive level of this characteristic than do managers in other functions. This suggests that compared to marketing or personnel managers, manufacturing managers are required to demonstrate less symbolic influence behavior, but this behavior is nonetheless related to effectiveness as a manufacturing manager.

SUMMARY ON THE GOAL AND ACTION MANAGEMENT CLUSTER

Summary of Findings

The results indicated a strong relationship between the competencies in the goal and action management cluster and the effectiveness of a manager. There appears to be a strong and consistent trend of superior managers having more efficiency orientation, proactivity, diagnostic use of concepts, and concern with impact than do average or poor managers. This is supported by information from the motive level, the skill level, and the social-role level (i.e., managers' role perceptions of what is important to doing well in the job). These competencies can, therefore, be included in a model of the generic characteristics of an effective manager. The elements of these competencies are summarized in Table 4-1.

Private sector managers appear to demonstrate more of the skills of these competencies than do public sector managers. This can be understood in terms of the differential opportunities, goals, and available performance measures of organizations in each sector. The term "opportunities" should not be confused with probability of advancement, but taken to mean the relatively easier access to explicit performance measures. This allows for the establishment of clear goals in terms of desired

TABLE 4-1   The Goal and Action Management Cluster[a]

Competency	Motive	Trait	Self-Image	Social Role	Skills
Efficiency orientation	*n Achievement*		I can do better	*Innovator*	*Goal-setting skills*
			I am efficient		*Planning skills*
					Skills in organizing resources efficiently
Proactivity		Sense of efficacy	I am in control of what happens to me	*Initiator*	*Problem solving skills*
					Information seeking skills
Diagnostic use of concepts			I am systematic	*Scientist*	*Pattern identification through concept application*
					Deductive reasoning
Concern with impact	*n Power*		I am important	Status-oriented roles	*Symbolic influence behavior*

[a]Levels of each competency for which results indicate a relationship to managerial effectiveness are italicized.

outcomes. The establishment of clear goals and standards of excellence and performance provides the arena for goal setting, assessing return on various forms of investment, taking personal responsibility for the consequences of actions, and obtaining identifiable results from problem-solving activities.

With regard to concern with impact, private sector managers may have more access to and flexibility in selecting and using symbols of power within their organizations than do public sector managers. For example, most public sector managers have experienced the frustration of attempting to get some new furniture for their offices. Not only is their choice often constrained by what is available, but also by the "government issue" style of furniture and furnishings. For the sake of cost effectiveness and standardization, large quantities of the same style furniture are purchased, and then managers must use what is available. Although managers in large private sector organizations experience similar frustrations, they often can purchase a new style of furniture or furnishings as long as they are within budget limitations.

This relatively greater flexibility available to private sector managers results in their having greater control over the use of symbols of power. The flexibility regarding office furniture and furnishings is merely an example of one form of symbols of power; the same relative flexibility is reflected in other types of symbols of power to which managers have access.

This relationship is further supported by the observation that public sector managers have a higher motive level of this characteristic than do private sector managers. A higher motive level and yet relatively lower demonstration of related behavior suggests that organizational or environmental constraints are limiting the ability of public sector managers to utilize the characteristic of concern with impact. The relationship to effectiveness as a manager is indicated within the public as well as private sector for the motive and skill level of concern with impact. Therefore, regardless of relative constraints or opportunities to demonstrate this characteristic, effective managers find ways to express concern with impact.

Among public sector managers, superior performers show significantly more proactivity at the skill level than do average or poor performers. Although public sector managers may not have as much access to measures of performance as do their counterparts in the private sector, they still have the opportunity to solve problems and take initiative. In fact, it has been suggested that the ability to perceive the opportunity and take initiative in a management job in a public sector organization—which is usually bureaucratic and heavily burdened with policies, procedures, and paperwork to document and justify any activity—distinguishes those managers who get the job done most effectively and efficiently.

As with proactivity, superior performing managers in the public sector do demonstrate more diagnostic use of concepts and concern with impact than do their less effective counterparts. There is a curvilinear relationship between the motive or trait levels of proactivity, efficiency orientation, and concern with impact and effectiveness. This suggests that managers in the public sector with the motive and trait levels of the competencies in the goal and action management cluster stand out.

They may be viewed as superior or poor performers, but not average. The difference between these superior and poor performers may be a result of whether or not they learned "how" to express these motives and traits in public sector organizations. That is, the poor performers have learned how to express the motives and traits in ways that are not "socially and politically" acceptable to the organization: they violate the norms, or rules of behavior, of the organization.

While no significant trend appears between proactivity and various levels of management, efficiency orientation, diagnostic use of concepts, and concern with impact bear some relationship to level of management. Entry level managers appear to demonstrate more efficiency orientation and diagnostic use of concepts at the skill level than do executives. On the other hand, the former seem to have less of the motive level of efficiency orientation and concern with impact. They also demonstrate less concern with impact at the skill level than do executives. The findings with regard to efficiency orientation may not be as contradictory as they seem. Executive managers must be sensitized to and internally concerned about performance toward a standard of excellence and maximizing return on investment of any resource. At the same time, they are not in a job that requires daily or weekly establishment of personal goals, nor is the information on personal performance according to such measures as readily available to them as it is to managers at an entry or even middle level management job.

Findings on all four competencies in the cluster indicate that effective managers in middle and executive level management positions demonstrate more of the competencies at the motive, or skill levels than do their less effective peers.

Managers in manufacturing functions appear to demonstrate fewer of these competencies than do managers in marketing or personnel functions. An observation that may help the interpretation of these findings is that manufacturing managers often receive plans and goals that others have developed, such as new product designs, modifications, or new delivery schedules. They are placed in a position of reacting to changes in their operations imposed by others (i.e., marketing, engineering, or others). Concerns about smooth, continuous operations and quality control would result in these managers resisting changes and attempting to minimize risks due to changes in operations. If this is occurring, the competencies in the goal and action management cluster are not required as frequently from manufacturing managers as other managers. The findings suggest that superior manufacturing managers do not accept this type of role and utilize the competencies in the goal and action management cluster. They probably seek an active involvement in planning, problem solving, and exploring innovations. The superior performing manufacturing managers are probably in an environment that recognizes, or at least does not punish, such action.

Another observation that may aid the interpretation of these findings is that manufacturing managers are not required to spend as much of their time and energies as marketing or personnel managers are in addressing the relationship between their organizational unit and other units in the overall organization or in the environment external to the overall organization. Personnel managers must deal with the availability of appropriate labor in the work force, government regulations, top management, and each of the functional units within the organization. Marketing managers must deal with various clients, competitors, internal research and development units, and manufacturing.

While manufacturing managers must deal with other organizational units in terms of integrating their activities, the major components of the external environment that they must address are government agencies that regulate and monitor many aspects of their functioning and the sources of their raw materials. Relationships with these two components of the external environment are often handled by special corporate units that manage the interface between the manufacturing operations, government agencies, and the sources of the raw materials.

It is understandable, therefore, that manufacturing managers do not need nor demonstrate as much of these competencies as do managers of other corporate functions. The evidence indicates that superior manufacturing managers do demonstrate more of each of the competencies than do their less effective counterparts. Even though they may, as a group, need to demonstrate these competencies less often, efficiency orientation, proactivity, diagnostic use of concepts, and concern with impact are still important to the manufacturing managers in doing their jobs well.

Interactions at the Skill Level

In terms of a cluster of competencies, these four competencies can be said to have primary relationships to each other. To set goals, establish plans, and organize resources efficiently (i.e., efficiency orientation), a manager must have skills in applying concepts or frameworks to determine what goals are appropriate and feasible, how to reach them, and what organization of resources is most efficient (i.e., diagnostic use of concepts). Skills in goal setting and planning (i.e., efficiency orientation) also provide a basis for application of diagnostic skills to understand how well the organization is doing (i.e., diagnostic use of concepts) and determining what could be done to improve performance (i.e., diagnostic use of concepts and proactivity). This includes an ability to detect and correct relatively small errors or deviations from a plan and act on this information. The manager with this cluster of competencies does not have to wait until the end of a planning period to determine the degree of desired progress toward a goal. It would be relatively inefficient and potentially ineffective for a manager to take initiative, seek information, or solve problems (i.e., proactivity) without doing so on the basis of certain goals, plans, and ideas as to how the organization should function and strive to achieve its goals (i.e., efficiency orientation and diagnostic use of concepts).

The manager must have a desire to impact on others (i.e., concern with impact) to get others to accept and work toward goals and plans (i.e., efficiency orientation), or to solve problems and collect needed information (i.e., proactivity). It is also essential that the manager be able to discriminate between relevant and irrelevant information and know what is critical (i.e., diagnostic use of concepts) to the image or reputation of the products and organization (i.e., concern with impact). Only with these skills will he or she be able to identify improvements on them, identify what can be done to attain these improvements (i.e., efficiency orientation), and begin to actively improve them (i.e., proactivity).

CHAPTER FIVE

The Leadership Cluster

To activate the human resources of the organization, the manager must stimulate people. After deciding which resources (human, financial, technical, or physical) are to be used, the manager must decide how they are to be organized to achieve the desired goals. Communicating the goals, plans, and rationale for the organization of resources to the personnel is an important aspect of stimulating their interest and involvement. A manager is also called on to motivate, or inspire, his or her personnel to have an interest in their work and the organization in other ways. The manager is often asked to represent the organization to outside groups, such as financial analysts, bankers, community and civic organizations, professional and trade associations, and government agencies. The objective of such meetings is often for the manager to stimulate an understanding and possibly interest and commitment of people concerning his or her organization. To perform these aspects of management jobs, managers should be leaders.

There are a number of popular images of leaders. One image is John F. Kennedy asking, in his Inaugural Address, for a renewed commitment to the country. Another image is Martin Luther King, Jr., saying "I have a dream," or walking at the head of a freedom march. One image is that of the commanding officer, on the bridge of the ship, preparing the troops for the battle about to begin. All of these images involve inspirational acts.

Although we do not usually think of the divisional general manager jumping in front of the personnel and leading them cheering and shouting to the water cooler or company cafeteria, managers are required to be inspirational in a less dramatic way than political, social, or military leaders. Sometimes they must be as dramatic as these popular images, such as a number of chief executive officers who recently have given the

99

"Now we are about to enter battle" speech to their staff before the annual stockholders' meeting. Not only have Frank Perdue and Lee Iacocca sought to present their companies' products in relatively dramatic ways, but many United States Presidents have used television as a vehicle to communicate and stimulate interest. What personal characteristics enable some managers to be inspirational and others not?

For managers to be inspirational to those inside and outside their organization, among other things, they must also be insightful. They must present ideas, concepts, beliefs, or goals that others find interesting, intriguing, or stimulating. This aspect of leadership has been called "articulating the common vision" (Berlew, 1974). This common vision may be shared objectives, values, or concerns of the personnel. It may also be a new direction, goal, or mission that others would like to follow. Numerous managers have propelled their organizations to success through identification of market needs, design of a new product, or a statement of the strategic direction of the organization.

To be insightful does not necessarily refer to being "smart" in the traditional use of the term. The analytic or cognitive skills of an effective manager may or may not be related in any systematic manner to a generalized concept of intelligence (McClelland, 1973), often referred to as intelligent quotient (IQ), which is why IQ measures do not consistently relate to effectiveness in many occupations (McClelland, 1973).

It is not enough to indicate that effective managers have analytic ability (Drucker, 1954, 1973), conceptual skills (Hersey & Blanchard, 1969), general mental ability or intelligence (Bray et al., 1974; Levinson (1980) or that they think. Bray et al. (1974) and Levinson (1980) have reported several intellectual skills that appear related to managerial effectiveness. A number of studies have shown that a variety of intellectual or cognitive skills are related to effective performance in college (Winter et al., in press) and in various occupations (Klemp, 1977). The important question is: How do insightful and effective managers think that is different than the way their less effective counterparts think?

Four underlying characteristics that enable a manager to be inspirational and insightful, as described, were identified through the cluster analysis of the managers in this study. They were labeled the *leadership cluster*. The four competencies are: (1) self-confidence; (2) use of oral presentations; (3) logical thought; and (4) conceptualization. Managers with this set of competencies see themes and patterns in the common or shared objectives, values, problems, products, concerns or performance of people and groups within the organization. They communicate them to others in a forceful and impressive manner.

Possession of the competencies in this cluster is similar to general leadership and representation skills described by Stogdill (1974). They enable a manager to represent the organization and its products to others (Morrison, 1980). This cluster of competencies is similar to characteristics that Levinson (1980) called articulateness, good impression, and vision, and which Bray et al. (1974) called personal impact.

These competencies are critical to the manager who wants to or must think strategically about his or her products and organizational performance. As Kotter (1982) indicated, identification of patterns of product performance and changes in the marketplace, and the communication of these observations internally, are characteristic of the effective general manager. Identification of the business within which an organization is functioning, which is different from the concept previously believed by management, emerges from the use of the competencies in this cluster; such behavior can be labeled strategic thinking.

Before continuing the discussion of how this cluster of competencies is related to effective management, it is important to examine the relationship of each of the four competencies to managerial performance in detail.

SELF-CONFIDENCE

Self-confidence is a competency often called decisiveness or presence. People with self-confidence feel that they know what they are doing. They also feel that they are doing it well. People with this characteristic have a positive self-esteem. In social or organizational contexts, such people move into the role of natural leader. People who adopt this social role on the basis of this characteristic may also be viewed as charismatic. These people demonstrate self-presentation skills.

People who have self-confidence act in certain ways. They express little ambivalence about decisions that have been made. This is not to say that they are arrogant or defensive about their decisions. Such managers might still be able to identify the pros and cons of a particular decision, but have no reluctance in making a decision and living with it. Whenever managers are with others, those with self-confidence demonstrate "presence." They seem, when they have a great deal of this characteristic, to exude or be surrounded with an aura. In behavioral terms, these people appear to be forceful, unhesitating, and impressive in verbal and nonverbal actions. They have a belief in the likelihood of their own success.

For example, one of the managers in the sample was manager of a research and development group (i.e., product design group) in an industrial products company. She was asked to make a presentation to the vice president of new business development and the vice president of marketing about a new product idea that had emerged from her group. She was asked to make the presentation before engineers in the R&D group felt they had enough data. She felt confident and walked into the meeting with a belief that she had an idea that was important to the organization even though it had not been completely examined. Throughout the presentation to the vice presidents and the discussion of the idea, she showed assurance of the quality of the idea.

When the vice president of marketing came up with a product safety problem in the proposed design, the R&D manager addressed the issue. She told him that the product safety issue looked relevant, and that her staff would work on redesigning the product to avoid the safety problem. She did not doubt that the safety problem could be overcome.

Compare this with an R&D manager making the same presentation who did not have the self-confidence competency. Even though the technical quality of the product presentation was high, the manager would probably hesitate in answering questions. He might have slouched in a chair or hung his head when a vice president came up with an issue that challenged the utility or marketability of the product. Regardless of how the manager felt about the product idea, if he was not presenting himself confidently, the vice presidents and others present might have interpreted such hesitation or "foot shuffling" as a lack of confidence in the product.

Results at the Skill Level

Self-confidence (referred to as SELF) as coded in the interviews appeared significantly related to effectiveness as a manager ($F = 6.558$, $df = 2$, $p = .002$), and showed a significant linear trend favoring the superior managers ($F = 12.903$, $df = 1$, $p = .0005$). Comparison of the groups with t-tests, shown in Figures 5-1 and 5-2 (see Appendix A for detail), indicated that:

1. Superior and average managers demonstrated significantly more SELF than did poor managers, and superior managers demonstrated more SELF than did average managers at a near significant level.

2. Among public sector managers, superior performers demonstrated significantly more SELF than did average and poor performers, and average performers demonstrated significantly more SELF than did poor performers.

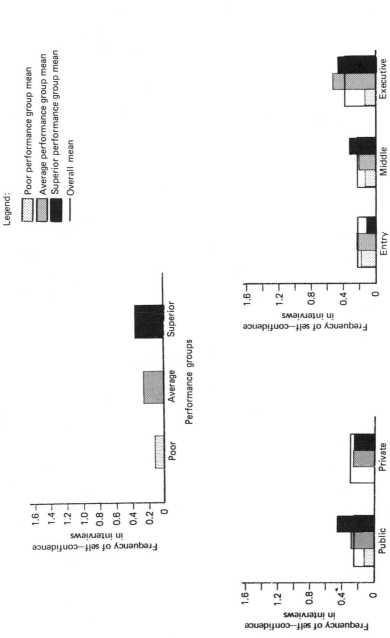

Figure 5–1. Skill level of self-confidence.

103

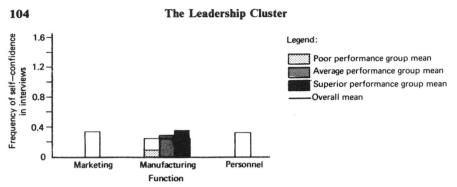

Figure 5-2. Skill level of self-confidence by function.

3. Executive level managers demonstrated significantly more SELF than did middle and entry level managers.

4. Among middle level managers, superior performers demonstrated significantly more SELF than did poor performers and more than average performers did at a near significant level.

5. Among executive level managers, superior and average performers demonstrated significantly more SELF than did poor performers.

6. Marketing managers demonstrated more SELF than did manufacturing managers at a near significant level.

7. Among manufacturing managers, superior and average performers demonstrated significantly more SELF than did poor performers.

Results at the Social-Role Level

In all seven studies of managers' perceptions, items relating to self-confidence were listed as required for performance as a manager. In six of the studies, these items were perceived by managers as characteristics distinguishing superior performance as a manager. This included items such as: "ability to inspire confidence," "confidence," and "decisiveness."

Interpretation

Self-confidence appears strongly associated with managerial effectiveness. Executive level managers appear to demonstrate more of it than do entry or middle level managers. Executives are often called on to represent the organization and its products to internal groups, as well as to groups outside the organization. Often, they must provide "inspiration" to people. It is also possible that the position of the executive imbues him or her with a certain "prestige" or aura that contributes to others' deriving inspiration from things the executive says or does. The strong relationship between superior performance and self-confidence within the middle and executive level managers suggests that merely being in the job is certainly not enough to lead others to conclude that the manager has this characteristic. Marketing managers demonstrate slightly more self-confidence than do manufacturing managers. This may be a function of aspects of the marketing task as compared to the manufacturing task. Marketing activities include presenting the product and the organization to others in an unhesitating and impressive manner. A manufacturing manager is less frequently called on to present the daily production information or solve an operating problem in a production process with a comparably unhesitating and impressive manner. Even though manufacturing managers may not be required to demonstrate self-confidence as often as are marketing managers, when it is called for or relevant, the superior managers demonstrate more of it than do their less effective counterparts.

USE OF ORAL PRESENTATIONS

Use of oral presentations is a competency with which people make effective verbal presentations, whether these presentations be in one-on-one meetings or an address to an audience of several hundred people. These people see themselves as able to verbally communicate effectively. In social or organizational contexts, they adopt roles as communicators, often summarizing or restating what others have said or are trying to say. They demonstrate verbal presentation skills.

People who use the oral presentations competency behave in certain ways. They are able to use symbolic, verbal, and nonverbal behavior to reinforce or interpret the content of the message and to ensure that the presentations are clear and convincing. When possible, they ask questions to ensure that individuals understand what is being said. They often utilize visual aids and graphics to get the message across to the audience.

For example, financial managers with this characteristic may have handouts and prepared charts of financial information and analysis when presenting productivity information to divisional executives. They stage the presentation of the information so that the audience is led up to the key results at a pace that not only allows them to understand the preliminaries and assumptions, but also maximizes their interest when the most important findings are discussed. These managers probably stand at critical points to emphasize the importance of these points. They only use language that the operating managers in the audience understand. If these financial managers have prepared the visual aids appropriately, the measures of productivity that the operating managers in the audience use in their jobs would be carefully translated to financial measures with which they might not deal often.

Results at the Skill Level

The use of oral presentations (referred to as UOP) as coded in the interviews was related to effectiveness as a manager ($F = 5.393$, df $= 2$, $p = .005$), with a significant linear trend favoring superior managers ($F = 10.697$, df $= 1$, $p = .001$). Comparison of the groups with t-tests, shown in Figures 5-3 and 5-4 (see Appendix A for detail), indicated that:

1. Superior managers demonstrated significantly more UOP than did average and poor managers, and average managers demonstrated significantly more UOP than did poor managers.
2. Private sector managers demonstrated more UOP than did public sector managers at a near significant level.
3. Among public sector managers, superior performers demonstrated significantly more UOP than did average and poor performers.
4. Among middle level managers, superior performers demonstrated significantly more UOP than did average and poor performers, and average performers demonstrated significantly more UOP than did poor performers.
5. Among executive level managers, superior performers demonstrated significantly more UOP than did poor performers.
6. Personnel managers demonstrated significantly more UOP than did marketing and manufacturing managers.
7. Among manufacturing managers, superior performers demonstrated significantly more UOP than did poor performers.

Results at the Social-Role Level

In all seven studies of managers' perceptions, items relating to use of oral presentations were listed as required for performance as a manager.

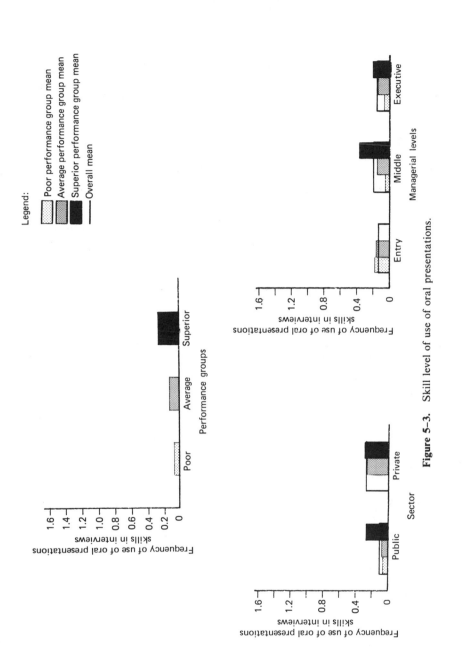

Figure 5-3. Skill level of use of oral presentations.

107

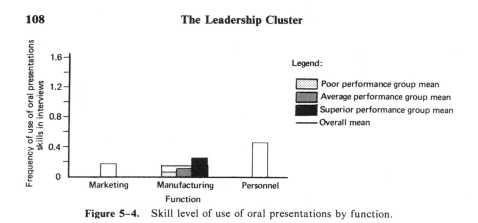

Figure 5-4. Skill level of use of oral presentations by function.

In six of these studies, these items were perceived by managers as characteristics distinguishing superior performance as a manager. This included items such as: "public speaking ability," "ability to present data to others," and "precision in communication."

Interpretation

Use of oral presentations is a competency that is strongly related to effectiveness as a manager. This does not merely refer to talking to others, but to the quality of the verbal communication and the aids used to enhance the message. Private sector managers demonstrate more of this characteristic than do public sector managers. A manager in the private sector may be called on to make more verbal presentations to subordinates, other managers, groups from the external environment of the organization, and top management than are managers in the public sector. Verbal presentations, such as press conferences and congressional hearings, to groups outside the immediate organizational unit in the public sector have meaning and include implications that affect the entire organization and the position of the government. The potential liabilities of such presentations and the concern for standardization of perspective or position on issues limit the public sector manager's opportunities to demonstrate the use of oral presentations competency. The findings show that superior but not average managers in the public sector demonstrated about the same use of oral presentations as do managers in the private sector. This suggests that the difference between sectors may not be a result of major differences in the nature of the organizations or their environments, but merely that even average managers in the private sector are often required to make verbal presentations.

Personnel managers demonstrate more of this characteristic than do managers in other functions. This may be the result of the fact that almost all activities of personnel managers (i.e., not only responsibilities as a manager but also the nature of the work being managed) involve talking with people. If they cannot verbally communicate effectively, little of their work will get done.

LOGICAL THOUGHT

Logical thought represents a thought process in which the person places events in a causal sequence. This sequence is based on the perception of a series of cause-and-effect events; that is, the person views certain events as preceding or causing other events, which in turn precede or cause other events. People with this characteristic see themselves as orderly and systematic. In the context of an organization or social group, they will adopt the role of systems analyst. These people demonstrate skills in organizing thoughts and activities and in sequential thinking.

People who possess the logical thought competency tend to behave and speak in certain ways. For example, they would describe a course of action with a list of actions or events arranged in an order reflecting a rational, causal sequence. The particular rationale they use for ordering the actions or events may vary, but a list or chart will result regardless of the framework used. The list may or may not represent the most effective or efficient approach, just as these people may or may not be moving toward an explicit goal. These aspects of "quality" or "utility" of the list are a function of logical thought in the context of other characteristics possessed by the individual. For example, people with both the logical thought and efficiency orientation competencies probably would identify the objective explicitly. They also would assess the appropriateness of the actions or events in the list in terms of efficiency.

The following examples from managers in the sample illustrate the demonstration of logical thought in their jobs.

I left the meeting and talked to my boss. I told him that I'd been asked to facilitate the meeting and he asked me why. I checked back with the manager who said he thought he'd dominate the meeting. In talking with my boss again, he asked if it was the best way to handle the situation. I said maybe not. If the manager were running it he'd be doing a lot of writing and wouldn't have a chance to dominate the meeting. I went back to the manager and told him that I wasn't going to run the meeting.

A meeting happened where money situation programming was being discussed. The advantage of using a particular sum of money from Congress was it would save problems in the current fiscal year and the service would look good for receiving the money. The disadvantage was that it would disrupt many of the service's people's lives. I took the position that disrupting people's lives was counterproductive in the long run as the service people would remember and resent the move. It would be best for retention rates in the long run not to use the money.

An idea emerged from several of my discussions with employees at the water cooler for flexy time. Some of the companies around town were experimenting with it. I wrote a proposal to the general manager and he agreed to try it as a pilot. One of my staff worked a detailed procedure manual and sent it to the general manager and he agreed to try it as a pilot. One of my staff worked a detailed procedure manual and sent it to the general manager. He sent it to the union rep and there it sat. He said it wouldn't work. I got mad as hell. He finally agreed to try it and sent it back to the general manager with his OK. That's my approach to making changes here: (1) Use the old boy network as a technique for selling my idea; (2) When I am not effective at step 1, then I lose my temper. Reps and mid-level managers cannot take four-letter words and if you insult them they usually do something for you; then (3) If neither step 1 or 2 works, then basically I try to get myself transferred out so I can start fresh in a new position. But most of the time I don't get to step 3.

Results at the Skill Level

At the skill level, logical thought as coded in the interviews was not related to overall effective managerial performance. The only significant differences worthy of comment were among middle level managers. Among middle level managers, superior and average performers demonstrated significantly more logical thought than did poor performers (mean scores: .482, .540, and .263, respectively, see Appendix A for detail).

Results at the Social-Role Level

In five of the seven studies of managers' perceptions, items relating to logical thought were listed as required for performance as a manager. Managers in all five studies perceived these items as distinguishing superior performing managers from less effective managers. This included items such as: "ability to think logically," "identifies the list of activities that the group must perform," and "ability to state which problem must be solved first to solve other problems."

Interpretation

Although managers perceive logical thought to be related to effective performance as a manager, results at the skill level support this perception only for middle level managers. What relationship there is suggests that poor middle level managers use less logical thought than do average or superior middle level managers. Since there are no other strong relationships, this characteristic can at best be labeled a threshold competency; that is, logical thought is probably needed to perform a manager's job adequately (at least for middle level managers), but demonstrating more of it does not necessarily result in better performance. This is a good illustration of the limitations of the self-report method of measurement as compared with Behavioral Event Interviewing. Many agreed that logical thought was important for managers, but the characteristic seldom distinguished superior from poor managers in action.

Managers must be organized in their thinking. These results indicate that mere organization of thought and activities is not enough to generate superior performance.

CONCEPTUALIZATION

Conceptualization is a thought process in which the person identifies or recognizes patterns in an assortment of information; that is, the individual develops a concept that describes a pattern or structure perceived in a set of facts. The concept seems to emerge from the information. This has been termed an imaging cognitive process, or an iconic learning style (Kolb, 1971; Kolb & Fry, 1975; Kolb, 1976). People with this skill develop a concept to interpret or understand certain events and information. Part of the self-image of people who conceptualize well and easily is a sense of being creative. In an organization or social group context, these people adopt the role of inventor, where "inventor" means developer of something new, whether the "thing" developed is an idea, concept, insight, or solution to a problem. Such people demonstrate skills in pattern recognition through concept formation and skills in finding themes or patterns.

People who conceptualize behave and speak in certain ways. When presented with a series of events, a variety of facts, or a phenomena, they can identify a theme that gives a pattern to the information (Levinson, 1980). They can also label the pattern so as to communicate the meaning of the concept. They can examine an issue or problem and provide meaning to it by differentiating it into its constituent parts, while using a new concept as the basis for the differentiation. A person who uses conceptualization is more likely than others to use a metaphor or analogy as an aid to interpreting or understanding an experience, a set of events, ideas, or observed phenomena. When a group of people is exposed to a seemingly unrelated set of events, it is the people who use conceptualization who come up with a concept to explain certain aspects of the events and how they are associated. In all likelihood, the concept identified is different from any used previously by the same group.

For example, one of the managers in the sample was a manufacturing manager in a consumer products company. She noticed that although weekly averages of the number of units off her production lines were similar, the variation in daily averages was substantial. In particular, she noticed that Mondays and Fridays were slow. She made an effort to walk through the plant each day at 8:30 a.m. and 8:30 p.m. for two weeks. These particular production lines operated on two shifts, Monday through Friday. She noticed that on Monday mornings people seemed to spend a lot of time rearranging the work stations. The line did not go "up" as early as it did on other days. She also noticed that an unusually large number of different people were at the work stations on the two Friday shifts. She asked the plant personnel manager about both issues. He claimed that Monday morning crew had to clean up and restock supplies. He also added that a number of the regular production line workers missed work on Fridays, or at least came in late. The absences and tardiness were not caused by the same people week after week. In reviewing some other aspects of the production line's operation, she realized that paychecks were distributed at the end of the Thursday shift. She identified the pattern in the daily variations in performance as a function of distributing the checks on Thursdays. As a result of her analysis, she was able to shift the distribution of the paychecks to the end of the Friday shift, and require that people clean and restock their work stations before leaving on Friday. Within two weeks of making these changes, the variation in performance disappeared.

The following examples from managers in the sample also illustrate the demonstration of conceptualization in their jobs.

I get a particular satisfaction out of acing out the competition by using strategies, past histories; tracking what the competition will do in a given situation; using that kind of information against them. Most people, as you know, have a signature. One particular strategy that comes to mind is when we were bidding 183 pieces of component parts. We had been in competition with SYSCOMP. By taking a look at their bidding history and their track record, at the eleventh hour before the bid was to go in, I decided to drop our bid by $3 per piece because I honed in on the price I thought they would bid. It turns out that by doing that we got the order because we were lower by $1.75 per piece. I did it by going back through history of bids of SYSCOMP against us over the past three years. I put myself in their shoes and asked what would they do in this situation. I concluded that they would drop their initial price by 6 percent at the end, which would have been $3 per piece. Fortunately, we were just about dead on.

We have gone through a difficult period, with me as manager of manufacturing engineering, where we had not been getting yields in quality we normally get. I asked myself, "Why could this phenomenon be taking place?" I consider it a phenomenon rather than a production screwup. I checked everything as much as possible—it took a long time. I then analyzed the problem into a number of components. One Saturday morning I was sitting here thinking of graphite and its properties. I got to thinking about the dry weather. Don't ask me why those two thoughts went through my mind except that it was damnably hot in here. I began to think about moisture, dryness, and graphite, and the way I began to put it together was relating it to a far-removed phenomenon. I began to think about the flying fortresses of World War II that flew at great heights. They began to find gun turrets and electrical systems going out. It was the brushes on the generators burning out and it was an emergency situation, 14 labs were put on the problem and they solved it. I read about this because I am a pilot. The long and the short of it was, when you get to great heights . . . graphite lubricates because of the presence of moisture, but at great heights they are getting to the point where there is no moisture in the air. Well, literally, like Archimedes running down the street yelling "Eureka," I ran out and found a technician. I got him to get water in the air of some of the chambers. It worked after some tests to find the right amount and yields went back up.

Results at the Skill Level

At the skill level, conceptualization (referred to as C) as coded in the interviews is significantly related to effective managerial performance ($F = 2.951$, df $= 2$, $p < .05$), and showed a significant linear trend toward superior performance ($F = 5.846$, df $= 1$, $p < .02$). Comparison of the groups with t-tests, shown in Figures 5-5 and 5-6 (see Appendix A for detail), with t-tests showed that:

1. Superior managers demonstrated significantly more C than did poor managers, and more C than did average managers at a near significant level.

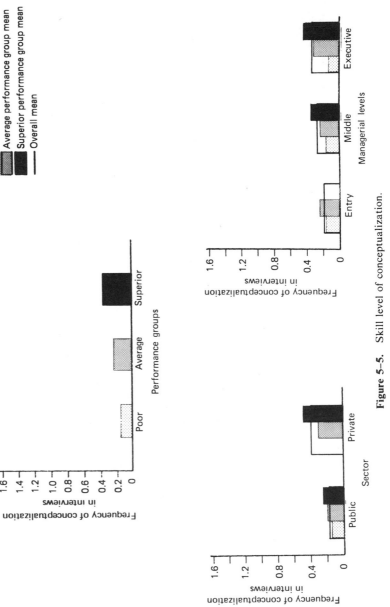

Figure 5-5. Skill level of conceptualization.

Legend:
- Poor performance group mean
- Average performance group mean
- Superior performance group mean
- Overall mean

114

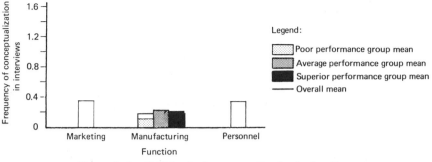

Figure 5–6. Skill level of conceptualization by function.

2. Private sector managers demonstrated significantly more C than did public sector managers.

3. Among entry level managers, average performers demonstrated significantly more C than did superior performers.

4. Among middle level managers, superior performers demonstrated more C than did poor performers at a near significant level.

5. Among executive level managers, superior performers demonstrated significantly more C than did poor performers.

6. Marketing managers demonstrated significantly more C than did manufacturing managers, and personnel managers demonstrated more C than did manufacturing managers at a near significant level.

7. Among manufacturing managers, average performers demonstrated more C than did poor performers at a near significant level.

Results at the Self-Image Level

Conceptualization was measured at the self-image level by the concrete experience and the reflective observation learning styles (Kolb, 1976). These styles involve people actively participating and then sitting back to reflect on what has occurred. These are aspects of a person's self-image that are conducive to conceptualizing, or collecting much data and identifying a theme to understand the data. The overall relationship between these learning styles and the performance of managers was not statistically significant (see Appendix A for detail). Since the samples on which this was assessed were all within middle level management and in one function, managerial level and function comparisons were not possible. There were no significant differences between managers in the two sectors. Among public sector managers, superior and average performers had higher scores on the concrete experience learning style than did poor performers, both at a near significant level. Among private sector managers, poor performers had significantly higher concrete experience learning styles than did average performers, and were higher than superior performers at a near significant level.

Results at the Social-Role Level

In two of the seven studies of managers' perceptions, items relating to conceptualization were listed as required for performance as a manager. In only one study did managers perceive these items to be related to superior managerial performance. This included items such as: "critical thinking as the ability to see information patterns in ambiguous situations; ability to see trends; and ability to see the forest for the trees."

Interpretation

At the skill level, conceptualization appears to be related to superior performance as a manager, particularly at the executive level. Managers often find themselves in situations in which a great deal of information is available and they must make sense out of it. Those managers who can perceive the patterns or themes in such information are able to function more effectively than those who cannot. Conceptualization enables an executive to identify and clarify strategic issues. An executive with this competency can answer important questions such as: What is our business? What is the expected condition of our industry in the future? This competency is critical for the executive to perceive and think at the strategic, not just tactical, level.

Although the self-image level of conceptualization does not distinguish between better and poorer performers, it has been shown that managers in different functions, as well as people in various occupations, have significantly different learning styles (Kolb, 1976). People in personnel occupations, counseling, and the arts have been shown to have higher concrete experience and reflective observation scores than others (Kolb, 1976). The managers in this study, especially those at the executive level of management, demonstrated skills in conceptualization more frequently than did their less effective counterparts even though they did not describe themselves as approaching situations in this way.

The higher degree of conceptualization demonstrated by private sector as opposed to public sector managers may be a function of the proscriptions and prescriptions given to public sector managers regarding what information they can examine and how they should examine it. It is understandable that these relative "constraints" on public sector managers have evolved from years of attempts to standardize procedures throughout government organizations.

Marketing and personnel managers demonstrate more conceptualization at the skill level than do managers of manufacturing. To the extent that marketing managers must interpret and understand actions of the various client groups in the marketplace and of their competition, they face situations calling for conceptualization. They must understand patterns in both their clients' and their competitors' behavior to develop effective marketing strategies and tactics. Personnel managers, in dealing with a wide variety of people in an organization, must be able to understand individuals well enough to respond to their needs, even when those needs are not articulated adequately or accurately. Although manufacturing managers appeared to demonstrate less skill in conceptualization, poor manufacturing managers appeared to demonstrate fewer of those skills than did average performers. This suggests that conceptualization skills may not be required often in manufacturing managers' functions, but are required at times.

SUMMARY ON THE LEADERSHIP CLUSTER

Summary of Findings

The competencies in the leadership cluster are related to effective management at middle and executive levels only. For inclusion in the competency model of management, self-confidence, use of oral presentations, and conceptualization can be considered competencies. Logical thought should be considered a threshold competency. The results are summarized in Table 5-1.

There was no evidence that the demonstration of these competencies was required for or related to effectiveness for entry level managers. With respect to conceptualization, it was found that average performers demonstrated significantly more of it than did superior performers at the entry level. Managers at middle and executive levels are exposed to a greater diversity of situations, information, and sources of information than most entry level managers. Procedures and practices are often more specified and routinized for entry level managers. In addition, entry level managers are not often asked to participate in strategic analysis. Given these observations, it is not surprising that conceptualization would be related to managerial effectiveness at middle and executive levels only. For these reasons, as well as the observation that entry level managers are not often required to represent the organization to outside

TABLE 5-1   The Leadership Cluster[a]

Competency	Motive	Trait	Self-Image	Social Role	Skills
Self-confidence			I know what I'm doing and will do it well	*Natural leader*	*Self-presentation skills*
Use of oral presentations			I can verbally communicate well	*Communicator*	*Verbal presentation skills*
Logical thought			I am orderly	*Systems analyst*	*Organization of thought and activities[c]* *Sequential thinking[c]*
Conceptualization			I am creative	Inventor	*Pattern identification through concept formation[b]* *Thematic or pattern analysis[b]*

[a]Levels of competencies for which results indicate a relationship to managerial effectiveness are italicized.
[b]At middle and executive management jobs only.
[c]At middle management jobs only.

groups, the leadership cluster is not as relevant to entry levels managers as it is for middle and executive level managers.

Manufacturing managers demonstrate less of these skills than do managers of marketing or personnel. The complexity and diversity of information that must be processed and understood in manufacturing management jobs does seem comparatively less than that in marketing or personnel management jobs. This could be because manufacturing functions are better understood than are marketing or personnel functions. To the extent that manufacturing functions have been studied, written about, and examined in more detail over the years, a current manager of such functions may need to exercise less of each of these competencies. It is important to point out, however, that poor manufacturing managers do demonstrate less of the conceptualization, use of oral presentations, and self-confidence competencies than do the average or superior manufacturing managers. Although managers in manufacturing may need to demonstrate these competencies less frequently than do managers of marketing or personnel functions, the demonstration of these competencies does distinguish the more effective manufacturing managers.

Although performance group comparisons could not be made within the personnel and marketing functions on these competencies, personnel managers demonstrated more logical thought, conceptualization, and use of oral presentations than did managers in other functions. Marketing managers demonstrated more self-confidence and conceptualization than did manufacturing managers. In both cases, these competencies appear closely related to the type of analysis and the format of presenting information required of managers in personnel or marketing.

Private sector managers appear to demonstrate more of the conceptualization competency than do public sector managers. This may be a function of the many different sources and types of information to which a private sector manager is exposed as compared with a public sector manager. It may also be a function of the relatively greater structure placed on information coming to public sector managers through the detailed and comprehensive policies and procedures within which a public sector manager must function. For example, information frequently comes to a public sector manager in a certain form (on forms designed in a certain manner for consistent use across functional groups) and is supposed to be examined and analyzed using a certain method (using procedures designed for consistent use across functional groups). Although many large private sector organizations may benefit and possibly suffer from similar bureaucratic attempts at standardization and consistency, this dynamic is not observed as frequently in the offices of private sector managers. The way information is provided to a manager and the proscriptions and prescriptions about how it is to be examined and analyzed may constrain the demonstration of this intellectual competency by public sector managers.

Interactions at the Skill Level

These four competencies can be said to have primary relationships to each other. To demonstrate a presence (i.e., self-confidence), a person must speak clearly, concisely, and convincingly (i.e., use of oral presentations). At the same time, it would be difficult to speak in such a manner without the competency of self-confidence. To effectively lead, represent the organization, and inspire others, a manager must be able to: (1) identify the common objectives, values, and mission of the people and groups within the organization and identify themes and patterns in the performance of the organization (i.e., conceptualization); (2) present himself or herself convincingly and with a presence (i.e., self-confidence); (3) communicate these ideas, themes, and patterns to others (i.e., use of oral presentations); and (4) understand how various elements of the organization or its processes affect each other (i.e., logical thought). It would be difficult for a manager to present these themes or patterns which he or she had identified without a degree of self-confidence in his or her ideas and thought processes.

Although the competencies in the goal and action management cluster and the leadership cluster did not group together, the two clusters showed a strong relationship to each other ($r = .456$, $N = 253$, $p < .001$). This suggests that the competencies in the goal and action management cluster have a secondary relationship to the competencies in the leadership cluster. That is, a manager could demonstrate the competencies of one cluster without possessing the competencies of the other cluster, but that possession of the competencies in one cluster would enhance a manager's ability to demonstrate the competencies in the other cluster. For example, a manager could set goals and plans, take initiative in making things happen, identify problems, and desire impact on others without being able to identify themes or patterns not previously observed, or giving inspiring and convincing presentations. Likewise, a manager could give inspiring and convincing presentations and identify themes or patterns not previously observed without setting goals, establishing plans, taking initiative, or seeking additional information, as is often evident in speeches by candidates running for political office. On the other hand, a manager's impact on the organization would be enhanced if the themes or patterns and presentations were in the context of goals, plans, and identified actions that could be taken to make things happen. Similarly, a manager's ability to diagnose what is occurring, determine goals, establish plans, and identify problems and initiatives would be enhanced if the manager could identify themes or patterns not previously observed, and communicate them in a clear, convincing, and inspiring manner.

CHAPTER SIX

The Human Resource Management Cluster

Besides death and taxes, the other thing managers can be assured of is that they must work with people. The others with whom they must interact may be subordinates, a boss, peers, a board of directors, stockholders, customers, suppliers, or representatives of regulatory agencies. About a year after a promotion, an executive recently confided to the author, "I really love my job, but the people are killing me!" Unfortunately, he was still struggling with understanding that marshaling human resources is an essential part of his and most managers' jobs. The specific requirements of *how* they must work with people will vary among management jobs.

A great deal of precision with regard to competencies is lost when a manager is labeled as sensitive, people-oriented, or interpersonally competent. Attempts to diagnose the "people problems" in an organization often result in statements that are too general to be of help. For example, "communication problems" has been a diagnostic dumping ground in organizations for years. Is this a symptom or a problem? Although access to and transmission of information may be a problem in organizations, it is more likely that the lack of certain competencies by managers in the organizations is the problem. This is most evident when a manager says, "What we have here is a failure to communicate," when he or she really means to say, "You do not see it my way."

Managing human resources in an organization involves many activities, but at a fundamental level it requires the coordination of groups of people. These groups may be work units, departments, divisions, or subsidiaries. The coordination may involve promoting cooperative efforts, resolving conflicts over the use of resources or operational difficulties, or groups exchanging information and goods. The manager has the responsibility of stimulating a degree of pride in the organization. This may take the form of loyalty, commitment to the organization, or an esprit de corps. However accomplished, it results in people working together toward the organization's goals.

Four underlying characteristics that enable a manager to respond to these responsibilities of the job were identified through the cluster analysis of managers in this study. They were labeled the *human resource management cluster*. The four competencies are: (1) use of socialized power; (2) positive regard; (3) managing group process; and (4) accurate self-assessment. Managers with this set of competencies have positive expectations about others; have realistic views of themselves; build networks or coalitions with others to accomplish tasks; use networks or coalitions to solve problems; and stimulate cooperation and pride in work groups. The use of the competencies in this cluster can be said to reflect an approach to management that McGregor (1960) called Theory Y. It is similar to what Maccoby (1976) called cooperativeness.

Before exploring how these competencies affect each other, a close look at each is important.

USE OF SOCIALIZED POWER

Use of socialized power is a competency in which the person uses forms of influence to build alliances, networks, coalitions, or teams. These people see themselves as members of a team; that is, they perceive themselves to be a part of particular groups. In social or organizational contexts, they adopt roles of team or organization members. They demonstrate skills in building alliances, networks, coalitions, or teams.

People who use socialized power behave in certain ways. To accomplish a certain task, they build a political coalition or network that did not exist previously (Kotter, 1982). They view their relationship with their boss as an important coalition (Kotter, 1979; Stogdill, 1974). They might attempt to build commitment of various people to certain standards of behavior through "modeling" desired behavior; that is, instead of describing the behavior and demanding compliance, these people would act in a manner consistent with the desired behavior and wait for others to appreciate its beneficial consequences. Perceiving themselves as team or organization members, they attempt to bring conflicting individuals or groups to a resolution of the conflict through building coalitions or using existing coalitions.

For example, one of the managers in the sample was a manager of training and development in the personnel department of a consumer products conglomerate. She decided that the time had come for the company to institute a career-development training program for administrative staff of the company. Instead of developing or purchasing a particular program and then presenting it to managers in various divisions of the company, she decided to establish the perceived need for it first. Since her group was conducting periodic surveys of attitudes and satisfaction within the various divisions, she asked each of the divisional vice presidents of personnel if her staff could include questions about the career mobility and opportunities for advancement within the division. She convinced each vice president that it was a growing concern in the work force. It did not seem a major deviation from typical procedures, so each divisional vice president agreed; actually, several thought it was long overdue. Once the survey information was collected, she had her staff process the information using the normal procedures, but withheld the career mobility and advancement information. One of her staff worked on a special analysis of this information for the administrative level employees. Another staff member began a search of the field and consulting groups for approaches to this issue. By the time the analysis was complete, members of her staff had developed a reasonably low-cost method for adapting some existing training programs to the organization's specific needs.

She began by presenting the information to two of the divisional vice presidents who were advocates of the effort. Once their agreement on the implications of the information and commitment to the design of the training program was obtained, she called a meeting of all vice presidents of personnel and their immediate subordinates. She presented the information, with elaboration from the staff members who had conducted the analysis. During the question and answer period, she allowed the vice presidents who were already committed to the program to address some of the reservations others were stating.

At a certain point in the meeting, she presented the proposed design of a training program and explained its potential benefits in terms of reduced turnover and increased motivation. She offered the divisions several options for implementing the program, each of which had various budget implications depending on whether corporate staff or divisional staff conducted the training. During all of the presentations and discussions, she kept speaking in terms of what was needed for the health of the organization as a whole. The program was adopted immediately by several divisions. Her expectation was that once success was demonstrated in several divisions, the others would follow. This manager built a network or coalition of key people who thought the idea was sound and who thought the program was needed. She did not attempt to make implementation a corporate policy, or to make the divisions use the program. Her use of socialized power helped this idea become an ongoing program within the company.

The following examples from managers in the sample also illustrate the demonstration of the use of socialized power in their jobs.

I was asked to sit in on a review project, to represent the marketing perspective. The manufacturing committee was set up to assess the status of our suppliers. I did some analysis on my own and felt that by focusing on one supplier for a commodity that was critical to our production we were foolish. What if they should fail? What if they could not grow fast enough to keep pace with our demand? I presented my argument to the manufacturing committee. They thought it was reasonable but started raising objections. They claimed that we had already spent a lot of money with two previous companies and had problems. They said that the current supplier was doing fine and working with them on delivery issues and quality concerns. I backed down at that point. I knew that several manufacturing engineers were on the committee. So I went to the design engineers and explained some of the dilemmas I saw in the situations. I explained to them the potential problems from a tooling standpoint, and they agreed. They also agreed to come to the next manufacturing committee meeting with me. It was a ploy in my negotiating with the committee. Having one engineer talk to another engineer can lead to an understanding sooner, it's a peer thing. It worked. The manufacturing engineers saw the point and pushed the rest of the committee to address my concern from several perspectives. Soon after, we started purchasing from several suppliers, which I think was the right decision for the company.

We were buying a basic component in our product from one of our other divisions. My manufacturing and engineering managers were complaining to me about problems in the delivery schedule. It was uneven, sometimes they hit it and sometimes they didn't. I called the division's general manager and told him about the problem. He checked with his people and said I was mistaken. So I went back to my managers and asked about the other division's salespeople. "How reliable are they?" I told them that there were no controls on the current procedure. There was no way to document who was telling the truth. I asked if the sales rep had been meeting the delivery plan. My manufacturing manager said, "What plan?" I told him to demand a written plan. Meanwhile, I told my engineering manager to demand written details on all of the specs of the material. Once the pressure was applied from several levels, the other division started to respond.

Results at the Skill Level

The use of socialized power (referred to as USP) as coded in the interviews was significantly related to effectiveness as a manager ($F = 9.092$, df $= 2$, $p = .0002$), with a highly significant linear trend favoring superior managers ($F = 18.173$, df $= 1$, $p = .0001$). Comparison of the groups with t-tests, shown in Figure 6-1 and 6-2 (see Appendix A for detail), indicated that:

1. Superior managers demonstrated significantly more USP than did average and poor managers, and average managers demonstrated significantly more USP than did poor managers.

2. Among public sector managers, superior and average performers demonstrated significantly more USP than did poor performers.

3. Among private sector managers, superior performers demonstrated significantly more USP than did average performers.

4. Among entry level managers, average performers demonstrated significantly more USP than did poor performers.

5. Among middle level managers, superior performers demonstrated significantly more USP than did average and poor performers, and average performers demonstrated significantly more USP than did poor performers.

6. Personnel managers demonstrated significantly more USP than did manufacturing managers.

7. Among manufacturing managers, superior and average performers demonstrated significantly more USP than did poor performers.

Results at the Social-Role Level

In six of the seven studies of managers' perceptions, items relating to use of socialized power were listed as required for performance as a manager. In five of these studies, these items were perceived by managers as characteristics distinguishing superior performance as a manager. This included items such as: "ability to gain cooperation," "ability to participate but not dominate," and "ability to work as a member of a team."

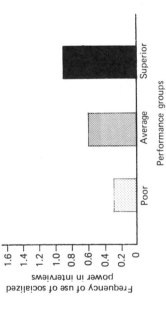

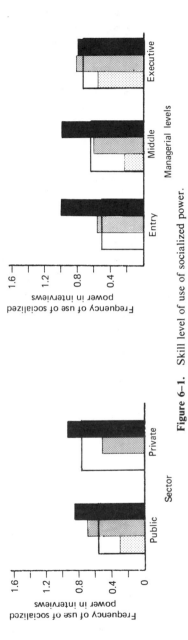

Figure 6–1. Skill level of use of socialized power.

126

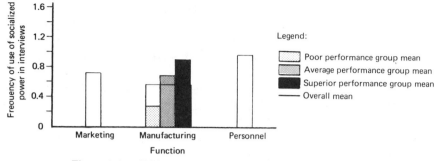

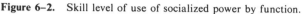

Figure 6–2. Skill level of use of socialized power by function.

Interpretation

Use of socialized power appears strongly related to effectiveness as a manager. The lack of differences between managers in the two sectors, or among managers at the various levels, suggests that this characteristic is a generic characteristic in almost any aspect of management. Using forms of influence that appeal to shared objectives and a common commitment to the organization contribute substantially to the effectiveness of a manager.

The observation that personnel managers demonstrate more use of socialized power than do manufacturing managers may be a function of their role in the organization. Personnel managers typically have fewer well-defined performance measures for their organizational unit, and also typically do not have as much "line authority" as do managers in other functions. For both of these reasons, in addition to the complexity of their subject matter (e.g., human resources), the use of socialized power may be their only option for influencing various members of the rest of the organization.

POSITIVE REGARD

Positive regard is a competency in which people believe in others. At the trait level, such people have a basic belief in others; that is, a positive belief that people are good. These people see themselves as good. It would be difficult for people to have this characteristic and not to assume that they are basically good while assuming that others are. In social or organizational contexts, such people adopt the role of optimist. They demonstrate verbal and nonverbal skills that cause others to feel valued.

People with positive regard behave in certain ways. They describe others as good or well-intentioned. They contend that, if given the chance, people will do "the right thing." Such people do not act in specific ways as much as they take a positive perspective on people around them.

The following examples from managers in the sample illustrate the demonstration of positive regard in their jobs.

> I had faith in this one man who applied for a staff job. I didn't have an opening at the time but sent him over to one of the other managers. The other manager didn't like him and thought that he didn't have the right background. Two months later, I had a job open up so I called the man and hired him. He did lack some of the experience we usually look for, but I thought he had the right attitude and could do the job.

> You can see how the problem would have been solved sooner if my boss had used his clout. I had to coach him into putting some pressure on the right people. He's a good buy, but just in the wrong job. He knows the technical stuff cold but needs some help on the people side.

Results at the Skill Level

Positive regard as coded in the interviews was not related overall to effectiveness as a manager. Middle level managers demonstrated significantly more positive regard than did executive level managers (mean score .268 versus .120, respectively; see Appendix A for detail). Among entry level managers, average performers demonstrated significantly more positive regard than did superior performers (mean score .231 versus 0.0, respectively). Among middle level managers, superior performers demonstrated significantly more positive regard than did average performers and demonstrated more of it than did poor performers at a near significant level (mean score .389, .200, and .184, respectively).

Results at the Trait Level

No measure of the trait level of positive regard was available in more than one of the studies in this aggregate sample. Therefore, no comment can be made concerning the trait level of positive regard.

Results at the Social-Role Level

In only one of the seven studies of managers' perceptions were items relating to positive regard listed as required for performance as a man-

ager. It was not perceived, even in this one study, that these characteristics distinguish superior performance as a manager. In the one study,
it included items such as: "having respect for one's subordinates; and
acceptance of others regardless of status."

Interpretation

Positive regard shows only a slight relationship to managerial effectiveness at the middle management level. It can, at best, be termed a
threshold competency at the middle management level only. The belief
that people can do their jobs effectively, which would seem to be related
to managerial performance, may not be the same as a basic belief in
people, which was coded as positive regard. The weak relationship to
effectiveness suggests that other aspects of work organizations may affect people's sense of being valued more significantly than does managers' behavior. Although it seems counterintuitive, it may also be that
people do not have to feel valued to perform effectively. None of the
interpretations can be confirmed with information available in this
study.

MANAGING GROUP PROCESS

Managing group process is a competency in which people can stimulate
others to work together effectively in group settings. Such people see
themselves as being able to make groups work well together. In social or
organizational contexts, these people adopt the role of collaborator or
integrator. They demonstrate group process skills and skills in using
instrumental affiliative behavior for group task accomplishment.

People who can use the managing group process competency behave
in certain ways. They communicate to a group the need for collaboration and cooperation. These people are able to get one work group to
cooperate with another work group.

They create symbols of group identity, pride, and trust which represent the team effort. People with this characteristic use personal contact
and friendliness as instrumental behavior in building the group members' commitment to the team and their task effort. They involve all
concerned parties in resolving a conflict within a working unit. They do
not take on or perform a task that should be a group effort.

For example, a manager in the sample who had this characteristic
worked in a consumer products company. In this company, once a new
product idea was developed to the prototype stage, a product-oriented
project team was established to carry it through all the stages of further

development and initial market testing until the product was ready for large-scale production. Many of the people assigned to the project felt that it interfered with their regular job responsibilities. The manager called frequent staff meetings of all personnel who might be involved early in the project. Even those people who would not be involved until the market testing phase were brought into a weekly meeting to discuss progress. The manager attempted to have the weekly meetings to solve problems, as well as report on progress. Each week, he made sure that there was some problem that the team could address and attempt to solve. He also stressed the importance of the various perspectives represented by the functional specialists within the team. Once the product was ready for market testing, he had a party for all the similar project teams in the company to "introduce" the new product. At the party, he introduced each member of the team and announced in a humorous style major contributions that each person had made to the team's progress.

The product was market tested, and the results were poor. The president of the company wanted to drop the product. The manager asked for two weeks to try to work out the problems. The team members all pushed for the extra two weeks. They got approval for only a week of extra work. The manager did not have to ask the team members for a major push—they all put in long hours that week. As a result of some creative problem solving and the perseverance of the team members, they changed the product design in two major ways. The new market test results were excellent. When the product went into production, the members of the team all requested that they be placed on another product team. What started as an assignment that a number of team members resented ended in a product and a group process that all members enjoyed and took pride in.

The following examples from managers in the sample also illustrate the demonstration of managing group process in their jobs.

I make it a point of going down to the floor area once a day, and I make it a point when I've got them in on Saturday to go down there and be highly visible. I walk up the back door and down the stairs and spend about 10 or 15 minutes. Unless it's absolutely impossible, I get in there. It gives them a chance to say hello, or ask a question. It also shows them, on Saturdays, that I'm not asking them to do something I won't do.

When I first started, I made a decision to talk with my staff. I saw the group as a unit and wanted everyone to do the same. I interviewed each one, asking about the inputs and outputs of their jobs. We are an electronics company, so I thought that would be a good way to get them to tell me about their jobs. I then had them review what they told me in a group meeting. I got a picture of the unit and understood what people were working on, and the connections to other groups within the organization. They got a sense of how everyone was fitting together.

Results at the Skill Level

Managing group process (referred to as MGP) as coded in the interviews was significantly related to effectiveness as a manager (F = 4.330, df = 2, p = .02), and showed a significant linear trend favoring superior managers (F = 8.589, df = 1, p = .004). Comparison of the groups with t-tests, shown in Figures 6-3 and 6-4 (see Appendix A for detail), indicated that:

1. Superior and average managers demonstrated significantly more MGP than did poor managers, and superior managers demonstrated more MGP than did average managers at a near significant level.

2. Private sector managers demonstrated more MGP than did public sector managers at a near significant level.

3. Among public sector managers, superior performers demonstrated significantly more MGP than did poor performers.

4. Among entry level managers, poor performers demonstrated more MGP than did superior performers at a near significant level, and average performers demonstrated significantly more MGP than did superior performers.

5. Among middle level managers, superior performers demonstrated significantly more MGP than did average and poor performers.

6. Among executive level managers, average performers demonstrated more MGP than did poor performers at a near significant level.

7. Personnel managers demonstrated more MGP than did manufacturing managers at a near significant level.

8. Among manufacturing managers, average performers demonstrated significantly more MGP than did poor performers.

Results at the Social-Role Level

Items relating to managing group process were listed in five of seven studies of managers' perceptions as required for performance as a manager. In only one study were these items perceived by managers as char-

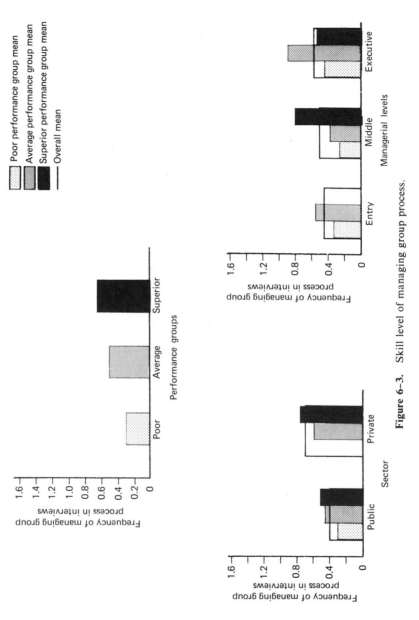

Figure 6–3. Skill level of managing group process.

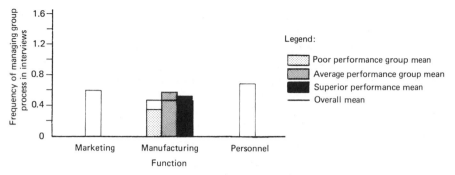

Figure 6–4. Skill level of managing group process by function.

acteristics distinguishing superior performance as a manager. This included items such as: "ability to manage groups; build team spirit; and create a group identity."

Interpretation

Managing group process appears related to effectiveness as a manager, except at the entry level. Most managers must spend time managing groups, whether the groups be their own staff (i.e., subordinates) or special temporary project teams. They must also spend time integrating groups from various units in the organization. Although the amount of time that a manager spends managing groups varies considerably from job to job, the results regarding the managing group process competency confirm the observation that groups are a basic element in a manager's human resource management system, particularly at the middle and executive levels of management.

Private sector managers appear to demonstrate slightly more managing group process than do managers in the public sector. This may be a function of the relatively greater number of constraints placed on public sector managers regarding options for human resource management. It is relatively more difficult for a public sector manager to bring together people from various units in an organization to create working groups or teams than for private sector managers. Civil service guidelines, detailed job descriptions, and caution to avoid overstepping one's territorial boundaries all contribute to constraining a manager in the public sector from forming and managing groups and stimulating collaboration and commitment with the flexibility that many private sector managers can. Although the constraints in the public sector may affect a manager's ability to demonstrate this characteristic, superior performers within the public sector manage group process more than do their less effective counterparts.

Personnel managers demonstrate slightly more of this characteristic than do manufacturing managers. This may be a function of the context in which certain types of activities occur. Personnel managers involved in training and development activities usually deliver such services in groups. In addition, feedback from surveys, problem-solving sessions, and other such responsibilities of personnel managers frequently take place in group settings. In the context of their jobs, personnel managers appear to have more opportunity to use the managing group process competency. Although manufacturing managers may not have as much opportunity, average performers do demonstrate more of the characteristic than do poor performers within the manufacturing function.

ACCURATE SELF-ASSESSMENT

Accurate self-assessment is a competency in which people have a realistic or grounded view of themselves. These people see their strengths and weaknesses and know their limitations, a characteristic that Bray et al. (1974) called self-objectivity. These people can demonstrate self-assessment skills and reality testing skills; that is, skills in testing their perceptions and judgments about themselves against some other view.

People who possess accurate self-assessment behave in certain ways. For example, they are able to describe and evaluate the effectiveness of their performance in a particular situation. Results of specific actions taken are attributed to personal strengths or weaknesses. Such people would not necessarily be labeled as humble, nor showing humility, because they readily admit their strengths. At the same time, these strengths are not aggrandized or overestimated. The strengths are in the context of admitted limitations or weaknesses. People with accurate self-assessment usually identify and seek help or activities to remedy their weaknesses. This behavior can be observed most frequently in someone who has both accurate self-assessment and proactivity.

For example, marketing managers asked by a subordinate about the meaning of technical specifications of a product might respond in a number of ways. If the managers have accurate self-assessment, they readily admit that they do not understand the meaning of these specifications. They probably then add that they will find the information, or they encourage the subordinate to ask someone else in the organization who has the information. Marketing managers who do not have accurate self-assessment may "tap dance" and make up an answer on the spot. They might also point out that the meaning of the particular specifications in question are not important. They might contend that the approach taken in marketing the product should be a function of the customer's perception of the product, or some other technical aspect than the one being questioned.

The following examples from managers in the sample illustrate the demonstration of accurate self-assessment in their jobs.

I knew how I would judge it, by price, performance, and delivery. I didn't say anything, though. I listened. The reason for that is, by sheer experience, I could outnegotiate or steer them in the wrong direction by giving inputs. I could give them information as to what a clause is and they would trust me as an authority and then sign the contract. But I listened and found out what they wanted.

I'm frustrated that I just haven't gotten a handle on everything in this job. The situation I was just describing is an example of how I'm just not as knowledgeable of the total program as I'd like to be.

I felt effective because I had helped surface the issues. I opened up communication and surfaced what could have been a performance problem before it got to that point. I felt that it was a positive learning experience for the new supervisor by showing her how important it is to communicate with the employee rather than being totally task-oriented, which didn't allow for good communication. I felt helpful on a personal level with the new employee, who was having trouble with the company's system. I think a lot of the specific questions I asked each of them and the way I stayed calm and didn't pass judgment helped them to see a better way to handle these types of problems.

Results at the Skill Level

At the skill level, accurate self-assessment (referred to as ASA) as coded in the interviews was barely related to effective performance as a manager, and showed a near significant linear trend favoring the better managers ($F = 3.166$, df $= 1$, $p = .076$). Comparison of the groups with t-tests, shown in Figures 6-5 and 6-6 (see Appendix A for detail), showed that:

1. Superior managers demonstrated significantly more ASA than did poor managers.

2. Among entry level managers, average performers demonstrated significantly more ASA than did poor performers.

3. Among middle level managers, superior performers demon-

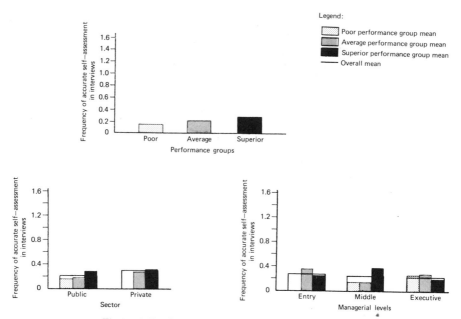

Figure 6–5. Skill level of accurate self-assessment.

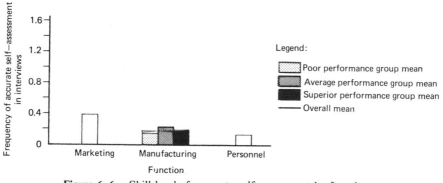

Figure 6–6. Skill level of accurate self-assessment by function.

136

strated significantly more ASA than did average and poor performers.

4. Marketing managers demonstrated significantly more ASA than did manufacturing and personnel managers.

Interpretation

Accurate self-assessment appears somewhat related to effective performance as a manager, particularly in middle level management. There were no results at the social role level. Due to these evident but weak results, accurate self-assessment could be considered a threshold competency. The results suggest, with some caution, that managers should have a degree of maturity that allows them to see themselves accurately, identifying and admitting strengths and weaknesses. It would certainly be difficult for managers to stimulate this characteristic in their subordinates if the managers do not demonstrate it.

The fact that marketing managers demonstrate more accurate self-assessment than do manufacturing or personnel managers could be a function of the relative uncertainty and diversity of the environments in which the former operate. Uncertainty of product changes by the organization, changes in marketplace demand, and changes in competitive edge may require marketing managers to have more reality-based perceptions of themselves. The consequences of inaccurate assessment of strengths and limitations in these aspects of the marketing manager's environment could be from minimal to disastrous for the entire organization.

SUMMARY ON THE HUMAN RESOURCE MANAGEMENT CLUSTER

Summary of Findings

The competencies in the human resource management cluster appear related to managerial effectiveness, but with some qualifications. The use of socialized power is a competency for managers in general. Managing group process is a competency for managers except for those in entry level jobs. Accurate self-assessment is a threshold competency primarily for middle level managers, but with a slight relationship to effectiveness for entry level managers. Positive regard is a threshold competency related to effectiveness for middle level managers only. The findings are summarized in Table 6-1.

TABLE 6-1   The Human Resource Management Cluster[a]

Competency	Motive	Trait	Self-Image	Social Role	Skills
Use of Socialized Power			I am a member of a team	*Team member* *Organization Member*	*Alliance producing skills*
Positive Regard		Belief in People	I am good	Optimist	*Verbal and nonverbal skills that result in people feeling valued*[b]
Managing group process			I can make groups work effectively	*Collaborator* *Integrator*	*Instrumental affiliative behaviors*[c] *Group Process Skills*[c]
Accurate self-assessment			I know my limitations, my strengths and weaknesses	Sounding board Reality tester	*Self-assessment skills* *Reality testing skills*

[a]Levels of each competency for which results indicate a relationship to managerial effectiveness are italicized.
[b]At middle level management jobs only.
[c]At middle and executive management jobs only.

The only sector difference noted within this cluster regarded the managing group process competency. Managers in the private sector appeared to demonstrate more of this competency than did managers in the public sector. Forming task groups, facilitating collaboration, and building group identity and pride within the public sector may violate statutes and regulations regarding the functioning of specific agencies. For example, from a total federal organization standpoint, it would be most efficient to bring together a group of specialists to address an emergent and serious problem, such as a dramatic increase in urban homicide. To call together a task force of representatives from the FBI, Treasury Department, CIA, military police, state police, and municipal police departments may be efficient for problem identification and problem solving, but would violate stipulations regarding territory, span of influence, and jurisdiction, which are part of the operating objectives and policies of these various organizations. Other members of the federal government and the populace that they are serving would probably object as well. While these constraints may be appropriate, reasonable, and needed within public sector organizations, they do result in decreased opportunities and flexibility for demonstration of certain competencies by managers. Again, despite relative opportunity differences, effective managers in the public sector do demonstrate more managing group process than do their less effective counterparts.

Every one of the competencies in the human resource management cluster is related to managerial effectiveness in middle level management jobs. Managing entry level managers and often other middle level managers involves some demonstration of positive regard in stimulating effective performance of subordinates. Since middle level managers are farther from the actual production work, and performance objectives and measures are less clear, middle level managers must utilize a greater number of interpersonal competencies as represented in the human resource management cluster than must entry level managers.

The only competency in this cluster that showed a relationship to effectiveness for executive level managers was managing group process. The use of socialized power and accurate self-assessment showed a relationship to effectiveness for entry level managers. None of these three findings could be considered strong. They are important to note because they may help to describe the changes needed in certain interpersonal competencies used by effective managers as they move from entry level to middle level to executive level management jobs.

Personnel managers demonstrated more of the managing group process and use of socialized power competencies than did manufacturing managers. The various responsibilities for negotiating, training, counseling, and explaining organizational policy require that these managers build networks and alliances throughout the organization, as well as within their own unit. Much of this activity takes place in groups. Also, the lack of formal "line" authority involved in performing most of their duties results in a necessity that personnel managers use alternate forms of influence, as reflected in the use of socialized power competency. Although demonstration of these competencies may not be required as often by manufacturing managers, effective ones demonstrate more of both of these competencies than do their less effective counterparts.

Interactions at the Skill Level

These two competencies and two threshold competencies can be said to have primary relationships with each other. To build team spirit, group identity and pride (i.e., managing group process), managers must be able to form networks and coalitions (i.e., use of socialized power). Likewise, it would be difficult to form networks or coalitions (i.e., use of socialized power) without being able to stimulate cooperation and collaboration on tasks and on approachs to issues (i.e., managing group process). To stimulate group pride, spirit, and collaboration (i.e., managing group process), to build coalitions and model desirable behavior (i.e., use of socialized power), a manager must have a realistic view of his or her strengths and limitations (i.e., accurate self-assessment). Without this realistic view of himself or herself, people in the networks, coalitions, or groups would see the person as a threat to the group's integrity, or at best as a marginal member, thereby severely limiting the person's ability to influence group members. At the same time, it is difficult for a person to get a realistic view of his or her strengths and limitations (i.e., accurate self-assessment) without collaborative relationships in which the person can see or hear about his or her strengths and limitations (i.e., managing group process and use of socialized power). Without the skill to build such relationships, the individual may get a biased view of himself or herself, seeing only strengths or weaknesses. To build networks and coalitions and to promote team spirit and collaboration (i.e., use of socialized power and managing group process), a manager must have faith in people's ability to change and to demonstrate appropriate behavior when given the opportunity (i.e., positive regard). Without it, such attempts would be viewed by others as artificial and manipulative. Similarly, having collaborative relationships and being a part of networks and coalitions contributes to and confirms a person's positive expectations of others.

To have positive expectations about others (i.e., positive regard), a person must have a realistic view of himself or herself (i.e., accurate self-assessment). Otherwise, the person's expectations about others may be naive or lack sincerity. Without positive regard, a person's view of himself or herself will tend to exaggerate his or her strengths or weaknesses (i.e., overestimate or underestimate one's capability).

Although the competencies and threshold competencies in the human resource management cluster did not group together with the competencies in the goal and action management cluster nor the leadership cluster, they showed a strong positive relationship to the former ($r = .432$, $N = 253$, $p < .001$) and a positive relationship to the latter ($r = .277$,

$N = 253, p < .001$). This suggests that the competencies and threshold competencies in the human resource management cluster have a secondary relationship to the competencies in both the goal and action management and the leadership clusters. That is, a manager could demonstrate the competencies and threshold competencies in the human resource management cluster without possessing the competencies in the goal and action management or leadership clusters, but possession of the competencies in these other clusters would enhance a manager's ability to demonstrate those competencies in the human resource management cluster. Setting goals, establishing plans, and initiating activity toward them (i.e., the goal and action management cluster) would provide a manager with the purpose and context for establishing coalitions, building collaborative work groups, stimulating work group pride and spirit, and obtaining a realistic view of himself or herself (i.e., the human resource management cluster). Having a realistic view of himself or herself and building such coalitions and work groups would enhance a manager's ability to initiate action, establish plans, and have impact on others.

Similarly, identifying themes and patterns in the organization and communicating them to others clearly, convincingly, and in an inspiring manner would enhance a manager's ability to form coalitions and networks, and build collaborative relationships in a work group, while stimulating pride and team spirit in the work group. Forming and being a part of such work groups and coalitions would provide a manager with the opportunity to make important presentations, and with additional information with which to identify themes and patterns regarding concerns, objectives, views, and performance of people in the organization.

CHAPTER SEVEN

The Directing
Subordinates Cluster

The two most direct methods a manager can use in guiding or controlling the activities of his or her subordinates is providing performance feedback and interpreting the feedback and its consequences. Feedback is a term borrowed from electrical engineering that refers to a flow of electrical impulses back to a source of those pulses. In management and organizational jargon, feedback has come to mean the return of information to a source. In its purest form, such information would concern only the result of a person's or an organization's actions, such as "Our branch hit a sales volume of $3,750,000 this month," or "Our division realized profits of $14,000,000 this month," or "The financial analysts were impressed with the presentation given by the treasurer."

Usually, the feedback includes an interpretation of the information. The interpretation may be in terms of variances to plan or budget, variances to organizational policies or tradition, or variances to someone's beliefs or preferences. The interpretation often results in a person feeling rewarded or punished. If performance was better than the plan, a manager's positive feedback (i.e., favorable interpretation of variance to plan) to the subordinate is rewarding. Similarly, if performance was over budget, a manager's negative feedback (i.e., unfavorable interpretation of variance to budget) to the subordinate is punishing. Often, the interpretation is necessary for the information have meaning, especially when the variances concern actions and consequences that are difficult to measure, such as "Too much humor was used at the Board of Directors meeting."

This explanation concerning feedback may appear overly simplistic to most managers, but many managers confuse the feeding back of performance information with the interpretation of it. Providing the information without interpretation concerning a person's or a group's performance is a potent managerial act. Providing information on performance, interpreting what the information means to the subordinate, and placing positive or negative values on the performance not only directs subordinate activity but also can be motivating to subordinates. Unfortunately, some managers think that feedback and the motivation to improve performance should be imparted with force. They walk around the office or plant as if they have steel-toed wing tips poised, ready to provide feedback. Although giving orders and disciplining subordinates is sometimes required in management jobs, a kung-fu management style (i.e., a style emphasizing the martial arts and not the spiritual aspect of kung-fu) does not produce performance improvement over long periods of time. What is it about some managers that enables them to guide and control their subordinates toward improved performance in a way that others cannot?

Three underlying characteristics that enable a manager to respond to these requirements of the job were identified through the cluster analysis of the managers in this study. They were labeled the *directing subordinates cluster*. The three competencies are: (1) developing others; (2) use of unilateral power; and (3) spontaneity. Managers with this set of competencies express themselves to others to improve subordinates' performance by giving directions, orders, commands, and performance feedback. Each of these competencies will be examined separately before continuing the discussion of their joint impact on managerial effectiveness.

DEVELOPING OTHERS

Developing others is a competency with which managers specifically help someone do his or her job. People with this characteristic see helping others as an essential part of the manager's job. They view themselves as helpful to others. In social and organizational contexts, such people adopt the role of coach or helper. They demonstrate feedback skills in facilitating self-development of others.

People with this competency behave in certain ways. They give others performance feedback with the intent of stimulating improved performance. They invite subordinates to discuss performance problems. People with this characteristic make training, expert help, and other resources available to others to help those individuals improve their skills and get their job done. While helping others, they are careful to allow the individual to take personal responsibility for making changes and testing his or her effectiveness.

Manufacturing managers who have this competency would provide a production supervisor with daily and weekly performance information. They might establish a chart or board in the work area of the production supervisor and have someone from operations post the number of products off the line on a daily basis. They may also have someone from the financial group post waste reduction or cost saving information on a weekly basis on the same chart. Periodically, these managers might discuss progress with the production supervisor in terms of production-line performance objectives. All of these steps might be taken with the intent that production supervisors manage their groups effectively and improve performance given the relevant information in a timely fashion.

The following examples from managers in the sample illustrate the demonstration of developing others in their jobs.

> There was a young man drafting some of the procedures in handling union grievances. Because management of grievances was a high priority, I tried to train this fellow. To give him some experience, I had him sit in on some of the grievance meetings and take minutes. Before this, I used to take the minutes. This exposed him to the situation and how the procedures unfolded in real life.

> I try to develop a team of people. I react differently to different people. One guy in particular, I get him motivated by giving him a challenge. For example, in the third quarter of this year I bet him a dinner that he wouldn't ship X number of dollars. It was a goal that I set that I thought was achievable. I lost the dinner, and I'm glad that I did. He likes little challenges as opposed to me going down and saying, you will ship X number of dollars by the end of June.

> I had a performance problem with this one worker that was getting pretty bad. I told him, 'I'll give you three weeks to try to work it out. At the end of that I, we, will either see a change or you must be transferred." I told him that he must think of himself more objectively and of his motives for doing things. The third week he came back and said that he had realized what he had been doing and changed. Yes, he is doing very well now.

Results at the Skill Level

Developing others (referred to as DO) as coded in the interviews appeared related to effectiveness as a manager ($F = 7.255$, $df = 2$, $p < .01$), with a significant nonlinear trend favoring average managers ($F = 13.364$, $df = 1$, $p = .0005$). Comparison of the groups with t-tests, shown in Figures 7-1 and 7-2 (see Appendix A for detail,) indicated that:

1. Superior managers demonstrated significantly more DO than did poor managers and significantly less DO than did average managers, and average managers demonstrated significantly more DO than did poor managers.

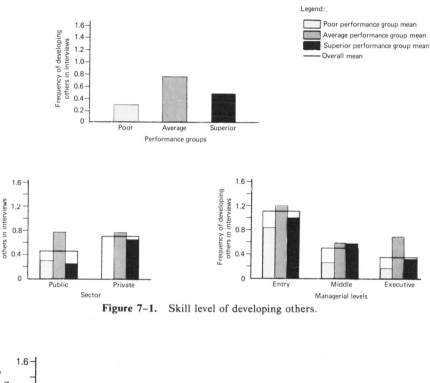

Figure 7–1. Skill level of developing others.

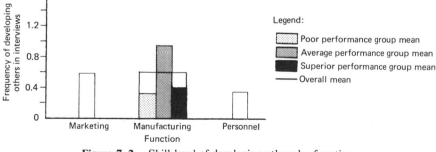

Figure 7–2. Skill level of developing others by function.

2. Among public sector managers, average performers demonstrated significantly more DO than did superior and poor managers.

3. Entry level managers demonstrated significantly more DO than did middle and executive level managers, and middle level managers demonstrated more DO than did executive level managers at a near significant level.

4. Among middle level managers, superior and average performers demonstrated significantly more DO than did poor performers.

5. Among executive level managers, average performers demonstrated significantly more DO than did poor performers and more DO than did superior performers at a near significant level, and superior performers demonstrated more DO than did poor performers at a near significant level.

6. Personnel managers demonstrated significantly less DO than did manufacturing managers, and less DO than did marketing managers at a near significant level.

7. Among manufacturing managers, average performers demonstrated significantly more DO than did superior and poor performers.

Results at the Social-Role Level

In six of the seven studies of managers' perceptions, items relating to developing others were listed as required for performance as a manager. In three of the studies, these items were perceived by managers as characteristics that distinguish superior performance as a manager. This included items such as: "giving subordinates feedback on their job performance," "helping individual workers with job-related problems," and "ability to counsel or advise subordinates about the job."

Interpretation

Developing others appears related to effective managerial performance; in particular, it is demonstrated by average performers overall, within the public sector, within middle and executive managerial levels, and within the manufacturing function. Although superior performers appear to have less of it than do average performers, they do demonstrate more of developing others than do poor performers overall, and within the middle and executive managerial levels. This suggests that, while it is important to have this characteristic to be effective as a manager, having a great deal of it does not necessarily relate directly to superior performance.

It may be that managers who spend a lot of time using the developing others competency substitute the development of subordinates as a primary goal of their organizational unit rather than keeping the development of subordinates in the context of organizational output or task performance goals. Certainly, developing subordinates within a unit should lead to improved unit performance. This relationship may not be as direct as it appears on the surface. While the managerial role is often described in terms of developing others, this may not be as important as such corporate values suggest. If developing others becomes a primary objective, decisions may be made and actions taken that help others develop but which do not result in maximum current productivity or performance.

For example, one of the managers in the sample was sales manager of a consumer products company. She was effective because, among other competencies, developing others was one of her interpersonal competencies. The sales personnel reporting to the manager performed more effectively toward their sales targets because they knew the targets, received performance feedback on a timely basis, and the manager made training or expert resources available to facilitate performance improvement. At one point, a recently hired subordinate's sales performance during the first three months was below the target established for new sales personnel. The manager discussed the performance problem with the subordinate. The subordinate felt that he needed some extra training because the nature of the product being sold was different than any he had handled previously. The manager provided the subordinate with additional training and had the subordinate go along with some of the superior performers to observe effective techniques. During the second three months, the subordinate's performance improved over the first period, but it was still below targets established for comparable sales personnel. The manager contended that the person was improving and must have another chance to demonstrate that he was acquiring the needed skills. The subordinate was not to be fired or transferred because the manager wanted to keep this person on and give him a chance to improve. Unfortunately, this decision was not consistent with the best interests of the organization, as her boss pointed out to her. The vice president of sales felt that it would not facilitate the maximum performance of the retail business, since this salesperson is one of a total sales force of five people. The manager explained that turnover of sales personnel is costly and that if this particular salesperson could be developed, the company would have an effective performer who was committed to the organization. The vice president went along with her position on the issue but expressed his reservations about the burden it placed on the other sales personnel. Developing others can be related to effectiveness as a manager, but may not have a positive impact on corporate performance if the manager has too much of it.

Entry level managers demonstrate more of developing others than do middle and executive level managers, and middle level managers show more of it than do executive level managers. This suggests that the developing others competency may be proportionately more important the closer one's management job is to the actual accomplishment of the work (i.e., the production of the product). As managers increase the span of control, their arena of responsibility, and the various layers of management reporting to them, the importance of developing others may decrease. Other competencies, such as those in the leadership cluster, would emerge as increasingly relevant.

The fact that personnel managers demonstrated developing others less often than did managers in marketing or manufacturing may seem counterintuitive; after all, working with people is their job. It is more accurate to say that working on human resource issues, rather than working with people, is their job. A compensation manager may have less interaction with others than does a production manager. This may also support the often made observation that it is relatively more difficult for personnel managers, as opposed to marketing or manufacturing managers, to assess and give performance feedback to their subordinates on measurable aspects of performance. Marketing and manufacturing managers have access to performance measures that are observable, explicit, and timely (e.g., sales per week, number of units off the production line). Personnel managers often have a difficult time measuring, and therefore informing their subordinates about the effectiveness of a training program, a career pathing system, or a new compensation system.

USE OF UNILATERAL POWER

Use of unilateral power is a competency with which people use forms of influence to obtain compliance; that is, managers act to stimulate subordinates, or others, to go along with their directions, wishes, commands, policies, or procedures. These people see themselves as being in charge. In social or organizational contexts, they adopt roles of being in charge of the group or certain functioning of the group. They demonstrate influence skills that produce compliance of others.

People who can use unilateral power behave in certain ways. They give orders, commands, or directions based on personal authority, positional authority, or the policies of the organization. Such people give directions, orders, or commands without necessarily soliciting the input of others, even in situations in which input has been solicited previously.

For example, a production supervisor in a plant at an industrial products company had established certain procedures and methods of operation on a newly established production line. These procedures were to ensure safety of personnel, not only to comply with government regulations, but also to protect workers from the hazards of chemicals with which they worked. He carefully instructed the personnel on specific activities to be performed and procedures to be followed. One of the production workers stopped wearing protective gloves in the second week of operation of the production line. The production supervisor told him to wear the gloves one morning. That afternoon the supervisor noticed that the worker was still not using the gloves. When he approached the worker to restate his directive, the worker insisted that there was no danger from the chemicals and that he could operate his machine better without the gloves. The production supervisor replied, "This is not a point of discussion. Wear the gloves and that's all!"

The following examples from managers in the sample also illustrate the demonstration of use of unilateral power in their jobs.

> I can remember the first meeting I ever had with the union. They had seven people lined up to have an overwhelming presence . . . . We had several months of meetings after that, but at one of the meetings the chief steward had asked me a question and I was trying to answer it, when the president of the union asked me another question, and I said, "Let me answer this one and I'll get to that one." He started doing a singsong of "I want an answer. I want an answer. I want an answer." At that point, I said, "I cannot work in this kind of situation. So, goodbye." That shocked them. I had to leave three meetings that way before we could get to the issues in a reasonable manner.

> Delivery performance of one of our suppliers was down. So I went on a trip with the buyer as back up support. We got there and met with two people who were incompetent. Their VPs had assured me that these two guys had the information. I was mad. I called the executive VP. It was gutsy because I went over the two VPs' heads and I was doing it rather than our buyer. I told him that we had a contractual agreement and that the performance of his company was horrible. I said that they were not paying attention to spares and that we didn't want to shut off the new contract but might have to if we didn't get the parts we needed. He gave me the party line and said he would remedy it. Well, the next day one of the VPs

called me and was Mr. Humble. We got the parts and the delivery performance improved.

Results at the Skill Level

Use of unilateral power (referred to as UUP) as coded in the interviews was related to effectiveness as a manager ($F = 4.078$, df $= 2$, $p = .02$), with a significant nonlinear trend favoring average managers ($F = 8.115$, df $= 1$, $p = .005$). Comparison of the groups with t-tests, shown in Figures 7-3 and 7-4 (see Appendix A for detail), indicated that:

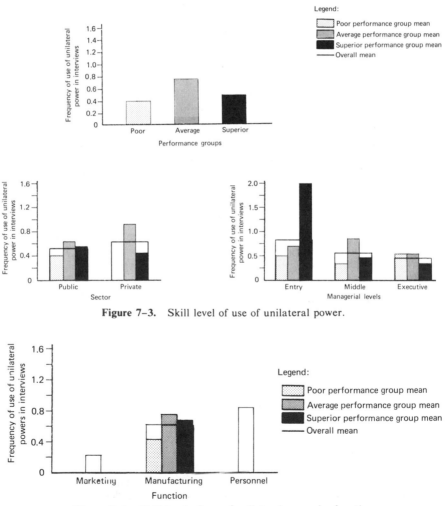

Figure 7–3. Skill level of use of unilateral power.

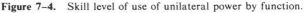

Figure 7–4. Skill level of use of unilateral power by function.

1. Average managers demonstrated significantly more UUP than did superior and poor managers.

2. Among public sector managers, average performers demonstrated significantly more UUP than did poor performers.

3. Among private sector managers, average performers demonstrated significantly more UUP than did superior performers.

4. Entry level managers demonstrated significantly more UUP than did executive level managers.

5. Among entry level managers, superior performers demonstrated more UUP than did average and poor performers at near significant levels.

6. Among middle level managers, average performers demonstrated significantly more UUP than did superior and poor performers.

7. Marketing managers demonstrated significantly less UUP than did manufacturing and personnel managers.

8. Among manufacturing managers, average performers demonstrated significantly more UUP than did poor performers, and superior performers demonstrated more UUP than did poor performers at a near significant level.

Results at the Social Role Level

In five of the seven studies of managers' perceptions, items relating to the use of unilateral power were listed as required for performance as a manager. In only one of these studies were these items perceived by managers as characteristics distinguishing superior performance as a manager. This included items such as: "ability to assume command in emergency situations, ability to give orders and direct subordinates, and ability and willingness to follow orders."

Interpretation

In entry level managerial jobs and in manufacturing management, use of unilateral power appears to be related to effective performance. In other situations, this characteristic appears related only to average performance. Use of unilateral power should, therefore, be considered a threshold competency with particular relevance in entry level management jobs. In entry level and manufacturing management jobs, compliance may be appropriate to ensure safety of workers, quality control standards in products, adherence to union stipulations, and maintenance of equipment and facilities. For jobs that demand this type of adherence to specific procedures and methods of operation, the use of unilateral power appears to be an interpersonal competency that contributes to the effectiveness of a manager. In other types of management jobs (i.e., other functions and other levels), managers seeking compliance may avoid missing a deadline or may "get the product out the door," but may lose the loyalty, commitment, or sense of personal responsibility of their subordinates or colleagues.

The fact that personnel managers demonstrate more use of unilateral power than do marketing managers fits within this interpretation. Personnel managers are responsible for ensuring that selection, promotion, compensation, and firing procedures comply with consistent organizational policy and government guidelines. Personnel managers also are often responsible for ensuring that union and management relations do not cause work stoppages. They must monitor and require the compliance of both union members and representatives with contract stipulations, as well as management's compliance. Both of these types of duties require substantial use of unilateral power, given the current status of the relationship between organizations, unions, and government agencies.

SPONTANEITY

Spontaneity is a competency with which people can express themselves freely or easily. These people see themselves as being able to act freely in the present (i.e., the here-and-now). In social and organizational contexts, they may find themselves in the role of a provoker (i.e., attempting to "provoke" someone) or a jester (i.e., attempting to elicit laughter). People with spontaneity demonstrate a variety of self-expression skills.

People with spontaneity tend to speak and behave in certain ways. They may express themselves with distinctly more emotion (i.e., positive or negative emotion) than others in various situations. They may act directly and without first thinking about the potential impact of these statements on others. They may be surprised when someone responds adversely. When people make quick or snap decisions, they may be demonstrating spontaneity.

Spontaneity does, in some sense, reflect impulsivity and is, therefore, opposite to self-control. It also represents a sense of freedom and an ability to express oneself that is not necessarily in conflict with self-control. For example, when their boss presents them with a new approach to a problem, managers may have difficulty articulating why they think the new approach will lead to more problems than the approach that has been used. Managers with spontaneity are more likely to find some mode of expressing this reservation and concern. The characteristic of spontaneity does not address the effectiveness of the expression that is covered in the competency called the use of oral presentations (see Chapter 5, The Leadership Cluster). Spontaneity is merely the individual's ability to feel secure or mature enough to recognize and express any thoughts, feelings, or opinions.

The following examples from managers in the sample illustrate the demonstration of spontaneity in their jobs.

> We had been working on a problem in the furnaces. Some of the engineers had figured out that a chemical reaction was taking place and producing a gas that we didn't want in the furnace. We were working on it flat out. One afternoon we were taking stock. One engineer had presented a theoretical idea as to what was happening. Another guy came up with an alternative way of setting up the furnace. Another engineer had an idea about a different alloy that wouldn't cause the same reaction. We were bouncing these ideas around. We were confused but pretty worked up about the problem. Finally, I said, "Enough talk. By God, let's just go out and squeeze some of that stuff and try it out." This eventually led to the solution to this problem that the plant had had on and off for four or five years.

> The general manager liked to have a lot of meetings. He expected everyone presenting information to use lots of graphs and would ask questions about details endlessly. I had recommended that we streamline the meetings to several agenda items and limit the number of graphs per agenda item. One day the general manager was complaining to me in my office that he thought people weren't doing enough preparation for the meetings. He had so missed the point that I told him that the staff saw those meetings as a real pain in the ___. He was mad and left. Several days later he came into my office to chew me out about some detail that he thought I had not followed up on. I had had it. I let loose and we had a real screaming session. Because I don't usually get that upset, the general manager finally calmed down and started to listen. The next day, he had a staff meeting and ran it very differently. He discussed only two subjects and said something to me at the end about having "gotten the message."

Results at the Skill Level

Spontaneity (referred to as SPON) as coded in the interviews is only related to effective performance as a manager at a near significant level ($F = 2.762$, df $= 2$, $p = .065$), with a near significant linear trend favoring average and superior managers ($F = 3.414$, df $= p = .066$). Comparison of the groups with t-tests, shown in Figures 7-5 and 7-6 (see Appendix A for detail), revealed that:

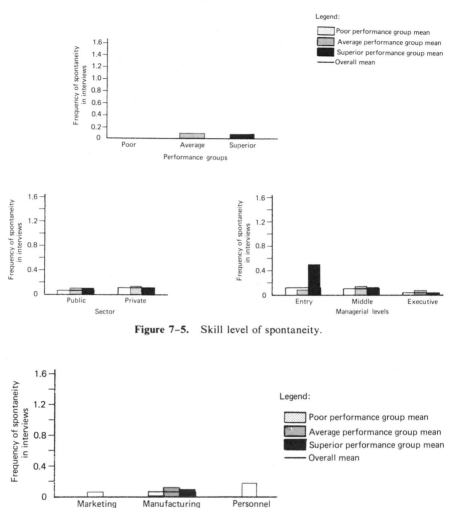

Figure 7-5. Skill level of spontaneity.

Figure 7-6. Skill level of spontaneity by function.

1. Superior and average managers demonstrated significantly more SPON than did poor performers.

2. Among public sector managers, superior and average performers demonstrated significantly more SPON than did poor performers.

3. Middle level managers demonstrated significantly more SPON than did executive level managers.

4. Among entry level managers, average performers demonstrated more SPON than did poor performers at a near significant level.

5. Among middle level managers, superior and average performers demonstrated significantly more SPON than did poor performers.

6. Personnel managers demonstrated more SPON than did marketing and manufacturing managers at near significant levels.

7. Among manufacturing managers, average performers demonstrated significantly more SPON than did poor performers, and superior performers demonstrated more SPON than did poor performers at a near significant level.

Interpretation

The evidence suggests a slight relationship of spontaneity to performance as a manager. It was not often evident in the interviews. The relationship to managerial performance appears to result primarily from the complete absence of spontaneity in the poor performing managers. This suggests that managers may need spontaneity to be effective, but that an increase in spontaneity does not necessarily lead to an increase in their performance. It could, with some caution, be considered a threshold competency. There was no supporting evidence at the social role level.

The relatively low amount of spontaneity demonstrated by executives is probably a function of the representational aspects of executives' jobs. Executives are not as "free" to express personal feelings, opinions, and thoughts without considering the consequences to the organization. An executive is in a position where expression of personal views that are contrary to a "management position" would create confusion, disruption, or even conflict rather than merely be seen as that person's view.

SUMMARY ON THE DIRECTING SUBORDINATES CLUSTER

The three characteristics in the directing subordinates cluster appear related to managerial effectiveness with certain qualifications. Developing others, the use of unilateral power and spontaneity are merely threshold competencies. The findings about these competencies are summarized in Table 7-1.

Developing others shows an overall relationship to effectiveness, but in a curvilinear manner. Overall, average and superior managers

TABLE 7-1 The Directing Subordinates Cluster[a]

Competency	Motive	Trait	Self-Image	Social Role	Skills
Developing others			I am helpful to others	*Coach* *Helper*	*Skills in feedback to facilitate self-development*
Use of unilaterial power			I am in charge	*Person in charge*	*Compliance producing skills[b]*
Spontaneity			I can act freely in the here and now	Provoker Jester	*Self-expression skills*

[a]Levels of each competency for which results indicate a relationship to managerial effectiveness are italicized.
[b]At entry level management jobs only.

demonstrate more developing others than do poor managers, but average managers show more of the characteristic than do superior managers. Developing others appears particularly relevant to entry level, marketing, and manufacturing management jobs. At the same time, superior and average managers in the middle and executive levels of management demonstrate more of it than do poor performers.

The competencies in the directing subordinates cluster appear particularly relevant for entry level managers. Entry level managers appear to demonstrate more developing others and use of unilateral power than do middle or executive level managers. In addition, among entry level managers, effectiveness was associated with the use of unilateral power and spontaneity. The entry level manager is often in direct contact with people performing tasks that result in the "product" of the organization. Managing these individual contributors, such as production line workers, clerks, salespeople, and so forth, allows for more use of the developing others competency. The jobs performed by these individual contributors usually provide the opportunity to get performance information in readily measurable terms. Subordinates can be given performance feedback with minimal interpretation as to what the measures mean, and performance objectives can be clearly stated. These managers are also in the position, as they are closest to the actual production work, to ensure quality control, appropriate safety procedures, attention to detail, and consistency of operating procedures. Their use of unilateral power is reflected in their requiring and obtaining compliance with these issues and procedures.

Developing others is less relevant to personnel managers because the specifics of their subordinates' performance, as well the effectiveness of their performance with other units in the organization, are not as clearly quantifiable as in marketing and manufacturing functions. Neither the performance objectives nor the assessment vehicles are as clear nor as invulnerable from various interpretations as they are in other functions. Although the name given to this competency makes the finding appear counterintuitive, the competency refers to behavior in which the manager provides others with specific performance feedback that can result in improved performance. With this definition of developing others, personnel managers do have less opportunity to demonstrate the competency than do managers in functions that have performance measures and objectives that are more explicit, less open to interpretation, and clearer (such as sales, number of units off the production line per day, cost savings from waste reduction).

Interactions at the Skill Level

Although the three threshold competencies are clustered together, there appeared to be only two primary relationships. Spontaneity and the use of unilateral power appeared to have a one-way primary relationship. To give directives, commands, and orders (i.e., use of unilateral power), a manager must be able to express himself or herself freely and not inhibit these orders because of a concern about how others will feel (i.e., spontaneity), but the opposite is not necessarily true. Use of unilateral power and developing others also appeared to have a one-way primary relationship. It is impossible to give someone positive and negative performance feedback (i.e.; developing others) without stating or implying a desired level of performance to which the manager expects the subordinate to conform (i.e., use of unilateral power). It can be said that the constructive impact of using the developing others competency can only occur if the manager is explicit in stating the degree of performance expected from the subordinate. The opposite is not necessarily true. That is, a manager can give orders and commands without involving the use of the developing others competency. Spontaneity and developing others each demonstrated some relationship to the use of unilateral power, thereby forming the cluster, but did not demonstrate any relationship to each other. It was the only relationship between two competencies within this or the three other clusters discussed which was not statistically significant.

The directing subordinates cluster showed a positive relationship of some strength to the goal and action management cluster ($r = .300$, $N = 253$, $p < .001$), but did not show a relationship of much strength to the leadership cluster nor the human resource management cluster. This suggested that the only secondary relationship that could be identified was between the directing subordinates cluster and the goal and action management cluster. Giving others performance feedback and giving them directives would be enhanced in the context of having set goals, established plans, and diagnosing the quality of performance and problems which need to be solved. Similarly, a manager would enhance his or her ability to get others to work toward goals, work on plans, and respond to initiatives if he or she could express himself or herself freely, provide performance feedback to others, and give explicit directives to subordinates.

CHAPTER EIGHT

The Focus On Others Cluster

Although stereotypes are changing, many people assume before they meet him or her, that an executive, will be someone with grey hair. In the early stages of the development of society, the people who "managed" the village, tribe, or family group were usually the elders. Merely surviving long enough to become an elder was evidence that the person had certain skills. His or her experiences became the collective wisdom of the tribe, family, or village. Although some of these attributions may still be relevant to those executives who survive internecine boardroom battles, no longer do most people expect that executives and even managers will be grey-haired. However, there is still the expectation, or at least the hope, that managers will have some degree of wisdom or perspective on events, the organization, and life. Sometimes, this characteristic is called maturity.

The maturity of a manager refers to the level of psychological development or ego strength he or she has attained. It specifically refers to the "sense" that people have of themselves, and to psychological and social aspects of their relationship to the surrounding world and life. It is expected that, as people pass through various life stages, they emerge with some greater degree of maturity. The characteristics involved in this development are not totally dependent on age or breadth of experience although both usually contribute to it. Some people develop aspects of maturity at a relatively early age in their adulthood. Other people, though they encounter successive life stages (Sheehy, 1976; Levinson, 1978), do not adequately deal with the issues or crises involved, and therefore do not advance in their maturity.

The aspects of maturity examined in this study do not directly include moral development (Kohlberg, 1969) or cognitive development (Brunner, 1966). Although moral and cognitive development are not addressed directly and should be a topic for further study, it is assumed that possession of the various competencies examined in this study could be associated with higher stages of moral and cognitive reasoning.

Of all the characteristics of managers examined in this study, aspects of maturity are perhaps the most elusive. That is, they are more difficult to identify in specific behaviors than are other competencies. How do mature managers act?

Four underlying characteristics of managers examined in this study were identified in the cluster analysis that correspond to the concept of maturity. This has been labeled the *focus on others cluster*. The competencies in this cluster are: (1) self-control; (2) perceptual objectivity; (3) stamina and adaptability; and (4) concern with close relationships. Managers with these competencies would take a balanced view of events and people. They would withhold their personal views, needs, and desires in service of organizational needs and concerns of others. They would be concerned with understanding all sides (e.g., opinions and feelings) of an issue or conflict. They would attempt to build close relationships with others. They would not be self-centered or narcissistic, and, therefore, have a focus on others in their environment.

For example, manufacturing managers who have these competencies might demonstrate a balanced perspective on events by "taking in stride" a new government environmental regulation that affects their production process, or a product liability regulation that identifies one of the constituent chemicals in a product as dangerous to customers. Although all reasonable managers are upset by such regulations that force a dramatic change in manufacturing operations, managers with these characteristics do not assume that the prophesied apocalypse has come or that the plant will be closed down. They would probably see it as another in the series of challenges that are presented to the organization and that will be overcome. Managers with fewer of these characteristics in such a situation may "dust off" their resumes and call some executive recruiters. The former type of manager may inform his or her employees that the employees' jobs are not in danger and that the organization will address the problem appropriately. These managers, although continuing to view government encroachment as a danger to private enterprise, are more likely than their less mature counterparts to examine the environmental or safety issues from a societal perspective. They may disagree with the specifics of the government regulation and its implementation, but they are likely to take a broader view of the issues and admit the validity of the environmental or safety issue. Each of the four characteristics should be examined separately before continuing the discussion of the cluster.

SELF-CONTROL

Self-control is a competency with which people inhibit personal needs or desires in service of organizational needs. At the trait level, self-control is impulse control (McClelland et al., 1972; McClelland, 1975). People with this trait consistently weigh the costs and benefits to themselves and to the social group, organization, or other system of which they are a part before expressing or acting on personal needs or desires. System-wide issues, such as concern for justice and equity, are often of primary importance to people with this trait. In contrast, people without this trait think of immediate gratification or satisfaction in an individual or self-centered manner. Individuals with self-control see themselves as disciplined people. These individuals demonstrate what might be called self-control skills.

People with self-control tend to avoid certain behaviors. When verbally attacked or aggressively confronted by someone, people with self-control do not necessarily react with corresponding anger or defensiveness. They remain "cool under stress" (Maccoby, 1976), whereas people without self-control are likely to defend themselves by attacking in return. For example, managers with self-control, when confronted by a subordinate who is angry or upset about a decision, first attempt to calm the subordinate or find out why he or she is angry. These actions are taken before attempting to explain the rationale for the decision. Of course, managers with self-control are more likely than their less mature counterparts to explain the rationale for such a decision to the subordinate rather than revert to an "I made the decision and that's the way it is" type of statement.

Managers with self-control are likely to make personal sacrifices when an organizational need presents itself (McClelland, 1975; Levinson, 1980). For example, such managers may change their approach to solving a problem, the agenda of a meeting, or the priorities of work assignments when an organizational need arises. To maintain consistency or equity across organizational units, they implement or follow through with an organization-wide procedure, even if they do not feel it is the most appropriate method for their unit.

The following examples from managers in the sample illustrate the demonstration of self-control in their jobs.

Four or five months ago two of my best supervisors were down in the mouth. With the expansion of product lines, they were not getting in on everything that was happening. Their feelings were hurt. They used to get in on everything. I had lost contact with the people. I was angry. How did I miss out? How do I make it right? I can't kiss their ___. So I asked each one what was the trouble and just listened. I bit my tongue about 10 times, but their problems were what I had guessed.

I was going to assume the investment responsibility for this new type of product. I guess I'm still certain today that Bob and I had agreed that I would have this responsibility. He was going on vacation and just a couple of hours before he left, we had a meeting about trying to finalize the business details in which Bob said that he was assigning this task to another guy. I was literally speechless. I was internally so upset that I did not speak or discuss the subject with him.

As a part of the project, I had to travel a lot. Even though I was away from home for awhile during those months, I never caroused or had heavy meals. I wanted to make sure that I'd wake up fresh each morning. Discipline is the key. I can't drink and be awake. So no matter how much I wanted to go out and relax or raise hell, I didn't.

Results at the Skill Level

There was no statistically significant relationship between effectiveness as a manager and the skill level of self-control as coded in the interviews (see Appendix A for detail). Managers at the entry and middle levels demonstrated significantly more self-control than did managers at the executive level (mean score .194, .141, and .040, respectively). Among middle level managers, superior performers demonstrated significantly more self-control than did average performers (mean score .222 versus .060, respectively).

Results at the Trait Level

Self-control was assessed at the trait level by the Activity Inhibition (referred to as AI) score from the Picture Story Exercise. Comparison of the groups with t-tests, as shown in Figures 8-1 and 8-2 (see Appendix A for detail), showed that:

1. Superior managers had significantly higher AI than did average managers;

2. Private sector managers had significantly higher AI than did public sector managers;

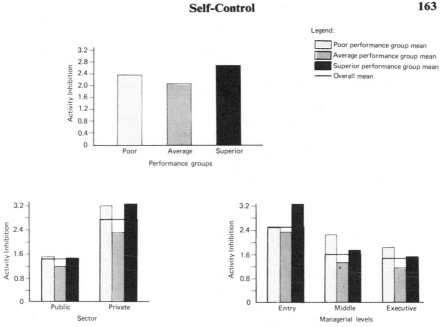

Figure 8-1. Trait level of self-control.

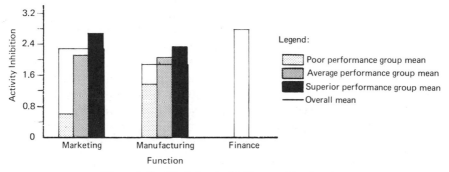

Figure 8-2. Trait level of self-control by function.

3. Among private sector managers, superior and poor performers had significantly higher AI than did average performers;

4. Entry level managers had significantly higher AI than did middle and executive level managers;

5. Among entry level managers, superior performers had significantly higher AI than did average performers, and higher AI than poor performers at a near significant level;

6. Among middle and executive level managers, poor performers had higher AI than did average performers at a near significant level;

7. Finance managers had significantly higher AI than did manufacturing managers;

8. Among marketing managers, average performers had significantly higher AI than did poor performers;

9. Among manufacturing managers, superior performers had significantly higher AI than did poor performers, and average performers had higher AI than did poor performers at a near significant level.

Interpretation

It appears that the skill level of self-control as coded from the interviews is not related to managerial performance. The trait level of self-control is related to effective performance as a manager only at the entry level. The lack of supporting evidence for the skill level of self-control for entry level managers may occur because people who have the trait level of self-control do not appear to be exercising self-control nor do they talk about it during interviews. They do not clench their fists, openly count to 10, or report how they had to constrain themselves.

Public sector managers have less Activity Inhibition than do private sector managers. This may be a consequence of the high degree of control, in terms of policies and procedures, that public sector organizations have developed to enforce individualized impulse control. While this may be labeled bureaucratic practices, it can be seen as a result of the mission of the public sector organizations: As functioning organizations in the government, they are supposed to uphold and implement laws and regulations for the good of society as well as perform services for the entire population of the country.

Entry level managers show greater amounts of self-control at the skill and trait levels than do middle or executive level managers. It is important to note that superior performers show higher Activity Inhibition than do average or poor performers at the entry level. While the relationship to effective managerial performance is supported at the entry level, it appears that entry level management jobs require more self-control than do middle or executive level jobs. This may seem counterintuitive. It might seem that people in higher levels of management encounter more situations in which they must maintain justice and keep the organization's objectives and policies in mind than do people in entry level management. The middle and executive level management jobs are designed such that these issues are implicitly built into the jobs. The responsibilities, activities, and performance measures of people in the higher level management jobs prescribe inhibition of personal needs for the benefit of the organization. They are so interwoven into the structure of the jobs that self-control at the trait level may not be as relevant as it is in entry level managerial jobs. People at the entry level are often viewed as being "on the firing line." Such a perception suggests that they are exposed to and must deal with many operational problems from which the middle or executive level manager is protected. The frequency with which self-control is required and called on may be substantially greater for entry level managers as a result of these factors. This may also occur because executive level managers may not worry as much as entry level managers about losing their jobs if they exhibit anger openly.

Although more effective managers appear to have higher Activity Inhibition as compared to their less effective counterparts within the marketing and manufacturing functions, finance managers have higher trait level self-control than do manufacturing managers. This may be a function of the nature of the work. It is more likely that finance managers will have to inhibit a strong personal urge (such as wanting to change a current asset to a fixed asset) than manufacturing managers will have to inhibit a personal desire.

PERCEPTUAL OBJECTIVITY

Perceptual objectivity is a competency with which people can be relatively objective and not limited in view by excessive subjectivity or personal biases, prejudices, or perspectives. This has been called social objectivity by Bray et al. (1974) and sensitivity to others by Levinson (1980). At the trait level, perceptual objectivity is the disposition to view an event from multiple perspectives simultaneously. These multiple perspectives may represent different levels of perception or conflicting views of a particular event or issue. These people demonstrate affective distancing skills; that is, the ability to remove themselves from emotional involvement in the specific situation or event and view it with relative objectivity. The term "relative objectivity" is used to avoid the philosophical discussion as to whether or not any person can be truly objective. Relative objectivity is, therefore, taken to mean the opposite of relative subjectivity.

People who possess perceptual objectivity tend to speak and behave in certain ways. For example, when presented with a conflict among subordinates, they are able to accurately describe each subordinate's "side" or view of the issue. Even if these people are involved in the conflict, they can accurately describe the other person's views and position. In discussing a possible decision, people with perceptual objectivity are likely to identify pros and cons of each alternative decision that could be made, a characteristic that Maccoby (1976) called openmindedness.

Managers encounter few situations or issues on which they do not have an opinion, thought, feeling, or position. Managers with perceptual objectivity have a level of socioemotional maturity that enables them to remove a degree of personal involvement, or the strength of their personal position, from examining the issue or event. They can minimize personal "projection" of their views onto a situation (Zaleznick, 1966). For example, a personnel manager confronted with a grievance from the shop steward must understand the nature of the grievance and determine what the issue really is, regardless of the manager's personal view as to the importance, pettiness, reasonableness, or unreasonableness of the grievance. If his or her personal view on the issue is expressed or affects the discussion of the issue, either the shop steward feels as if he or she is confronting an enemy and will be forced to escalate the consequences of the grievance (if the personnel manager takes a straight "management" position), or the manager's boss feels that the manager has "gone over to the other side" and the boss will treat the personnel manager as an enemy (if the personnel manager takes the "union" position).

The following examples from managers in the sample illustrate the demonstration of perceptual objectivity in their jobs.

> The plant manager came up to me one day, bypassing my boss, and told me that he had a report from the personnel manager that one of my data entry clerks had been sleeping on the job. It surprised me because the clerk he mentioned was a good worker. So I told him that something else must have been going on and I would check into it. Later that day I walked by Betsy's station and saw her mumbling and occasionally hitting her console. So I asked, "What's bothering you?" She said that she had been having a problem with access to one of the subroutines. Every time she thought she had the problem solved either the machine went down or she was placed in line for access. I asked her if she had mentioned it to one of the computer operators or programmers. She said, "No, I wanted to figure it out by myself. But I'm not doing so hot." I told her to relax, and then she logged off, put her arms on top of the console and put her head down. She mumbled, "I guess you're right. I'm getting too worked up about it." Obviously, the personnel manager had walked by at a time

when she was doing the same thing, out of frustration, not because she was sleeping. I had a few words ready for the personnel manager.

When I got the job as personnel manager for the plant, I had heard about the admin. manager being a real monster, always demanding, wanting things done in a short period and not tolerant at all. But I'm an eternal optimist—I like to find out for myself about monsters. So I made a courtesy call to the admin. manager. I showed him that I had a lot of experience and expertise. I told him about some of the staff joining me from my prior firm. I told him that I understood that the general manager placed a lot of demands on him about good communications and smooth operating systems. I told him that I felt he really wanted to please the general manager and assured him that I would do my job and that would help him. He had been a monster to people who were not doing their jobs. I knew where he was coming from, and he was no monster to me.

Results at the Skill Level

Perceptual objectivity (referred to as PO) at the skill level as coded in the interviews was related to effective performance as a manager ($F = 4.936$, df $= 2$, $p = .008$), with a significant linear trend ($F = 3.907$, df $= 1$, $p = .049$) favoring superior managers and a significant nonlinear trend ($F = 5.966$, df $= 1$, $p = .015$) favoring superior and poor managers. Comparison of the groups with t-tests, shown in Figures 8-3 and 8-4 (see Appendix A for detail), showed that:

1. Superior managers demonstrated significantly more PO than did average managers, and more PO than did poor managers at a near significant level;

2. Poor managers demonstrated more PO than did average managers at a near significant level;

3. Among private sector managers, superior performers demonstrated significantly more PO than did average performers;

4. Executive level managers demonstrated more PO than did entry level managers at a near significant level;

5. Among middle level managers, superior performers demonstrated significantly more PO than did average and poor performers;

6. Personnel managers demonstrated significantly more PO than did manufacturing managers;

7. Among manufacturing managers, superior performers demonstrated more PO than did average managers at a near significant level.

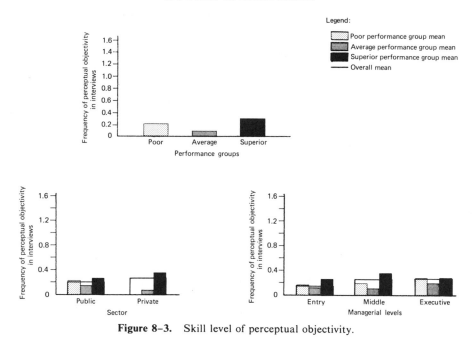

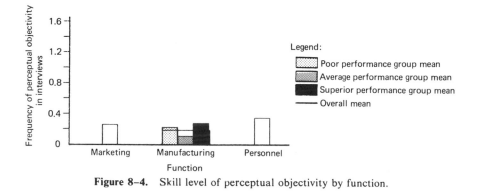

Figure 8-3.   Skill level of perceptual objectivity.

Figure 8-4.   Skill level of perceptual objectivity by function.

Results at the Trait Level

No single measure of the trait level of this characteristic was used in more than one of the studies that constituted the aggregate sample used in this study. No results, therefore, can be reported on this level.

Interpretation

Perceptual objectivity appears related to performance as a manager. In particular, it distinguishes superior performance within the private sector, within middle level management, and among manufacturing managers. Without having perceptual objectivity, managers find it difficult to balance the many perspectives—of subordinates, other managers within the organization, or the various groups in the external environment—involved in almost every issue or event. To make decisions, resolve conflicts, or develop policies and procedures that seem fair requires that a manager have perceptual objectivity.

Executive level managers demonstrate slightly more perceptual objectivity than do entry level managers. The nature of executives' jobs requires balancing perspectives from substantially diverse groups within the organization, as well as numerous groups in the external environment. Executives are called on to demonstrate perceptual objectivity relatively more often than are managers in other levels of management—in particular, entry level managers.

Personnel managers demonstrate more perceptual objectivity than do manufacturing managers. Personnel managers are frequently in situations that require perceptual objectivity, such as mediating labor-management disputes or at least managing that relationship. They are also the focus of employee concerns and problems that may conflict with corporate policies and procedures, not to mention government regulations regarding personnel practices. Personnel managers usually deal with the most subjective material or tasks within the realm of organizational functions. Positions taken on production processes or marketing strategy are usually not at the mercy of as many different perspectives and interpretations as are issues involved in personnel policies, procedures, and practices. Even though personnel managers may be called on to demonstrate perceptual objectivity more often than are manufacturing managers, the superior manufacturing managers do demonstrate somewhat more of this characteristic than do their less effective counterparts.

STAMINA AND ADAPTABILITY

Stamina and adaptability is a competency with which people have the energy to sustain long hours of work and have the flexibility and orientation to adapt to changes in life and the organizational environment. At the trait level, there are two aspects of this characteristic. One aspect is the physical stamina to sustain long hours, and often to maintain high performance under consistently high stress. Another aspect is the orientation that allows for flexibility in responding to stress and changes in the situations encountered, as well as the ability to adapt to the changes. This aspect of the trait level is termed developmental Stage of Adaptation (Stewart, 1977). These people see themselves as diligent and hard workers, but flexible. They demonstrate adaptation and coping skills.

People with stamina and adaptability behave in certain ways. They can be seen working long hours when this is needed. They can maintain a high quality of performance through 14-hour days and 70-hour weeks. Throughout such a prolonged or arduous task, they maintain their usual degree of attention to detail. They have characteristics that Bray et al. (1974) called energy and resistance to stress. These people also remain relatively calm or patient during such periods. This posture is maintained even in shorter time spans as well as on those occasions when they experience a high degree of stress for a number of days, weeks, or even months in a sequence. Whether in response to stressful events or long hours, people with this characteristic can be observed to pace themselves; that is, they designate periods of time to certain activities, allowing for some distribution of periods of intense output and relatively lighter periods. They engage in activities specifically chosen to reduce the effects of the stress or fatigue. These people respond to changes in the job demands or the environment by making appropriate changes in their behavior or approach. The flexibility needed to adapt to these types of changes is apparent as a pattern in their behavior. This characteristic has been called behavioral flexibility (Bray et al., 1974), tolerance of uncertainty (Bray et al., 1974; Stogdill, 1974), and stamina and adaptability (Levinson, 1980).

The following examples from managers in the sample illustrate the demonstration of stamina and adaptability in their jobs.

It's a do or die period. For example, on the high pressure air system, we were up 48 hours working on the valves. In one case we repaired a valve 13 times and it still leaked. The repair of the final valve was done 2 hours before we were supposed to leave and the system go back up.

That trip was tough. I was on the road for almost every working day for three months and some weekends. I always kept my watch on eastern standard time, so no matter where I was I could be in touch with what time my head was at. Bouncing back-and-forth between time zones was rough on my body but even rougher on my head. I also ate by my own eastern standard time and went to sleep by it. It helped me avoid jet lag and kept for me alert for all those meetings.

Results at the Skill Level

At the skill level, stamina and adaptability as coded in the interviews was not related to effective performance as a manager nor was it frequently reported in the interviews. Middle level managers demonstrated significantly more stamina and adaptability than did entry level managers (mean score .183 versus .083, respectively).

Results at the Trait Level

Physical stamina was not measured in any of the studies in the aggregate sample, and therefore cannot be addressed at this level. There was information on the developmental Stage of the Adaptation aspect of this characteristic. Information on this variable was not available for managers in some of the samples. A person receives four scores with this measure, one for each of the four developmental stages. The four stages reflect the behavioral and dispositional characteristics associated with dominant theories of personality development (Freud, 1933; Erikson, 1963; Stewart, 1977). Stage I represents a concern with dependencies, often called the oral stage. Stage II represents a concern with self-discipline, often called the anal stage. Stage III represents a concern with asserting oneself on the environment, often called the phallic stage. Stage IV represents a concern with one's place in the larger order of the universe and life, often called the generativity stage. The mean stage scores are shown in Table 8-1 (see Appendix A for detail).

Poor managers were significantly higher in Stages I and II than were average managers. Poor managers were higher in Stage I than were superior managers at a near significant level. Superior managers were significantly higher in Stages II and III than were average managers.

Managers in the private sector were significantly higher in Stages I and III than were managers in the public sector, but public sector managers were significantly higher in Stage IV than were private sector managers. The public sector manager sample was too small to conduct a comparison of performance within it. Among the private sector managers, poor performers were significantly higher in Stages I and II than were average performers. They were higher in Stage IV than were average performers at a near significant level. Superior performers were significantly higher in Stage II and III than were average performers, and higher in Stage IV than were average performers at a near significant level.

Entry level managers were significantly higher on Stages I and III

TABLE 8-1   Trait Level of Stamina and Adaptability

		Mean Stage Score			
		Stage I	Stage II	Stage III	Stage IV
Performance groups	Poor	4.89	1.87	1.09	1.96
	Average	4.17	1.46	.85	1.63
	Superior	4.35	1.78	1.24	1.81
Public sector		1.80	1.53	.27	3.07
Private sector	Poor	4.89	1.87	1.09	1.96
	Average	4.26	1.44	.87	1.52
	Superior	4.54	1.82	1.30	1.84
Entry managerial level	Poor	4.92	1.78	1.23	1.53
	Average	4.35	1.39	.87	1.15
	Superior	4.66	1.75	1.41	1.61
Middle managerial level	Poor	4.60	2.60	0.0	5.40
	Average	3.00	1.93	.71	4.71
	Superior	2.82	1.94	.35	2.82
Marketing function	Poor	4.60	2.60	0.0	5.40
	Average	3.74	1.77	.92	2.77
	Superior	3.91	1.86	.86	2.37
Manufacturing function		4.41	1.52	.91	1.28
Finance function		4.86	1.42	1.25	1.33

than were middle level managers. Middle level managers were significantly higher in Stages II and IV than entry level managers. No data were available on executive level managers. Among entry level managers, poor performers were significantly higher in Stages II and III than were average performers, and higher in Stages I and IV than were average performers at a near significant level. Superior performers were significantly higher in Stages II, III, and IV than were average performers. Among middle level managers, poor performers were significantly higher in Stage I than were average performers, significantly lower in Stage III than were average performers, and higher in Stage IV than were average performers at a near significant level. Poor performers were significantly higher in Stages I and IV than were superior performers, but significantly lower in Stage III than were superior performers. Superior performers were lower in Stage III than were average performers at a near significant level, and significantly lower in Stage IV than were average performers.

Marketing managers were significantly lower in Stage I than were manufacturing managers, significantly higher in Stage IV than were manufacturing managers, and higher in Stage II than were manufacturing managers at a near significant level. Finance managers were significantly higher in Stage I than were marketing managers. Finance managers were lower in Stage II but higher in Stage III than were marketing managers, both at near significant levels.

Among the marketing managers, superior and average performers were significantly higher than were poor performers in Stage III, and significantly lower in Stage IV than poor performers.

Interpretation

While stamina and adaptability does not appear related to performance as a manager at the skill level, at the trait level it does appear related to effective performance. There is probably no specific behavior that a manager displays that can be easily pointed to as evidence of greater stamina and adaptability. Effective managers do not necessarily describe the long hours they put in or their flexibility and adaptation in response to changes; they merely do these things. If they have this characteristic, managers can be expected to perform under stress and deal with rapidly changing aspects of the environment without showing signs of difficulty or fatigue.

The information provided a specific clue as to the nature of the trait level that is associated with effectiveness. The poor managers appear to be high in Stages I and II, while the superior managers appear to be high in stages II and III. This suggests that less effective managers are at a stage of adaptation in which they look to others in the hierarchy for decisions, rely on the judgment and opinions of others, or perceive the people around them in terms of dependency relationships. In addition, they deal with changes in their surroundings in terms of perceptions that call for people to "take care of themselves" and focus on self-control or self-discipline as an adaptive response to stress. Meanwhile, more effective managers perceive themselves as part of many competitive relationships that require assertiveness. Like warriors entering battle, these people see many encounters as challenges and opportunities, or as chances to prove themselves, in which beneficial outcomes result only from individual action and assertion. At the same time, they focus on self-control or self-discipline as an adaptive response to stress. If a conflict emerges with other managers in the organization or with elements of the external environment, less effective managers (with high Stages I and II) are more likely to wait for "management" to make a decision, state a policy, or point toward a direction than are their more effective counterparts. More effective managers (high in Stages II and III) see the conflict as a contest. Although these managers probably check the "rules of the game" before taking action, they neither wait nor expect someone else to take care of the conflict.

The observation that superior managers do not, as a whole, appear relatively higher on Stage IV than do their less effective counterparts could be a function of Stage IV modes of adaptation (with the corresponding perspective). It may not be appropriate in American industrial organizations. Cultural values may preclude someone high in Stage IV (i.e., generativity) from becoming effective in organizational settings, especially in the role of a manager. It may be that effective performance in a staff job (e.g., a functional specialist) may be related to Stage IV. In such jobs, where the decision-making and leadership aspects of management are not a primary responsibility, assertiveness may be less adaptive and generativity may be more adaptive to stress and demands for flexibility.

Private sector managers have higher Stages I and III scores, while public sector managers have higher Stage IV scores. This may be a function of the societal service aspects of organizations in the public sector. Managers in the public sector must internalize this aspect of the organizational mission, among other aspects, to perform in the context of changing administrations and changes in public opinion and government spending.

Entry level managers have higher Stage I scores than do middle level managers. Entry level managers must depend on other levels of management for more decisions and guidance than do middle level managers. This difference could be interpreted as a result of the differences in their positions in the hierarchy. It should be remembered, though, that poor performers at both levels appear to have higher Stage I scores than do their more effective counterparts.

Entry level managers have higher Stage III scores than do middle level managers. This could be interpreted as a demand on entry level managers to enable them to progress up the managerial ladder. Both poor and superior performers at the entry level have high Stage III scores. This suggests that although a Stage III orientation to adaptation may be important for promotion to higher levels of management, merely having more of it does not indicate that performance in the present job will be effective. In contrast, among middle level managers, superior and average performers have higher Stage III scores than do poor performers.

In a manner opposite to that observed with Stage I, middle level managers have higher Stage IV scores than do entry level managers. Middle level managers are in positions that require more concern about systems maintenance, the general welfare and health of the organization, and a more comprehensive perspective on the organization than entry level managers must have. Although middle level managers appear higher in Stage IV, the poor performers have the highest Stage IV scores as compared to their more effective counterparts. The point made earlier concerning cultural appropriateness of Stage IV should be considered in interpreting the results among performance groups within middle level management.

In comparing managers in various functions, it appears that marketing managers are low in Stage I and high in Stages II and IV. Superior and average performers in marketing functions have higher Stage III scores and lower Stage IV scores than do poor performers. Marketing managers are directly exposed to and must contend with a considerable number of changes. They must deal with changes in product line, changes in customers' buying behavior, changes in competition, changes in government regulations, and changes in organizational strategy. Compared to manufacturing and finance managers, their immediate environment appears to be less certain and to change more rapidly. This difference requires that marketing managers have a greater degree of flexibility and function at higher stages of adaptation than do their counterparts. This is not to say that flexibility and adaptation are not important to manufacturing or finance functions, but that they appear relatively more critical to functioning as a manager in marketing.

CONCERN WITH CLOSE RELATIONSHIPS

Concern with close relationships is a competency that people care about and build close relationships with individuals. The types of relationships sought and built can best be described as friendships. At the motive level, this is termed the *n* Affiliation. People with the *n* Affiliation spend their time talking with others (i.e., make many long-distance telephone calls to friends and write letters), and prefer to work in groups and with people they know (Boyatzis, 1973; Boyatzis, 1974; Atkinson, 1958). These people see themselves as likeable and caring. In social and organizational contexts, they adopt the role of friend or family member. They demonstrate nonverbal skills that cause people to feel cared for, and friendship-building skills.

People with the characteristic of concern with close relationships behave in certain ways. They spend time talking with subordinates and co-workers when there is no particular task requirement. They make friends with specific others. They are also likely to ask others what they think or feel about certain things.

Managers who spend a certain amount of time each week talking with subordinates about their families, sports, or hobbies probably have this characteristic. These conversations are not held for instrumental purposes of understanding or motivating the subordinates, but for the purpose of getting to know and being friends with them.

Results at the Skill Level

Concern with close relationships as coded in the interviews did not appear related to managerial performance. Managers in the public sector demonstrated significantly more concern with close relationships than did managers in the private sector (mean score .286 versus .131, respectively, see Appendix A for detail). Among private sector managers, average performers demonstrated more concern with close relationships than did superior performers at a near significant level (mean score .205 versus .083, respectively). Among executive level managers, average performers demonstrated significantly more concern with close relationships than did poor performers (mean score .533 versus .105, respectively), but also demonstrated more of it than did superior performers at a near significant level (mean score .533 versus .171, respectively). Managers in manufacturing demonstrated significantly more concern with close relationships than did managers in marketing (mean score .280 versus .093, respectively) and more of it than did personnel managers at a near significant level (mean score .280 versus .158, respectively).

Results at the Motive Level

At the motive level, concern with close relationships was measured by the affiliation motive (referred to as n Aff or n Affiliation) for the Picture Story Exercise. Comparison of the groups shown in Figures 8-5 and 8-6 (see Appendix A for detail) with t-tests indicated that:

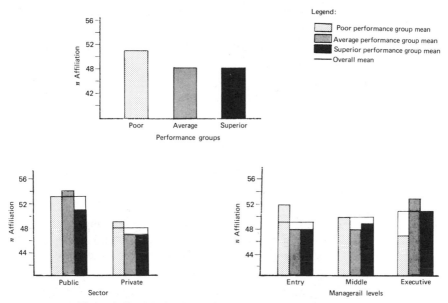

Figure 8-5. Motive level of concern with close relationships.

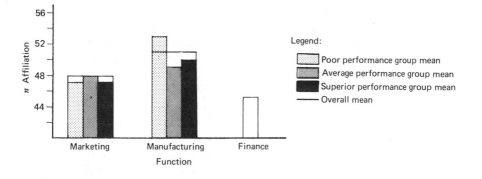

T score reflects adjustment for length of protocol

Figure 8-6. Motive level of concern with close relationships by function.

1. Poor managers had significantly higher n Aff than did average and superior managers.

2. Public sector managers had significantly higher n Aff than did private sector managers.

3. Among private sector managers, poor performers had higher n Aff than did average and superior performers at near significant levels.

4. Executive level managers had significantly higher n Aff than did entry level managers, and middle level managers had higher n Aff than did entry level managers at a near significant level.

5. Among entry level managers, poor performers had significantly higher n Aff than did average and superior performers.

6. Among executive level managers, average performers had significantly higher n Aff than did poor performers, and superior performers had higher n Aff than did poor performers at a near significant level.

7. Manufacturing managers had significantly higher n Aff than did marketing and finance managers.

8. Among manufacturing managers, poor performers had significantly higher n Aff than did average performers, and higher n Aff than did superior performers at a near significant level.

Interpretation

There was a slight relationship between concern with close relationships and managerial ineffectiveness (opposite to prediction) at the skill level, and a strong relationship to managerial ineffectiveness at the motive level with the one exception at the executive level. Even at the executive level, where the motive level did appear related to effectiveness, the skill level did not. This characteristic and the building of friendships may interfere with certain aspects of a manager's job, such as the need to give negative performance feedback, fire someone, or assign people to unpopular tasks. This characteristic cannot be viewed as a relevant element in a generic model of management.

In his study of general managers, Kotter (1982) observed that they often inquire as the the health and activities of a manager's family and the manager's leisure activities. Kotter noted that these interactions tended to be brief and often occurred when the executive was walking between meetings or between appointments. This may explain the findings with the n Affiliation at the executive level. It also suggests why the motive-level findings were not supported at the skill level. The affiliative actions are brief and are not a part of important events (i.e., the types of critical incidents examined in the interviews) at work.

Public sector managers not only demonstrate more of the skills of concern with close relationships, but also have a higher motive level than do private sector managers. Since it is not related to effectiveness in either sector, this suggests that the environment of the public sector provides more opportunity for having friendships and talking with others out of the context of task demands. This may be a function of the duration of employment that many have within the public sector, and the fact that they work with many of the same people from year to year.

Manufacturing managers have a high motive level compared to marketing and finance managers, and demonstrate more of the skills than do marketing or personnel managers. This may be a result of a structural aspect of their work. They often work with the same people month after month, and year after year. It may also be a function of the atmosphere in manufacturing facilities in which strong affiliation needs and friendly behavior of people working on production lines permeates the organization and becomes part of even managers' behavior patterns. Within the manufacturing function, there was no relation between this characteristic and performance at the skill level and an inverse relationship between performance and this characteristic at the motive level. Although it may be a part of the atmosphere or structural aspect of manufacturing organizations, concern with close relationships does not appear to contribute to the effectiveness of managers.

SUMMARY ON THE FOCUS ON OTHERS CLUSTER

Summary of Findings

The characteristics in the focus on others cluster appear somewhat related to effectiveness as a manager and are summarized in Table 8-2. Since all four of these characteristics were theoretically considered related to psychosocial development (i.e., maturity), it was not expected or predicted that a social-role level of these characteristics would exist. They are primarily intrapsychic characteristics.

At the trait level, self-control appears related to effective managerial performance at the entry level and stamina and adaptability at the middle level of management (no data were available at the executive level

TABLE 8-2   The Focus on Others Cluster[a]

Competency	Motive	Trait	Self-image	Social Role	Skills
Self-control		*Impulse control*[b]	I am a disciplined person I have a lot of self-discipline		Self-control skills
Perceptual objectivity		Multiple perceptions of events	I can keep an appropriate emotional distance		*Effective distancing skills*
Stamina and adaptability		Physical stamina *Developmental stage of adaptation*	I work hard and diligently I am flexible		Adaptation skills Coping skills
Concern with close relationships	*n* Affiliation		I am likable and caring		Nonverbal skills that result in people feeling cared for Friendship building skills

[a]Levels of each competency for which results indicate a relationship to managerial effectiveness are italicized.
[b]At entry level management jobs only.

for the latter), but at the skill level neither does. Perceptual objectivity does relate to effectiveness as a manager at the skill level.

Concern with close relationships does not show a relationship to effectiveness in any of the groups studied. It seems particularly relevant to public sector and manufacturing managers, at both the skill and motive level. Overall and among performance group comparisons there is either no relationship to performance or a negative relationship to performance at both the skill and motive levels; that is, in some of the comparisons, the poor performers show more of the characteristic than do the average or superior performers. The only exception to this is at the motive level of the characteristic with executive level managers. Even though average and superior managers in this group have more of the motive level than do poor performers, this was not reflected in the findings at the skill level.

These results suggest that this characteristic should not be considered an element of a generic model of management. Concern with close relationships may actually interfere with a manager's ability to perform aspects of his or her job. For example, having this characteristic might cause managers to have difficulty either firing or giving negative performance information to a subordinate. They see such actions as damaging to a close relationship or at least potentially damaging the relationship. Similarly, they regard delegation of responsibility and allowing a subordinate to work independently on a task as interrupting or precluding a certain amount of interpersonal interaction. Having this characteristic leads managers toward increased interpersonal contact regardless of task considerations (Boyatzis, 1973).

Interactions at the Skill Level

These four characteristics can be said to have only three primary relationships to each other at the skill level. To build close relationships, a person must be able to withhold personal feelings and desires at times (i.e., self-control). It is difficult to build a warm, close relationship if one of the people involved impulsively expresses all personal feelings, desires, thoughts, and needs without concern for the other person. Similarly, to identify and communicate each person's views or "sides" in a conflict or disagreement (i.e., perceptual objectivity), a person must be able to withhold his or her own views for a certain amount of time and at certain points during interactions. It is also difficult for a person to build close relationships unless he or she has a concern about others' feelings, and an understanding that multiple perspectives can exist in any event, in any relationship, or concerning any issue among people (i.e., perceptual objectivity).

At the skill level, stamina and adaptability did not show any statistically significant relationship to the other three characteristics in the cluster. A conclusion would be that there is no primary or secondary relationship between the stamina and adaptability characteristic at the skill level and any other competencies. Since no support was found for stamina and adaptability being included in the integrated competency model at the skill level, the lack of primary and secondary relationships is not surprising.

The focus on others cluster showed a positive relationship to the human resource management cluster (r = .229, N = 253, p < .001), but did not show a relationship of much strength to the other three clusters. This suggested that the only secondary relationship that could be identified was between the focus on others cluster and the human resource management cluster. Building coalitions, stimulating collaboration and team spirit in work groups, having positive regard and a realistic view of himself or herself (i.e., the human resource management cluster) would be enhanced if the person could inhibit personal needs, desires, and feelings in the context of work group or organizational needs, perceive the various positions and perspectives people may have on an issue or in a conflict, and make friends (i.e., the focus on others cluster). Since the opposite is not necessarily true, it would appear that this is a one-way secondary relationship.

CHAPTER NINE

Specialized Knowledge

Specialized knowledge refers to facts, principles, theories, frameworks, or models. Through the competency assessment approach, specialized knowledge has been further refined to mean *usable* facts and concepts. A model of performance in any job must include specialized knowledge in this sense. Although it may seem like a semantic quibble, the qualification of specialized knowledge as usable information rather than information is a more stringent clarification. The specific information of concern in assessing competence in certain jobs must be practical; if it is not usable, the possession of information is not related to performance. Although it is beyond the scope and data available in this study to provide elaboration of the structure of specialized knowledge or what knowledge is needed by managers, several points about this competency can be made.

A THRESHOLD COMPETENCY

In the various competency assessment studies conducted on specific jobs in particular organizations, which have been combined for the aggregate sample in this study, specialized knowledge was often identified as related to performance as a manager (Klemp, 1979). In some cases, the specialized knowledge appeared related to the managerial function being performed, the products being produced, the technology being utilized, or appeared as a level of other competencies. *None of these studies showed that superior performance as a manager was related to possession of more facts and concepts than average performance as a manager.* It did appear in several studies that both average and superior performing managers had and used certain facts and concepts that poor performing managers did not have or use. No set of facts or concepts (i.e., specialized knowledge) was identified as being consistently used by managers in the aggregate sample regardless of the performance group.

This may have been a function of the methods used in the studies (i.e., the Behavioral Event Interviews and tests). Neither the interviews nor the tests included questions about specialized knowledge needed during certain events.

Results at the social-role level (i.e., from the job element analysis) show that items related to specialized knowledge do appear in managers' perceptions. In six of the seven studies, managers listed them as required for performance in their jobs. Managers in only two of these studies perceived these items as distinguishing superior performing managers. This included items such as: "knowledge of international law," "high degree of technologic ability in a speciality," and "knowledge of codes, statutes, and policy."

This suggests that certain facts and concepts are needed by a manager to perform his or her job, but that having more of the specialized knowledge does not by itself contribute to superior performance as compared to average performance in the job. In this sense, *specialized knowledge can be considered a threshold competency.*

For example, marketing managers may need to know certain fundamentals about human motivation. They may be effective in the job if they know that people in marketing jobs (i.e., their subordinates) have a type of motivational disposition that suggests that rapid and specific performance feedback stimulates increased performance. They may also be effective if they know they should establish moderate risk performance goals for each subordinate to stimulate a maximum degree of striving toward a standard of excellence, rather than making the standard so high that the subordinate gives up, assuming that the goal is unattainable and therefore not worth attempting.

On the other hand, the level of specialized knowledge about human motivation reflected in a graduate degree in psychology may not result in better performance by marketing managers. As a matter of fact, this level of specialized knowledge may cause the manager to view this part of his or her job as so complicated that it interferes with other aspects of the job.

In addition to the potential limitation imposed by the methods in this study, there are three issues that complicate further inquiry into specialized knowledge. As a result of these issues, the only conclusion that can be made regarding a generic model of management is that specialized knowledge appears to be a threshold competency and that further research is needed before anything more elaborate can be said.

RELEVANT KNOWLEDGE OR KNOWLEDGE USED

One of the first problems encountered when addressing specialized knowledge is establishing a framework in which to describe it. Within the realm of the structure and sociology of knowledge, the focus of this study is relatively narrow. The concern here is about the specialized knowledge related to performance in the job of a manager.

The structure of specialized knowledge for management jobs may be a function of whom you ask. If you consult faculty at business schools, the curricula, textbooks, or the professional literature (i.e., information found in professional journals), you will discover a structure of specialized knowledge that can be said to have "perceived relevance" to the manager. These sources describe what they think "should be known" by a person in a management job. The perceived importance of certain information may be a result of the observations of these "experts," or it may be a result of particular values, traditions, or the folklore of a field.

A body of knowledge emerging from this perspective may constitute what Argyris and Schon (1974) called an "espoused theory of action." That is, professionals in the management field and even managers may think that they should know such information because it is expected that they know it, not necessarily because it has any utility in functioning as a manager. Such knowledge may be considered "credential oriented," and appear as the jargon, or buzzwords, of the field. It constitutes the social-role level of the specialized knowledge competency as explained in the model presented in this study.

Unfortunately, such knowledge cannot be cast aside with a pragmatic statement such as, "If it cannot be used, I do not need to know it." Although perceived relevant knowledge may be a fad, value position of the "experts" in the field, or their folklore, it may represent a contribution or advancement of the state of the art. That is, knowledge identified as relevant by such "experts" may fill a gap in understanding, which current managers do not presently see. In this manner, knowledge perceived to be relevant may satisfy a future need or a past need, but not be viewed as useful in the present.

Regardless of the past, present, or future merit and utility of such information, the structure of it develops on the basis of topics. For example, a study of course offerings and textbooks in management yields a framework that includes six major categories: (1) finance, including accounting and economics; (2) marketing, including sales and product development; (3) human resource management, including personnel, industrial relations, organization development, and organization structure; (4) production, including manufacturing engineering; (5) information analysis and systems, including quantitative analysis, operations research, and computer usage; and (6) general management, including business policy and strategy, legal, ethical, and social responsibilities, and international business.

The American Assembly for Collegiate Schools of Business (AACSB) has undertaken a project to clarify this structure as a part of its Accreditation Research Project (Laidlaw & Zoffer, 1979). In this project, the researchers have attempted to determine what knowledge should be covered by undergraduate and graduate business curricula and what knowledge should be retained by graduates of such programs. The research has divided the field of knowledge into thirteen major categories: accounting, economics, finance, human behavior and organization theory, information systems, international business, legal and social environment, management of human resources, management policy and strategy, marketing, quantitative analysis, operations research, and production and operations management. It is assumed that within each of these major areas there are basic requirements, as well as information that provides enhancement but is not required for performance in all management jobs.

This structure of knowledge can be made more specific by outlining topical domains within each major category. For example, the structure of knowledge in marketing, as observed in textbooks and course outlines, can be divided into eight domains: (1) marketing strategy; (2) consumer behavior; (3) product; (4) price; (5) promotion; (6) marketplace; (7) market research; and (8) management of the marketing function. The structure of knowledge in human resource management can, similarly, be divided into six domains: (1) the individual; (2) the group; (3) the organization; (4) the environment; (5) legal and ethical issues; and (6) management of the human resource function.

From the perspective of practicing managers, the structure of knowledge of management might look considerably different. They might present a structure based on "utility," which is organized in terms of decisions that have to be made or problems that have to be solved. This might be called a "functional use" perspective rather than a perceived relevance perspective. For example, marketing knowledge may be organized around such issues as: assessment and analysis of competitors; product-life cycles; or implications of changes in the national economic condition. In the human resource management area, knowledge may be organized around such issues as: selection and promotion systems; career pathing, career planning, and career guidance; appraisal and developmental assessment; and so forth. If a structure of knowledge in management were constructed from the functional utility perspective, it would probably constitute what Argyris and Schon (1974) have called a "theory in use."

Unfortunately, due to its nature, a structure based on the functional utility perspective would have a present and past focus. It would not necessarily include knowledge that has not been needed in the past, or is not needed currently, but will be needed in the years ahead. It would structure the current state of understanding in a field, whether the state is sophisticated or relatively ignorant, and make it difficult for testing or adoption of future developments.

Each perspective has limitations and contributions to understanding specialized knowledge needed and useful to people in management jobs. Facts and concepts emerging from either perspective can be *usable* and therefore incorporated as part of the specialized knowledge competency in a generic model of management. The dilemma is that if you choose or operate from one perspective your understanding of specialized knowledge will be constrained.

FUNCTION, PRODUCT, AND TECHNOLOGY FOCUSED

Most management jobs require that the managers have and use facts and concepts related to the particular function performed, the particular products produced, or the technology used by the organization. This was described by a product manager in the sample:

> There are several things I need to know about marketing. Now I'm differentiating between a product manager and the president of our organization, although some of these things may apply there. It's essential to have a knowledge of the product. That's almost a must. And you have to know your marketplace. I get a lot of joy and kicks out of knowing the product and knowing the marketplace. I don't feel that you can put an accountant in a job like this, for example. I think that the business aspects can be taught, or that you can hire some good financial people, but I think knowing the product and the marketplace is something like a sixth sense—it's not something you learn, it's just a sense.

This manager used his "sixth sense" to make product modification decisions, to respond to customers' demands or requirements, to make pricing decisions in attempting to build market share and "beat out" the competition, and so forth. Kotter (1982) reported that superior performing general managers that he studied had a long history and extensive knowledge of their industry and the specific products of their company. Information from this history of experience was crucial in making strategic as well as operational decisions.

Personnel managers must have access to or know guidelines related to affirmative action or equal employment opportunities. To evaluate a selection procedure, to do a quarterly check to ascertain compliance with an affirmative action plan, or to guide hiring plans, personnel managers must at least know the principles. Research and development managers in a company that develops and manufactures computer components must retain a certain body of knowledge of electronics and physics and have access to recent developments in the literature of the relevant fields. Without access to such information, R&D managers may have difficulty assessing the feasibility of certain research and development projects. Making decisions as to which projects to continue, which to disband, and which deserve an increase of resources requires such specialized knowledge. A manufacturing manager whose company produces plastic products must know static and ambient temperatures necessary to produce and stabilize the particular plastics used in his or her products.

Due to the nature of specialized knowledge and its relevance and utility to managers within certain functions and dealing with particular products and technologies, it may not be possible to identify common components for inclusion in a generic model of management. The only option may be to turn to each of the functional, product, and technology fields to accumulate the specialized knowledge relevant and useful to managers. Unfortunately, this could result in an encyclopedia of management larger than most managers' offices. The dilemma, therefore, is how to determine what knowledge should be known or is needed by managers, and what is extraneous.

RECOGNITION VERSUS UTILITY

The third issue complicating the inquiry into specialized knowledge is one of recognizing information versus the ability to use the information. In many professions, learning facts and concepts that are useful to the professional appears to be a process of learning to organize a system of references of the various facts and concepts. Possession of the knowledge then refers to knowing where to look for the specifics and details rather than retaining all of the information. For example, it is important that a personnel manager know about incentive plans. Does every personnel manager have to know the details of how a Scanlon Plan is structured and how it operates? It is probably adequate that the personnel manager knows that a Scanlon Plan is one of many types of incentive plans and that he or she knows where to look for the details. Does every marketing manager need to know what the Kondratieff Cycle is and where he or she currently is in the cycle? It is probably adequate for the marketing manager to know that there appear to be long-term business cycles and to have a sense as to where current conditions indicate the economy is in terms of such cycles.

Unfortunately, most assessment techniques used to measure specialized knowledge do not provide "credit" for a manager having his or her information organized and knowing what references to check for details. Many multiple choice and even a number of essay-type tests measure recognition of facts and concepts. Some measure the ability to use facts and concepts. Case analysis and some essays that are problem- or issue-focused measure a person's ability to use facts and concepts, not merely the recognition of them. Reports, open-book tests, and take-home examinations allow a person to utilize his or her organization of information and to consult various references.

Procedures used in standardized testing, by certain professions in licensing and certifying members, and by faculty in certain educational and training programs, only assess and base judgments on recognition of facts and concepts, not a person's ability to use them (McClelland et al., 1958). These assessment methods, although begun as an attempt to reduce discrimination and subjectivity and increase consensus of standards within professions, may be having the effect of constraining the understanding of what specialized knowledge is relevant and useful in a field and how it can be used most effectively (McClelland et al., 1958).

The impact of these issues contributes to the complications in understanding the specialized knowledge competency. The dilemma presented is: How do we know when we have identified facts and concepts that should be known by managers and how do we know that managers can use them?

MEMORY

A discussion of specialized knowledge is incomplete if it does not address the issue of memory. Memory is the accurate, appropriate, and rapid recall of certain events or information. Although memory was originally explored in the interview and job element analysis portions of this study, no evidence could be found to support its inclusion in the generic model.

Memory is not demonstrated as a separate, distinguishable characteristic at the skill level, and managers do not perceive memory as a separate item relevant to management jobs. This suggests that memory is not relevant in itself, and that it becomes relevant only in the context of other competencies. A person must remember certain "things" to utilize and demonstrate any of the competencies examined in this study. These "things" may be relevant facts and concepts (i.e., specialized knowledge), or they may be information needed to use one of the competencies at the skill level. To use logical thought, a person must remember causal relationships observed and discovered in previous experiences. To utilize and demonstrate conceptualization, a person must remember information about events to link together and recognize a pattern in that information. To generate metaphors or analogies, which is a part of conceptualization, a person must remember these metaphors and analogies. To utilize and demonstrate diagnostic use of concepts, a person must remember the concepts, theories, or frameworks to apply them in particular situations or events. It is understandable, therefore, that memory does not appear as a separate competency, but is so basic to performance as a manager that it is a precursor to demonstration of any of the competencies, just as being alive is necessary for a person to function as a manager. Because memory does not appear relevant unless in the context of other competencies, it does not seem functionally useful to incorporate it into a generic model of management.

SUMMARY

Although specialized knowledge appears related to effectiveness as a manager, it is probably a threshold competency. It has been suggested that specialized knowledge is easier to identify and describe for specific management jobs in specific organizations rather than as part of a generic model of management. Too much time and energy is devoted to specialized knowledge in many management education, development, and orientation programs. Such programs often ignore the competencies that will enable the manager to use the facts and concepts offered. They assume that information is the most critical component in helping someone be an effective manager. Although important, specialized knowledge is only one of the elements in enabling someone to be a competent manager.

CHAPTER TEN

An Integrated Competency Model

The need for a model of management, and one of its essential components, which is a competency model of management, was discussed in earlier chapters. It is worth repeating that the human organism is a complex system, just as organizations are, and that these systems cannot be understood by looking at only one part of either of them. You cannot understand a manager's competence by looking at one of his or her competencies or even at one of his or her competency clusters out of context of his or her other competencies. That would be similar to an attempt to determine if someone is alive by looking at one of his or her organs lying on a table after it has been separated from the other organs. Although in this case the mere examination process determines the conclusion, the point is that looking at one part of a system of parts, which are connected and depend on each other, does not provide an adequate understanding of the condition and functioning of the entire system.

Combining the findings about various competencies and clusters into an integrated competency model is similar to completing a jigsaw puzzle. The picture on the cover of the box was the basic model showing the relationship between an individual's competencies and effective job performance (see Figure 2-1). The conceptual framework describing the various levels of competencies and their relationship to each other (see Figure 2-2) was analogous to completing the border of the puzzle. Each of the competency clusters described and explained in Chapters 4–9 were similar to completing sections of the puzzle. That is, putting together the pieces forming the red house or the bowl of fruit. It is now time to place all of the sections of the puzzle within the border and fit them into place.

THE COMPETENCY MODEL

Causality

Before putting the pieces together, several points should be clarified regarding causality. It was stated in the definition of a job competency that the "underlying characteristic would *result in* effective and/or superior performance." It was explained that this meant that the use or demonstration of the characteristic would *lead to* effective actions, or behavior. It would be inaccurate to say that the person's competency causes the effective behavior, but that it is *a* cause. The competency is necessary but not sufficient for effective behavior. These relationships between the competencies and job performance have been examined in Chapters 4–9. Statistically speaking, the relationships examined through the findings in this study would mostly be called associational. In only two of the samples were the performance measures based on longitudinal information. In the other cases the performance information was collected at approximately the same time as the competency information. For a complete examination of the causal relationships, all of the performance information should be collected on future performance of a manager (i.e., his or her performance following the collection of information about his or her competencies). Even with some longitudinal and mostly associational information, causal relationships between the competencies and effective job performance were described and inferred in the earlier chapters.

In Chapter 2, effects that various levels of a competency may have on other levels of a competency were explored (see Figure 2-2 for the illustration of these effects). Even though there are causal relationships among the levels of competencies, to minimize confusion with the relationship between competencies and job performance, these relationships will be called "interactions."

There remains one additional type of relationship that may or may not be considered causal. What effect does the demonstration of one competency have on the demonstration of other competencies? Cluster analysis was used to determine these relationships among the competencies at the skill level. In describing the relationship among the competencies in each of the clusters, the term "primary relationship" was used. Because it is difficult with the information available to determine whether the relationship among the competencies within a cluster is causal or associational, primary relationship was used to mean a substantial and significant direct relationship. In such a primary relationship, the demonstration of one competency can be said to stimulate or precipitate the demonstration of the other competency (Klemp, 1979). In contrast, in a secondary relationship, the demonstration of one competency can be said to enhance the use of the other competency (Klemp, 1979).

For example, a primary relationship can be said to exist between the ingestion of certain nutrients and the functioning of the human body. Consider the nutrients in chicken. A person can ingest these in several forms and effectively feed his or her body. A liquid could be made of the chicken meat and pumped directly into a person's stomach. A person could roast a chicken, remove the skin, and eat the meat or a person could eat chicken kiev. Although a chef would disagree, the difference among these various forms of ingestion of the nutrients in chicken meat are found in secondary relationships to nourishment of the body. The "taste" of the chicken has a secondary relationship to the benefits of its ingestion. The sensation of tasting the roasted, plain chicken meat may make the ingestion experience interesting. The additional sensations of the butter, chives, tarragon, and deep-fat frying of the chicken kiev make the experience delightful. The spices and process of preparing the chicken kiev enhances the experience, makes it a richer human experience, and for most people increases the likelihood that they will eat chicken again.

The Integrated Competency Model

An integrated competency model would include the competencies and threshold competencies that appeared in the six clusters. Efficiency orientation, proactivity, diagnostic use of concepts, and concern with impact would be included from the goal and action management cluster. Self-confidence, use of oral presentations, conceptualization, and logical thought would be included from the leadership cluster. Use of socialized power, managing group process, positive regard, and accurate self-assessment would be included from the human resource management cluster. Use of unilateral power, developing others, and spontaneity would be included from the directing subordinates cluster. Perceptual objectivity, self-control (at the trait level only), and stamina and adaptability (at the trait level only), would be included from the focus on others cluster. Specialized knowledge would be included.

The integrated competency model at the *skill level* is presented in Figure 10-1. The primary and secondary relationships discussed in the text are noted. Self-control and stamina and adaptability do not appear

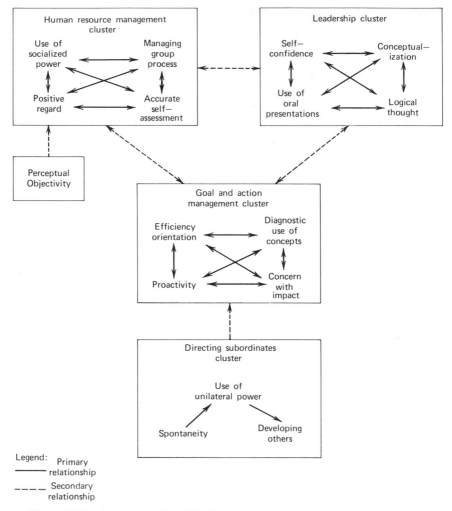

Figure 10-1. An integrated model of management competencies at the skill level.

in the figure because they cannot be considered competencies at the skill level. Since the cluster analysis was only conducted with the skill level of the competencies, it would be incorrect to include them in the figure. Specialized knowledge does not appear in the figure because, as was mentioned earlier, its impact on the other competencies is pervasive.

The model shows three of the clusters to be central to the interaction of competencies for managers: (1) the goal and action management cluster; (2) the leadership cluster; and (3) the human resource management cluster. A manager would be most effective if he or she possessed all of the competencies and threshold competencies in all of the clusters. It can be inferred from the model that it is far more serious if a manager lacks one or more of the competencies within a cluster than if the manager lacks an entire competency cluster. Due to the primary relationships, a manager who does not possess one of the competencies within a cluster will have his or her probability of effectively demonstrating the needed skills in the job related to that cluster potentially minimized, or threatened. In other words, lacking one of the competencies within a cluster will jeopardize the potential impact of the entire cluster as it affects his or her performance. On the other hand, a manager may not possess an entire competency cluster, potentially lessening the maximum possible impact of the other clusters on his or her performance, but not threatening minimal effective performance. It is also possible that some of the clusters are not relevant to specific management jobs (i.e., at certain managerial levels). If this were true, a manager could perform effectively at his or her level without possessing the competecies in a particular cluster (see Chapter 11 for further discussion of this point).

INTERACTIONS AT THE MOTIVE OR TRAIT LEVEL

Eight of the nineteen characteristics in the competency model exist at a motive or trait level as well as at the skill level. Possession of a specific motive or trait will increase the likelihood that people will incorporate certain related behaviors into their chosen self-image and social roles, and that these behaviors will emerge as patterns of behavior that are related to some performance goal.

The Impact on Behavior

People with the conscious and unconscious dispositions represented by the motives or traits respond to their environment and events in life in specific ways. This occurs because they think about their environment and life in certain ways and are sensitive to information in these events in a particular manner. The more people think about and perceive aspects of their lives in a certain manner, the more they integrate these consistent thoughts and observations into a self-image; that is, the thoughts and observations become a part of their concept of themselves and form the basis for their evaluation of that self-concept (i.e., self-esteem). Individuals choose and adopt roles in social and organizational contexts that are relatively consistent with this self-image and the precursory dispositions (i.e., motives and traits).

To the extent that the individuals' actions (i.e., demonstrated behavior) are consistent and are related to some performance goal, these individuals can be said to be demonstrating a skill. The behavior demonstrated by individuals is a function of these dispositions, their self-images, and social roles chosen in the context of stimuli or demands from their jobs and the environment in which the jobs exist.

Although information on motive, trait, and skill aspects of the same competencies was not available on the same individuals in this aggregate sample, prior research supports the conclusion that there are relationships between the motive, trait, and skill aspects of six of the competencies.

With regard to efficiency orientation, people with a high *n* Achievement have been shown to: set goals that reflect a moderate risk of success; seek feedback on their performance toward those goals; and take personal responsibility for performance toward those goals (McClelland, 1961; Heckhausen, 1967; Atkinson, 1958; Atkinson & Feather, 1966). These individuals have been shown to do well in jobs such as small business and sales, which provide the opportunity for direct measurement of their actions and offer relatively rapid feedback on performance (McClelland, 1961). Therefore, people with the motive level of efficiency orientation can be expected to demonstrate the skill level of efficiency orientation. Without the support of the motive, people may be concerned about efficiency and set goals, but they probably will not do it as consistently as people with the motive.

With regard to proactivity, people with Self-Definition and a sense of efficacy have been shown to: take initiative to solve their own problems; identify problem situations; seek information from their environment about things that concern them; and take personal responsibility for the results of these actions (Stewart & Winter, 1974; Rotter, 1966; Boyatzis, 1969; deCharms, 1968). They do not wait for things to happen to them. Therefore, people with the trait level of proactivity can be expected to demonstrate the skill level of proactivity.

With regard to self-control, people with Activity Inhibition have been shown to: drink less alcohol and get intoxicated less often; function more effectively in social systems in which others depend on their behavior; demonstrate altruistic behavior; and pay more attention to issues of equity and justice (McClelland et al., 1972; McClelland, 1975). People with this trait appear to act in such a way that opportunities for conflicts between themselves and others are minimized. While people with Activity Inhibition can be expected to exercise more self-control over their behavior than do others, they are not necessarily seen to exert self-control; that is, people exercising self-control effectively do not look tensed, constrained, or as if they are holding themselves back. Although more self-control behavior can be expected from someone with the trait level of self-control, these actions most likely are observed not in a specific situation but become apparent as a pattern when examined in context of a series of events.

With regard to stamina and adaptability, a similar dynamic to that discussed with self-control is expected. People with high scores on Stages of Adaptation have been shown to respond to their environment in a more interactive manner, and to function well in positions of responsibility in organizations (McClelland, 1975; Stewart, 1977). People who have this characteristic of adaptability to the environment demonstrate their flexibility in the environment or to stress, but are not likely to be observed to demonstrate specific skills in any particular situation. The corresponding behavior is evident as a pattern in the individuals' behavior when studied across many situations or events. People with the physical energy trait of the stamina and adaptability competency are likely to be seen to sustain an appropriate level of energy over long durations or in periods of stress. In any specific situation, they do not necessarily demonstrate more activity or movement than people with less of this trait.

With regard to concern with impact, people with n Power have been shown to: take leadership positions in organizations (especially volunteer, civic, or professional organizations); collect prestigeful possessions that enhance their symbolic influence on others; carry more credit cards as a symbol of financial potency; and show sensitivity to influence dynamics in situations (McClelland et al., 1972; Winter, 1973; McClelland, 1975; Atkinson, 1958). They act in such a way as to provide others with evidence of their potency, such as acting assertively (Winter, 1973; McClelland et al., 1972). Therefore, people with the motive level of concern with impact can be expected to express the skills of concern with impact.

With regard to concern with close relationships, people with high n Affiliation have been shown to make more long-distance telephone calls, write more letters, spend more time with subordinates, and prefer working with a friend to an expert who is a stranger (Atkinson, 1958; Boyatzis, 1973). Therefore, people with the motive level of concern with close relationships can be expected to express skills of concern with close relationships.

The Relationship to Other Motives and Traits

There are relationships among the motive and trait levels of the competencies. The correlation matrix of the motive or trait level of six of the competencies is shown in Table 10-1. Information was not included in

TABLE 10-1 Correlations of Competencies at the Motive and Trait Level

	MOTIVES		TRAITS					
	n Affiliation[a]	n Power[a]	Activity Inhibition	Self-Definition[a]	Stage I	Stage II	Stage III	Stage IV
MOTIVES *n* Achievement[a]	.024	.047	−.010	.110	.167**	.194***	.051	.315***
N	531	532	218	347	347	347	347	347
n Affiliation[a]		−.025	−.078	.116	.291***	.085	.013	−.021
N		608	608	217	347	347	347	347
n Power[a]			.106**	.145*	−.002	.127*	.340***	.062
N			609	218	347	347	347	347
TRAITS Activity Inhibition				.045	.073	.075	.173**	−.017
N				218	347	347	347	347
Self-Definition[a]					.109	.154	−.201	−.294
N					35	35	35	35
Stage I						.050	.031	−.103
N						363	363	363
Stage II							.190***	.176***
N							363	363
Stage III								−.035
N								363

[a]These scores were adjusted for length of protocol.

*p < .05 .

**p < .01 .

***p < .001.

this study on the trait levels of perceptual objectivity and positive regard because it was not available on more than one of the separate studies included in the aggregate sample. These results indicate a positive relationship between the motive level of efficiency orientation and the trait level of stamina and adaptability. This suggests that people with lower Stages of Adaptation set goals and make plans. These plans probably are about their individual behavior which others have determined as relevant to their jobs. The relationship with the highest Stage of Adaptation suggests that at this level of stamina and adaptability, people can set goals and plan at an organizational or system level. The motive level of efficiency orientation and the trait level of proactivity are not significantly related indicating that these two competencies are not strongly related at the motive and trait level.

The motive level of concern with close relationships shows a relationship to only the lowest stage of the trait measure of stamina and adaptability.

The motive level of concern with impact shows a positive relationship to the trait levels of self-control, proactivity, and stamina and adaptability. This suggests that people with the motive level of concern with impact view themselves as initiators, assertively respond to changes in the environment, but at the same time inhibit impulses or needs in service of organizational concerns or objectives.

The trait level of self-control appears related to a high Stage of Adaptation in the trait level of stamina and adaptability. This suggests that people with this higher Stage of Adaptation have the disposition to inhibit personal needs in service of organizational needs.

Previous research has shown that a particular pattern of a high n Power, a low n Affiliation, and a high Activity Inhibition score is related to managerial performance (McClelland, 1975; McClelland, 1979; McClelland, 1978; Winter, 1979; Howard, in preparation). This pattern is called the leadership motive profile. It is calculated by converting the two motive scores to t-scores after adjusting for length of the protocol. People are said to have the leadership motive profile if: (1) their t-score of the n Power is greater than 45; (2) their t-score of the n Power is greater than the t-score for the n Affiliation; and (3) their Activity Inhibition score is 2 or greater.*

---

*The Activity Inhibition score is not adjusted for length of protocol for the calculation of the leadership motive profile due to the J curve distribution that Activity Inhibition shows in most samples. With this type of distribution, having a score of 2 or more appears to account for the majority of the variance in the scores without further distinction as to specific frequency beyond 2.

Significantly more superior managers in the aggregate sample had the leadership motive profile than did others (34 percent of the superior performers as compared with 24 percent of the average performers and 20 percent of the poor performers), as shown in Table 10-2. Significantly more managers in the private sector had the leadership motive profile (31 percent) than did managers in the public sector (16 percent) ($x^2 =$ 17.731, $p < .001$). Within the public sector, significantly more superior managers (26 percent) had the leadership motive profile than did average (7 percent) or poor (11 percent) managers. At the executive level, more superior managers had the leadership motive profile (30 percent) than did average (8 percent) or poor (17 percent) managers, at a near significant level. Although there were no significant differences found among the marketing managers, significantly more of the superior manufacturing managers (32 percent) had the leadership motive profile than did average (20 percent) or poor (11 percent) manufacturing managers.

It is likely that motive and trait levels of the competencies have additional interactive effects on the behavior of managers other than the leadership motive profile. Unfortunately, the data in this aggregate sample did not allow for other joint effects to be tested.

DIFFERENTIATING PERFORMANCE GROUPS

Exploration of an integrated competency model would not be complete without examination of the predictive effect of the competencies, in the context of each other, on differentiating performance groups. To determine this, a multivariate analysis must be used. Since the classification into performance groups (i.e., designation as poor, average, or superior performers) was ordinal, discriminant function analysis was selected. Discriminant function analysis will yield one function (i.e., a set of competencies) that provides a maximum separation of the performance groups, taking into account the effect of all of the competencies on each other. It will also yield a second function (again, a set of competencies) that provides a maximum separation of the performance groups, for those competencies not associated (i.e., correlated) with those in the first function (Overall & Klett, 1972). A stepwise computation was used to determine the set of competencies to be included in the two functions. The procedure used was based on the maximum Rao's V to enter each competency, which accounts for variances explained by all competencies previously entered into the stepwise computation.

TABLE 10-2 Analysis of Leadership Motive Profile

		Number of Managers Who Did Not Have the Leadership Motive Profile	Number of Managers Who Did Have the Leadership Motive Profile	Percentage of Managers With the Leadership Motive Profile	χ^2	Significance Level of Chi-Squared
Perfor- mance groups	Poor	72	18	20		
	Average	184	59	24	6.803	.034
	Superior	88	46	34		
Public sector managers	Poor	40	5	11		
	Average	42	3	7	7.082	.030
	Superior	28	10	26		
Private sector managers	Poor	32	13	29		
	Average	142	56	28	2.675	n.s.
	Superior	60	36	38		
Entry level managers	Poor	47	13	22		
	Average	135	53	28	3.935	n.s.
	Superior	58	33	36		
Middle level managers	Poor	15	3	17		
	Average	16	3	16	1.488	n.s.
	Superior	14	6	30		
Executive level managers	Poor	10	2	17		
	Average	33	3	8	4.881	.088
	Superior	16	7	30		
Marketing managers	Poor	5	0	0		
	Average	35	17	33	2.622	n.s.
	Superior	21	7	25		
Manufac- turing managers	Poor	40	5	11		
	Average	123	31	20	7.327	.026
	Superior	50	23	32		

Ten competencies were included in the two discriminant functions. These were: self-control; spontaneity; perceptual objectivity; diagnostic use of concepts; developing others; concern with impact; use of unilateral power; use of socialized power; use of oral presentations; and concern with close relationships. The standardized canonical discriminant coefficients are shown in Table 10-3. The first function yielded a maximum separation of poor, average, and superior performers from each other. The second function yielded a maximum separation of poor and superior performers from average performers. Both functions yielded highly significant canonical correlations.

A comparison based on the two discriminant functions of the performance classification predicted by the competencies to the actual performance classification of the managers in the study is shown in Table 10-4. The competencies correctly classified 51 percent of the managers; a totally random prediction would have resulted in correct classification of only 33 percent of the managers. The prediction underestimated the performance classification of 33 percent of the managers, and overestimated the performance classification of 16 percent of the managers. This suggests that although the prediction based on the competencies is most likely to be accurate, there is a bias toward conservatively predicting a manager's performance. That is, of those incorrectly classified, there was twice as much chance that a manager would have been clas-

TABLE 10-3   Results of the Discriminant Function Analysis on the Entire Sample, $N = 253$

	Standard Canonical Discriminant Coefficients	
Competency	Function One	Function Two
Self-Control	.132	.322
Spontaneity	−.332	−.158
Perceptual objectivity	−.200	.382
Diagnostic use of concepts	−.487	−.167
Developing others	−.093	−.589
Concern with impact	−.168	.330
Use of unilateral power	.230	−.454
Use of socialized power	−.482	.067
Use of oral presentations	−.293	−.075
Concern with close relationships	.198	−.217
Canonical correlation	.395	.339

TABLE 10-4   Comparison of Predictions Based on Competencies with Actual
Performance

Actual Group Classification	N	Predicted Group Classification[a]		
		Poor	Average	Superior
Poor	63	42	10	11
		17%	4%	4%
Average	91	32	40	19
		13%	16%	8%
Superior	99	29	22	48
		11%	9%	19%

[a] Percentages are based on the total sample size, $N = 253$.

sified in a lower performance category than the criterion information collected on the manager indicated.

Examination of Table 10-4 shows that if we chose to predict merely effective performance (i.e., average or superior performance) as compared to poor performance, 68 percent of the managers would have been correctly predicted based on the competencies, with 24 percent of the managers having their performance underestimated, and 8 percent of the managers having their performance overestimated. In a similar manner, if we had chosen to predict superior performance as compared to average or poor performance, 68 percent of the managers would have been correctly predicted based on the competencies, with 20 percent of the managers having their performance underestimated, and 12 percent of the managers having their performance overestimated.

It is important to remember that the objective of the discriminant function analysis was to determine the degree of accuracy in predicting performance group classification based on the entire set of competencies in the context of each other. The method utilized to construct the discriminant functions takes into account the degree of association of the competencies once each competency is stepped into the analysis. This means that *the list of specific competencies in the discriminant functions is not as important to this analysis as the predictive accuracy of the entire set.* Given the theoretical hypotheses that certain competencies would be highly associated with other competencies, and the empirical confirmation of this with the cluster analysis, it is to be expected that the particular competencies that loaded onto the two discriminant functions represented a sampling from each of the clusters identified in the cluster analysis, and do not represent a list of the "most important" competencies.

The integrated set of competencies appeared effective in differentiating the superior, average, and poor managers. In addition, they accounted for about 27 percent of the variance in the performance measures (the sum of the squares of the canonical correlations). Considering that these were competencies common to managers in both the private and public sectors, and from entry, middle, and executive levels, in a variety or organizations and specific management jobs, the results are substantial. The competencies validated in this study were the same, or very similar to, about half (56 percent) of the competencies validated in the separate studies which composed this aggregate sample and several competency studies of managers completed after this study. The validated competencies in these separate studies tended to account for about one-half to two-thirds of the variance in the separate performance measures used in each. Therefore, *the competencies in the integrated model are, on the whole, about half of the competencies that are related to effective performance of managers in particular management jobs in specific organizations*, and they probably account for about the same variance in performance measures that the job- and organization-specific competencies do. These other competencies are characteristics that are related to performance in the context of the particular management jobs (with the corresponding variations in functional responsibilities referred to in Chapter 2) within specific organizations (with the corresponding variations in industry characteristics and organizational environment referred to in Chapter 2). This suggests that about one-third of the variance in performance of a manager can probably be accounted for by these generic management competencies, about one-third of the variance can probably be accounted for by job- and organization-specific management competencies, and the remaining one-third of the variance is probably due to situational factors (e.g., both day-to-day events in the job and aspects of the environment).

CHAPTER ELEVEN

Interpretation by Sector And Managerial Level

As a result of the nature of the aggregate sample, competent managerial performance could be examined in the contexts of: one aspect of the environment in which managers function (i.e., public and private sectors); and one aspect of the jobs in which they function (i.e., entry, middle, and executive levels). Although the purpose of the study was to develop an overall competency model of management, the available information can be used to further interpret the relationship between competencies and performance.

ENVIRONMENTAL DIFFERENCES IN TERMS OF SECTOR

In Chapter 2, it was proposed that a number of environmental factors would affect a manager's performance, in terms of how they affected the use of competencies. The environmental factors included the organizational climate of the specific organization in which the person works (i.e., policies, procedures, structure, norms, and values), the strategic condition of the organization, its products or services, the industry of which it is a part, and cultural issues. Whether the organization exists in the private or the public sector can be considered one of these environmental issues, but it is only one of them.

The Goal and Action Management Cluster

Managers in the private sector demonstrated more of each of the four competencies in the goal and action management cluster (i.e., efficiency orientation, proactivity, diagnostic use of concepts, and concern with impact) than did managers in the public sector, at the skill level. This suggests that the environment of organizations in the private sector demands, stimulates, or requires more of each of these skills, in general, than the environment of organizations in the public sector. Organizations in the private sector have access to indicators of performance that are easier to measure and assess on a timely basis, such as profits, sales volume, number of units off the production line, market share, cost savings due to waste reduction or innovation, and so forth. The nature of the work, the structure of jobs, and the measures of performance used in the public sector do not allow for easy and quick feedback to managers regarding performance. Without the availability of such measures of performance, it is more difficult to set goals, establish plans, initiate action, solve problems, diagnose difficulties, have impact on the image or reputation of the organization and its products or services, and, in general, manage with the competencies in the goal and action management cluster. In support of these findings, Bower (1977) indicated that public sector managers must accept goals set by organizations and operate structures designed by groups other than their own.

One observation of the findings indicates that this is not merely a function of self-selection of certain types of managers into private sector organizations. The observation is that managers in the public sector appeared to have higher motive and trait levels of the three competencies in the goal and action management cluster, which were hypothesized to have motive or trait levels than did managers in the private sector. If the findings at the motive and trait levels were opposite, then it could have been inferred that a self-selection process was operating.

People who have higher motive and trait levels on these three competencies (i.e., efficiency orientation, proactivity, and concern with impact) may select careers in the public sector because the career path is clearer and more established than in the private sector. People with these motives and traits are concerned about their careers from a long-term perspective and want to take action to "get ahead" (McClelland, 1961; Stewart & Winter, 1974; McClelland, 1975; Boyatzis, 1969). In many cultures, the most effective course of action to achieve upward mobility from the working class is to enter government service or the church as a career.

This concern with career advancement and upward mobility may be stimulating people relatively higher in these motives and traits to enter organizations in the public sector. Once they attain managerial jobs, they are not called on to demonstrate the corresponding skills as often as they would have been in the private sector. This would encourage such

managers in the public sector to stay in government service only until they have gained enough credibility or experience to move into the private sector. Due to the lucrative pension benefits for managers in the public sector, such managers would be expected to leave government service once they have reached the point of maximizing their pensions, and also maximizing the experience that is marketable in the private sector. This would result in public sector organizations having problems retaining their most experienced managers.

Another dynamic might also occur for managers with these motives and traits in public sector organizations. This dynamic is that once they have achieved a certain managerial position, they would satisfy their motives and traits involving the goal and action management competencies in activities outside the work setting. In this case, as well as the one mentioned above, public sector organizations potentially are losing the managerial resources they have regarding goal and action management competencies.

This can be a serious problem for public sector organizations because of the additional observation that effective and/or superior managers in the public sector demonstrated more of the skills of each of these four competencies than did less effective managers. The constraints, lack of inducements, and relative lack of opportunity to demonstrate these skills, which appear to be a part of the public sector environment, do not inhibit effective managers from demonstrating them. If the environment in which they function does not reward or encourage the demonstration of such skills, their length of employment, as well as the focus of their energies, may not be as extensive as it would be if the environment provided a different set of encouragements and opportunities.

An implication of these findings regarding the goal and action management competencies for public sector organizations is that managerial performance could be improved if the environmental demands placed on the organizations and managers were altered. The changes would have to allow for measurement of performance, establishment of goals and plans, diagnosis of performance problems and potential for improvement with the appropriate concepts, managerial initiative to implement changes, and the power to put them into effect. This is not merely a contention that managers in the public sector would be more effective if their environment were similar to the environment of private sector organizations. Remember, effective managers within public sector organizations demonstrated more of these competencies than their less effective peers.

This type of change in environmental demands would be complex and require careful thought and planning. Otherwise, the implementation of such changes would wallow in additional procedural regulation and lose effectiveness as the changes are imposed on public sector managers. Caution would have to be exercised so that legitimate and functional concerns with standardization and consistency were not violated. At the core of this implication is a massive effort to redesign public sector management jobs in terms of responsibilities, tasks, functions, span of control, performance measures, and commensurate rewards. Recent reforms in the civil service system (i.e., a merit-based bonus system for senior federal executives and new performance appraisal procedures) suggest the possibility that some of these changes have been recognized as desirable. The question remains whether implementation efforts are substantial enough and have been systematically designed and implemented with enough forethought to have the desired impact. There is also a question whether such programs have taken into account differences in time horizon, institutional response time, policy-directed objectives, and other factors that make public sector management different than private sector management (Bower, 1977).

The Leadership Cluster

Managers in the private sector demonstrated more of two of the competencies in the leadership cluster than managers in the public sector: conceptualization and use of oral presentations. The other competencies in this cluster, self-confidence and logical thought, appeared to be equally stimulated or demanded by organizations in both the public and private sectors. The difference in demonstration of the use of oral presentations may result from a different demand on managers in the public sector than on those in the private sector to make oral presentations to others in the organization, as well as to others outside the organization. Managers in public sector organizations are under certain pressure during such presentations to reflect "administration" policies and perspectives. The press and the public scrutinize such presentations by managers in public sector organizations carefully. Groups within the government (i.e., legislative committees and regulatory agencies) and those outside the government (i.e., special interest lobbies and the press) have access to and examine presentations by managers in the public sector. For these reasons, the frequency of demonstration of the use of oral presentations competency may be less than it would be with managers in the private sector. It is important to note, however, that effective managers in the public sector demonstrated more use of oral presentations and self-confidence than did their less effective peers. This suggests that although there are constraints on the presentations made by public sector managers, the effective managers can use these two competencies to make their presentations effective.

Regarding the third competency in the leadership cluster, conceptualization, managers in organizations in the private sector are demanded, required, or stimulated to demonstrate this competency more often than are managers in public sector organizations. In addition, effective managers in public sector organizations did not demonstrate any more of this competency than did their less effective peers. Managers in private sector organizations are often exposed to, and must respond directly to, many diverse groups and perspectives, both internally and externally. In responding to these perspectives, in solving complex problems, and by innovating to adapt to changes in technology and the marketplace, managers in private sector organizations need to be able to identify themes and patterns in such information for a variety of reasons. At the same time managers in public sector organizations, although exposed to many diverse perspectives, are required to analyze, document, and adapt to problems, issues, and changes in relatively standardized ways. The standardization of procedures within the public sector has emerged from the need to establish equitable and consistent methods of operation and problem solving across various branches, agencies and functional groups within the government. One result of this concern with standardization has been a plethora of forms, proscriptions, and prescriptions telling managers how to address, analyze, and document their operations. Such standardization, taken to this degree, does not allow managers to utilize the conceptualization competency. The observation that it was not differentially demonstrated by various performance groups of managers in the public sector suggests that it is not necessary as a competency for these managers.

Private sector managers are repeatedly required to make strategic decisions. They must identify trends in the marketplace, themes that differentiate them from their competitors, and patterns of internal resource utilization that will be most effective. All of these activities call for the use of the conceptualization competency. Bower (1977) claimed that this is the art of "the application of massive resources to limited objectives." Such resource decisions require the type of analytic thought reflected in the use of the conceptualization competency. On the other hand, Bower claimed that public sector managers must practice the art of "the application of limited resources to massive objectives." With a multitude of objectives and concerns about social responsibility, resource allocation decisions of the public sector manager require a great deal of analytic thought reflected in the use of the diagnostic use of concepts competency. They must assess, in a deductive manner, the degree to which any activity or resource allocation will work toward various objectives and social responsibility concerns. The identification of themes, trends, and patterns in public concern are usually made by the "top advisors" in the current or past administrations and handed to the managers as policy directives.

The Human Resource Management Cluster

One of the competencies (i.e., use of socialized power) and the two threshold competencies (i.e., accurate self-assessment and positive regard) in the human resource management cluster are apparently demanded, required, or stimulated to similar degrees from managers in organizations in both the private and public sectors. The other competency in this cluster (i.e., managing group process) was demonstrated more often by managers in private sector organizations than by managers in public sector organizations. This suggests that differences in the environment, in terms of sector within which managers function, do not make a difference as to the need to demonstrate the human resource management competencies and threshold competencies.

The one observed difference suggests that managers in private sector organizations have more opportunity for, and inducement to build work group identity, pride, and team spirit, as well as stimulate collaboration within the work group. This may result from rotation of managerial personnel within public sector organizations and from a need within public sector organizations not to establish too much identity, spirit, and cooperation among agencies and departments. Such behavior on the part of managers may result in the dilution of the basic system of checks and balances on which the government is based, and also may violate those aspects of public trust that require privacy and confidentiality regarding information obtained on individuals. The observation that effective public sector managers do demonstrate more of the managing group process competency than do their less effective peers suggests that effective managers may be able to establish identity, spirit, and cooperation within their work groups that does threaten to violate these other concerns about interagency or interdepartmental functioning.

Other Competencies

Three threshold competencies (i.e., developing others, use of unilateral power and spontaneity), which are the directing subordinates cluster, appear to be equally demanded, simulated, or required from managers in organizations in both sectors.

The one skill level competency within the focus on others cluster (i.e., perceptual objectivity) appears to be equally required, demanded, or stimulated from managers in organizations in both sectors.

The revelant competencies for managers in each sector are summarized in Table 11-1.

Differentiating Performance Groups

To assess the degree to which the complete set of competencies was effective in distinguishing among performance groups of managers (i.e.,

TABLE 11-1   Competencies Relevant to Performance and Effectiveness in Terms of Environmental Demand: Public Versus Private Sector[a]

For Managers in Organizations in the Public Sector	For Managers in Organizations in the Private Sector
Goal and action management cluster	Goal and action management cluster
Concern with impact	Concern with impact
Diagnostic use of concepts	Diagnostic use of concepts
Efficiency orientation	Efficiency orientation
Proactivity	Proactivity
Leadership cluster	Leadership cluster
Self-confidence	Conceptualization
Use of oral presentations	Use of oral presentations
Human resource management cluster	Human resource management cluster
Managing group process	Managing group process
Use of socialized power	Use of socialized power
Directing subordinates cluster	Focus on others cluster
Use of unilateral power	Perceptual objectivity
Spontaniety	Self-control (at the trait level)
	Stamina and adaptability (at the trait level)
Focus on others cluster	
Stamina and adaptability (at the trait level)	

[a]Relevance is defined as that competency which is demanded or required more for performance of that sector than for the other sector *or* that competency which is characteristic of effective managers within that sector of the environment.

poor, average, and superior managers), discriminant function analyses were conducted separately on managers in each of the sectors. Since the objectives of the analyses were the same as with the overall analysis described in the preceding chapter, the same procedures were followed.

The discriminant function analysis within the public sector yielded two discriminant functions, as shown in Table 11-2. These included eight competencies: self-confidence, self-control, spontaneity, proactivity, diagnostic use of concepts, developing others, use of socialized power, and use of oral presentations. The first function yielded a maximum separation of superior, average, and poor managers from each other. The second function yielded a maximum separation of superior and poor managers from average managers. Both functions showed highly significant canonical correlations.

A comparison based on the two discriminant functions of the performance classification predicted by the competencies to the actual performance classification of the managers in the study is shown in Table 11-3. The competencies correctly classified 59 percent of the managers; a totally random prediction would have resulted in only 33 percent of the managers. The prediction underestimated the performance classification of 27 percent of the managers, and overestimated the performance classification of 14 percent of the managers.

The discriminant function analysis within the private sector yielded

TABLE 11-2 Results of the Discriminant Function Analysis on the Public Sector Sample, $N = 154$

Competency	Standardized Canonical Discriminant Coefficients	
	Function One	Function Two
Self-confidence	−.404	−.234
Self-control	.377	.257
Spontaneity	−.584	−.113
Proactivity	.081	.519
Diagnostic use of concepts	−.311	.175
Developing others	−.074	−.789
Use of socialized power	−.367	−.230
Use of oral presentations	−.461	.343
Canonical correlation	.448	.432

TABLE 11-3　Comparison of Predictions Based on Competencies with Actual Performance in the Public Sector Sample

Actual Group Classification	N	Predicted Group Classification[a]		
		Poor	Average	Superior
Poor	63	50	8	5
		32%	5%	3%
Average	52	20	23	9
		13%	15%	6%
Superior	39	14	7	18
		9%	5%	12%

[a]Percentages are based on the total public sector sample size, $N = 154$.

one function, as shown in Table 11-4. This included eight competencies and one characteristic that did not warrant categorization as a competency: self-control, perceptual objectivity, stamina and adaptability, efficiency orientation, diagnostic use of concepts, concern with impact, use of unilateral power, use of socialized power, and concern with close relationships. The function yielded a maximum separation of superior and average managers, and showed a highly significant canonical correlation.

A comparison based on the discriminant function of the performance classification predicted by the competencies to the actual performance classification of the managers in the study is shown on Table 11-5. The competencies correctly classified 73 percent of the managers; a totally random prediction would have resulted in only 50 percent of the managers. The prediction underestimated the performance of 14 percent of the managers, and overestimated the performance of 13 percent of the managers.

As with the overall discriminant function analysis presented in the preceding chapter, the total set of competencies was highly effective in distinguishing among performance groups within each of the sectors. The slightly higher canonical correlations of the discriminant functions, and the percentage of managers correctly classified in the separate analyses within each sector as compared to the overall analysis was probably the result of controlling for one aspect of the organizational environment, namely the sector in which their organization is located. This also supports the contention that if other aspects of the environment were controlled for and if aspects of the functional requirements of the vari-

TABLE 11-4   Results of the Discriminant Function Analysis on the Private
Sector Sample, $N = 99$

Competency	Standardized Canonical Discriminant Coefficients
Self-control	$-.450$
Perceptual objectivity	$-.391$
Stamina and adaptability	$.282$
Efficiency orientation	$-.325$
Diagnostic use of concepts	$.447$
Concern with impact	$-.396$
Use of unilateral power	$.585$
Use of socialized power	$-.359$
Concern with close relationships	$.377$
Canonical correlation	$.510$

TABLE 11-5   Comparison of Predictions Based on Competencies with Actual
Performance in the Private Sector Sample

Actual Group Classification	N	Predicted Group Classification[a]	
		Average	Superior
Average	39	26	13
		26%	13%
Superior	60	14	46
		14%	47%

[a]Percentages are based on the total private sector sample, $N = 99$.

ous management jobs were controlled for by the research design (i.e., conducting the analysis on managers in one job within one organization), the percentage of correct classification would increase substantially.

It is worth reminding the reader that the discriminant function analyses were conducted to determine the predictive effect of the complete set of competencies at the skill level. The particular competencies listed in each of the discriminant functions represent those characteristics that, when entered into a function in a stepwise method, describe the maximum separation of performance groups while controlling for interactions with other characteristics. Because the characteristics are generic, human characteristics, it is not expected that they would have independent effects on performance as a manager (see the discussion in Chapter 2). Therefore, the particular characteristics listed in the discriminant functions *do not* constitute a critical list of competencies that aid in the understanding of differential environmental demands from the public and private sectors. They are merely a list of characteristics that, when taken as a set, have a maximum effect on distinguishing performance groups. For an understanding of the potential impact of each competency on managerial performance, the reader is referred to Chapters 4–9. To understand how the competencies affect each other, the reader is referred to Chapter 10. For an understanding of the differential environmental demands from the public and private sectors, the reader is referred to the previous discussion in this chapter.

JOB DIFFERENCES IN TERMS OF MANAGERIAL LEVEL

In Chapter 2, it was proposed that functional requirements and situational demands of specific management jobs would affect a manager's performance, in terms of how they affected the use of competencies. These factors included functional and task requirements, or responsibilities, of a particular job, as well as situational demands that might occur day-to-day. The aggregate study allowed for one general aspect of the functional requirements of management jobs to be examined in terms of competencies: the managerial level of the job.

The Goal and Action Management Cluster

The competencies in the goal and action management cluster appeared relevant to management jobs at all levels. Of the four competencies in the goal and action management cluster (i.e., efficiency orientation, proactivity, diagnostic use of concepts, and concern with impact), diagnostic use of concepts and efficiency orientation were demanded or required more from entry level managers than from other managers and concern with impact was demanded or required more from executive level managers than from other managers. Since there was no difference in the amount of proactivity demonstrated by managers at each of these levels, but the average frequency of demonstration of proactivity was relatively high for managers at each of the levels, it can be inferred that proactivity is demanded or required from all levels of managers. In addition, middle and executive level managers appeared to have higher scores of the motive levels of efficiency orientation and concern with impact than did entry level managers.

In terms of distinguishing effective managerial performance, efficiency orientation did so: for entry level managers at the motive level; for middle level managers at the skill level; and for executive level managers at both the motive and skill levels. Proactivity at the skill levels was demonstrated by effective managers at the middle and executive levels. Diagnostic use of concepts was demonstrated by effective managers at the middle and executive levels. Concern with impact was demonstrated by effective middle level managers at the skill level, and by effective executives at the motive level.

A competency can be said to be *relevant* to a particular management job if it is either demanded or required more by that job than by other management jobs, *or* if it is demonstrated or possessed by effective managers in that job and not by their less effective counterparts. With this definition of relevance to the job, it can be said that the competencies in the goal and action management cluster are relevant to all three levels of management jobs, with the exception of concern with impact, which is relevant at middle and executive levels only. The way in which they are relevant, or manifest themselves in behavior, is probably different at each of the management levels.

At the entry level, a manager is responsible for progress toward certain goals in accordance with certain plans. He or she provides feedback to subordinates, primarily as individual contributors, with respect to the goals, plans, and performance standards established for their jobs. It is likely that the entry level manager has been given the goals, plans, and standards of performance by managers at higher levels in the organization. This manager is concerned with diagnosing performance problems in the context of these goals and plans and is expected to take action to solve certain problems. It is understandable, therefore, that three of the competencies in the goal and action management cluster would be relevant to his or her job.

At the middle level, a manager is also responsible for progress toward certain goals in accordance with certain plans. He or she provides feedback to subordinates who are most likely entry level or lower middle level managers. This feedback is in terms of individual performance, as well as their work group's performance. Within the ranks of middle level management, the higher the manager is located in the structure, the more it would be expected that his or her feedback to subordinates is oriented toward performance of a work group, versus individual performance. This feedback, diagnosis of performance problems and initiation of actions to solve them is based on goals and plans that the middle level manager may have had some input in developing. Although the goals and plans may initially emerge from upper levels of management, or from the needs of the organization in terms of business plans (i.e., as communicated to this level of management by upper levels), the middle level manager confirms, if not develops, the goals and plans for his or her unit. This manager would be expected to influence subordinates to accept and follow the plans (i.e., using the competency concern with impact). Therefore, all four of the competencies in the goal and action management cluster are relevant to the middle level manager's job.

At the executive level, a manager establishes goals and plans for the whole organization, or large segments of the organization. These are established as part of a corporate business plan, even if the business plan is implicit in the mind of the executive. These goals and plans, and the types of feedback provided to subordinates, tend to focus on organizational units, such as divisions of business groups. The executive level manager must, to be effective, be concerned about the image and reputation of the organization as a whole. He or she must have impact on the managers who report to him or her about maintaining or building this image and stimulating performance. The executive must be able to diagnose problems and identify opportunities for the organization. He or she must initiate activities, solve problems, and seek needed information. Therefore, all four of the competencies in the goal and action management cluster are relevant to the executive manager's job.

Other Clusters Relevant to Entry Level Jobs

The major differences in jobs at the various levels of management begin to emerge from examining the relevance of other clusters of competencies to these jobs. At the entry level, a manager is focused on directing and guiding his or her subordinates. Since they are, on the whole, individual contributors, he or she must provide specific performance feedback in the context of specific standards of performance that have been established primarily by other levels of management. To get subordinates to perform to these standards and goals, the entry level manager uses two competencies: developing others and the use of unilateral power. Entry level managers are required to demonstrate more of each of these competencies than are managers at any other level in the organization.

For example, one of the entry level managers in the sample was a purchasing supervisor in a manufacturing operation. He described an incident in which he utilized two of the competencies from the goal and action management cluster (i.e., efficiency orientation and diagnostic use of concepts) and two of the competencies from the directing subordinates cluster (i.e., use of unilateral power and developing others).

> One of my guys came in for a contract review meeting. His objective was
> to hold the line on pricing but he was vacillating. I told him that holding

the line isn't good enough; we should drive the cost down. I told him to go back and offer a lower price of $3750 per unit. He came back and asked some questions. I said, "O.K., and now what?" Finally, the guy came back in a panic because the vendor hadn't responded. I said, "Fine. Don't do anything." I knew we had time to wait and that gave us an advantage. I told him that if the vendor said "No" we would send in another buyer and pretend that he had been put on another project. Finally, the vendor came back and said, "Yes." I feel good because as a corporation we lowered the price from the vendor. Also, the individual realized that setting tough objectives leads to better performance. I made inputs along the way, like a surgeon teaching a resident how to do surgery. He does the operation and I give tips and critique him. I've very technically proficient at negotiating, and I want to show my buyers how it's done.

Entry level managers are responsible for obtaining compliance with work procedures and adherence to progress on work plans. They must ensure that production line workers wear the required protective clothing. They must ensure that a bookkeeper does not change a fixed asset to a current asset because it seems to fit better. They must ensure that a salesperson does not provide special discounts to favored customers because of a personal relationship, but because such discounts are consistent with corporate policies and promotional strategies. In addition, the entry level manager exercises power on the basis of rules, orders, and established corporate procedures. The focus of the entry level manager is predominantly downward on his or her subordinates and their performance as individual contributors. The competencies in the directing subordinates cluster (i.e., developing others, use of unilateral power, and spontaneity) are, therefore, of primary importance to the entry level manager.

Although not demanded in the job, effective entry level managers also develop a focus regarding their peers. They build networks or coalitions among other entry level managers to enhance both their access to resources and their power bases. The use of the socialized power and accurate self-assessment competencies are crucial to accomplishing this function. In performing this function, these competencies from the human resource management cluster are relevant to the entry level manager's job.

To be effective, entry level managers should have certain competencies that enable them to relate to or manage their bosses. Effective entry level managers demonstrate the use of unilateral power competency, which suggests that they will follow orders, directives, and established procedures as they have been given to them. People who use rules, orders, and established procedures as a basis for their power or authority will often respect and comply with others on this basis of power or authority.

Entry level managers appeared to have higher trait levels of self-control and stamina and adaptability (i.e., Stage III scores) than managers at other levels. This further clarifies that in relation to their bosses, they will inhibit personal needs, desires, and feelings and be more likely to follow the directives and wishes of their bosses than managers with less of these traits.

For entry level managers, competencies in the goal and action management cluster and the directing subordinates cluster are of primary importance to the performance of their jobs, and to their effectiveness. In addition, several other competencies and threshold competencies appear relevant to performance of their jobs and their effectiveness. They are: use of socialized power, accurate self-assessment, self-control at the trait level, and stamina and adaptability at the trait level.

Other Clusters Relevant to Middle Level Jobs

At the middle level of management, a manager's focus is predominantly downward, toward the lower level managers who report to him or her. He or she provides feedback on performance to these other managers in terms of their individual performance, but also in terms of their work group's performance. Two of the competencies in the directing subordinates cluster are demanded of middle level managers: developing others and spontaneity. The middle level manager provides this feedback without the restraint of the effective entry level manager, but with a belief that his or her subordinates can develop and change (i.e., positive regard).

The effective middle level manager utilizes several competencies in the human resource management cluster to stimulate and foster the performance of the work groups reporting to him or her. That is, they build spirit, collaboration, and a coalition of these groups through the use of socialized power, managing group process, positive regard, and accurate self-assessment competencies. The lower level managers reporting to the middle level manager can feel they belong to an alliance, and experience the pride and spirit of belonging to the department or organizational unit headed by the middle level manager, because he or she is using the competencies in the human resource management cluster.

The effective middle level manager also uses these competencies to develop networks, coalitions, and collaboration with other middle level managers. The integrating function required to coordinate resource allocation and utilization, and to coordinate effort toward divisional or business group goals and plans is demonstrated, predominantly, through the use of the competencies in the human resource management cluster.

Other competencies help this "sideways" focus to be effective. One competency from the focus on others cluster (i.e., perceptual objectivity) aids in this integration activity by allowing the manager to understand the different perspectives on various issues that may be characteristic of other middle level managers. In addition, the use of the logical thought competency enables the effective middle level manager to perform these integrating activities in the context of a systems orientation, understanding the causal sequence required among events and activities. Effective middle level managers demonstrate the other competencies from the leadership cluster that help in the communication processes necessary for this type of integration and collaboration to occur (i.e., self-confidence, conceptualization, and use of oral presentations).

In relating to or managing his or her boss, the effective middle level manager utilizes some of these same competencies to have an impact. He or she uses self-confidence and use of oral presentations from the leadership cluster to present his or her points and thoughts to the boss. The concern with impact competency from the goal and action management cluster, shown by effective middle level managers, also helps in the process because the manager desires to have an impact and communicates concerns about the image and reputation of his or her organizational group and their performance.

For example, one of the middle level managers in the sample was the director of personnel for his division. He described an incident in which he utilized competencies from the goal and action management cluster (i.e., efficiency orientation, proactivity, concern with impact, and diagnostic use of concepts), the human resource management cluster (i.e., managing group process and positive regard), and the leadership cluster (i.e., self-confidence and use of oral presentations).

> When I came to Livingston, personnel was not very highly thought of and that was my department. I am proud that I was able to turn that impression around. When I came into the group, I came in over a guy who was already here and thought he would have gotten the job. My first action was to give the staff work to jump in on immediately. Prior to my arrival, the group was not working hard. Promotion and pay schedules were not being attended to and in fact members of the staff were often seen going home early.
>
> I changed this and put them immediately to work on meaningful projects. I established myself as boss right away. Two weeks later I held a staff

meeting. I outlined a series of objectives, stated the facts and assumptions about my staff and the department's work which I had and introduced a flipchart on which I asked people to write exactly what tasks they worked on.

At this point in the interview, Frank pulled out these charts and showed them to the interviewer. Throughout the next 30 minutes he kept referring back to the charts.

I told them at the meeting that I wanted them to change assignments. One major assumption I had is that the only people who will help us increase our credibility is we ourselves. There were three critical assumptions:

1. That people should specialize as well as be generalists;
2. Our credibility is bad, we need a lot of PR work to improve it; and
3. I would be a working manager, not just a manager of my subordinates, but actually involved in the same kind of tasks that they would be involved in.

I told them as a group and then named each individual as to how I thought that they were good in their jobs and that they could make the changes needed to change our image.

I then suggested how to respond to managers who come into the office and demand things without doing their part first. I told my staff to tell managers that they would only go so far, but the managers had to do their part and that they should be firm about this. I told them that I would back them up, if a manager complains about his or her treatment.

We also talked about how to find out whether we are being successful. I told them that I listen in the hallways, watch what mail comes in, see who comes into the office and what questions are asked. I told them that the information is everywhere. I told them that if we're reaching our objectives the information should confirm this.

I know that I've been effective in the past year. Among other things, the vice president and general manager comes in to ask my advice on numerous issues, which are not explicitly part of my job description, or his prior expectations as to what personnel could do for him in running the organization.

For middle level managers, competencies in the goal and action management cluster, the human resource management cluster, and the leadership cluster are of primary importance to the performance of their jobs, and to their effectiveness. In addition, several other competencies and threshold competencies appear relevant to performance of their jobs and their effectiveness. They are: developing others, spontaneity, and perceptual objectivity.

Other Clusters Relevant to Executive Level Jobs

At the executive level, a manager's focus is primarily toward the organization as a whole and toward groups external to the organization (i.e., outward from the organization). The job demands that the executive represent the organization and its products or services internally as well as externally. This is reflected in the observation that two of the competencies are demonstrated more by executives than by any other managers, namely self-confidence and concern with impact. The effective executive utilizes three of the competencies in the leadership cluster to accomplish this function. He or she demonstrates self-confidence, use of oral presentations, and conceptualization. In conjunction with the competencies in the goal and action management cluster, these enable the executive to represent the organization effectively to the world outside the organization, and to represent effectively the image of the organization, its mission, and its products or services. They also enable an executive to do the strategic thinking necessary to move the organization toward its goals.

Internally, the executive's focus is toward the organization as a whole. The basis of exercised power is in symbols of authority (i.e., concern with impact) and in the stimulation of commitment of personnel through inspiration (i.e., self-confidence and use of oral presentations). To have this impact, the effective executive must be able to identify themes or patterns in the organization's activity and performance, as well as in the common concerns and values of its personnel. This has been called expressing and communicating the common vision of the organization (Berlew, 1974).

The effective executive uses several other competencies to perform his or her functions. The executive level manager will use the managing group process competency to build a sense of identity, pride, spirit, and cooperation among the various divisions or managers of functional groups that report to him or her.

For example, one of the managers in the sample was a marketing executive. He described an incident in which he utilized competencies from the goal and action management cluster (i.e., efficiency orientation, proactivity, diagnostic use of concepts, and concern with impact) and the managing group process competency from the human resource management cluster.

> I had a customer situation. An extremely serious product problem in the field. The company's product was identified as the cause of an accident. We had been working on this problem for a number of months and hadn't

solved it. A high level guy from the client called the general manager and said, "You've got 72 hours to fix it or your unit is off the machine." I questioned the general manager about the client's seriousness. "He was serious," I was told in no uncertain terms. I hung up the phone. I was under a great deal of stress. It was Friday a.m. and it had to be fixed by Monday noon. The first thing I thought of was that people would be taking off. I pulled together the key people in the department and laid out the problem.

We named 10 guys we wanted for the job—those were the guys who could do it. We rounded them up in 20 minutes and told them the problem. We had to go to another site for any product modification testing. We got them on a charter plane and to the site that afternoon. We all wound up at the site by six o'clock that evening. . . .

We worked straight through. We got the solution. We spent a lot of time hypothesizing the problem as a group. I got them to come up with the two most likely causes and then we structured how we would solve each of them. I stressed we didn't have time to try all of the possibilities. We got lucky through brainstorming sessions which I was running. I asked them finally, "If you had to bet your life on it, which one would you pick?" We picked one and then just worked like hell. We all felt great about hitting the solution. Some of the group started to work out how to make the changes in the units that the client had.

Another executive, who was the commanding officer of a ship, described an incident in which he utilized competencies in the goal and action management cluster (i.e., proactivity and concern with impact), the leadership cluster (i.e., self-confidence, use of oral presentations, and conceptualization) and the managing group process competency from the human resource management cluster.

We were having a beach party. It was part of the liberty after a long cruise. Some of the guys were playing volleyball. Although we hadn't had any racial incidents on the cruise, the volleyball game was getting hot. There were several white sailors and several black sailors on both teams. I saw one of the black sailors tease another black sailor across the net. Then one of the white sailors said something in defense of his teammate, but I couldn't hear what it was. I could see that for the next few serves, people on each team seemed to be shouting at the other team. It didn't look like the usual razzing. I decided that we had a potentially bad situation here.

So I walked over to the game, and at the next serve I said, "Fellas, it looks like you're having a good game. Why let this racial garbage get in the way? You've worked well together on board." Both teams were silent.

Then one of the black sailors walked up to me and said, in a respectful way, "Sir, you tell us not to hype our differences and yet you're wearing an 'Italian Power' t-shirt." I had always been proud of my ancestry and was wearing a t-shirt that my wife had given me. But I realized that I was, even in humor, giving off a signal opposite to what I talked to them about several times. I said, "You're right."

I stepped over to a rock that was nearby, stood on top, and called all of the crew around. I said that I had been proud of their performance and that we could all take pride in our ship and the crew. I added that although I was also proud of my ancestry, the t-shirt did emphasize an unimportant difference among us. So I took off the t-shirt and said that I would not wear it. I then said that we all had something in common to be proud of—our ship. So I pointed to a group from another U.S. military service that was having a party down the beach and asked the crew if they would be interested in taking on this group in a volleyball game. I added something like, "Let's show them that we're as good on land as we are at sea." The group cheered.

I went down the beach and set up the game with the senior officer of the other group. We won!

The executive level manager is required to demonstrate more perceptual objectivity than do other levels of management. This aids in his or her understanding of the diverse perspectives represented by various internal groups. It also helps in his or her understanding of and ability to communicate that understanding effectively to groups external to the organization.

The effective executive demonstrates developing others, although he or she probably does it differently than entry or middle level managers (i.e., average performers demonstrated more of it than did superior performers, while both demonstrated more of it than did poor performers). Performance feedback does not necessarily focus on managers who are his or her subordinates as individuals, but on the performance of their organizational groups. In addition, superior performing executives probably spend less time providing such performance feedback directly and utilize other methods for having middle level managers or lower level executive managers obtain performance information on their own (i.e., through the use of management information systems and so forth). Since the subordinates of the executive level manager probably have substantial input into the establishment of goals and plans for their organizational groups, allowing subordinates to have independent access to performance feedback would enhance their sense of responsibility for, commitment to, and ownership of their organizational unit's performance.

For executive level managers, competencies in the goal and action management cluster and the leadership cluster are of primary importance to the performance of their jobs and their effectiveness. In addition, several other competencies appear relevant to job performance and effectiveness. They are: perceptual objectivity, managing group process, and developing others.

Summary and Implications

A summary of the competencies relevant to performance and effectiveness in terms of job demands at various levels of management is shown in Table 11-6. These findings contain a number of implications for maximizing competent performance in managerial jobs at various levels. Not only are different competencies relevant to the various levels of jobs, but the manifestations of the competencies (i.e., how they emerge in specific behavior and action) appear to be different. It has been pointed out that even the focus and orientation of the various levels of management jobs is different. This suggests that a transformation must occur within the individual to enable him or her to perform competently once a promotion to the next level of management is obtained. Demonstration of some of the competencies that indicated superior performance at one level, and probably aided the person in obtaining the promotion, might interfere with effective functioning in the new job.

The change in focus and orientation required is more than will occur simply because a person is handed a new job description. It is also more of a change than will probably occur naturally, or if left to chance. The changes needed by an effective entry level manager to be effective at a middle level management job are substantial, and probably reflect the most difficult transition in a person's career. For the entry level manager who has been promoted, the changes would not only be in orientation and focus, but also in the competencies needed to perform the job and to do it effectively. Although the changes needed for the middle level manager who has been promoted into an executive level job require a transformation of focus and orientation and a change in the manifestations of the competencies, the effective middle level manager is likely to have demonstrated many of the competencies needed at the executive level as part of effectively performing his or her prior job.

Since allowing the changes to occur "naturally" would be an inefficient use of human resources and potentially would threaten the effectiveness of key managerial talent, the organization should assist managers in these transitions through one of three options: training, career pathing, or special mentoring. The training must consist of more than

TABLE 11-6 Competencies Relevant to Performance and Effectiveness in Terms of Job Demands: Various Levels of Management Jobs[a]

For Entry Level Managers	For Middle Level Managers	For Executive Level Managers

Goal and action management cluster
  Diagnostic use of concepts
  Efficiency orientation
  Proactivity
	Goal and action management cluster
	  Concern with impact
	  Diagnostic use of concepts
	  Efficiency orientation
	  Proactivity
		Goal and action management cluster
		  Concern with impact
		  Diagnostic use of concepts
		  Efficiency orientation
		  Proactivity

	Leadership cluster
	  Conceptualization
	  Logical thought
	  Self-confidence
	  Use of oral presentations
		Leadership cluster
		  Conceptualization
		  Self-confidence
		  Use of oral presentations

	Human resource management cluster
	  Accurate self-assessment
	  Managing group process
	  Positive regard
	  Use of socialized power	

Directing subordinates cluster
  Developing others
  Spontaneity
  Use of unilateral power		

[a]Relevance is defined as that competency which is demanded or required more for performance of that level than for other levels *or* that competency which is characteristic of effective managers within that level of management jobs.

226

TABLE 11-6 *(Continued)*

For Entry Level Managers	For Middle Level Managers	For Executive Level Managers
Other competencies Accurate self-assessment Self-control (at the trait level) Stamina and adaptability (at the trait level) Use of socialized power	Other competencies Developing others Perceptual objectivity Spontaneity Stamina and adaptability (at the trait level)	Other competencies Developing others Managing group process Perceptual objectivity

educational programs intended to impart knowledge to the manager. They must have competency development as the objective, as will be discussed in the Chapter 12. A career pathing system, which would sequence a person through various managerial jobs within each level, should be designed to allow for the gradual development and refinement of the competencies needed in the management jobs toward which the person is headed. This requires, in addition to a well-developed and coherent human resource management system, detailed understanding of which competencies can be developed, practiced, and demonstrated in various management jobs.

Of course, a career pathing system by itself would not ensure that the appropriate competencies would be developed or refined. A developmental program that provided mentoring or counsel from relatively more experienced managers to the individuals involved would also be needed. The latter would help the individuals efficiently work toward competency development, receive assessment on their progress, and develop the new manifestations (i.e., specific behaviors and actions) of the competencies needed to be effective in various management jobs.

Managers must also resolve a dilemma posed when opportunities for promotion emerge. If the promotion involves entering a new managerial level, the best performer in his or her current job may not have the needed competencies. The typical example of this problem is the promotion of the best salesperson (i.e., an individual contributor) to a sales manager. A person may be highly effective at sales without possessing the developing others or use of socialized power competencies. Unfortunately, his or her ability to be effective as a sales manager requires these competencies. By promoting such a person without providing some developmental experience, the manager has increased the likelihood that this person will not be effective in the sales management job.

CHAPTER TWELVE

Summary and Implications

SUMMARY

The purpose of the study was to determine which characteristics of managers are related to effective performance in a variety of management jobs in a variety of organizations. These characteristics could be considered competencies in common to people in management jobs. An aggregate sample of over 2000 managers who were in 41 different management jobs in 12 organizations was used.

Of the 21 characteristics initially hypothesized to relate to managerial effectiveness, 12 were found to be competencies, as summarized in Table 12-1. They were: efficiency orientation; proactivity; diagnostic use of concepts; concern with impact; self-confidence; use of oral presentations; conceptualization, for middle and executive level managers only; use of socialized power; managing group process, for middle and executive level managers only; perceptual objectivity; self-control, at the trait level only; and stamina and adaptability, at the trait level only.

Seven of the characteristics were found to be threshold competencies. They were: use of unilateral power; accurate self-assessment; positive regard, for middle level managers only; spontaneity; logical thought; specialized knowledge; and developing others.

For two of the characteristics, and at the skill levels of two of the other characteristics, either no support was found or the results suggested an inverse relationship to managerial effectiveness. They were: concern with close relationships, at all levels of the characteristic; mem-

229

TABLE 12-1   Summary of Competency Results[a]

Cluster	Competency	Threshold Competency
Goal and action management cluster	Concern with impact (skill, motive) Diagnostic use of concepts (skill, social role) Efficiency orientation (skill, motive, social role) Proactivity (skill, social role)	
Leadership cluster	Conceptualization [b] (skill) Self-confidence (skill, social role) Use of oral presentations (skill, social role)	Logical thought (skill, social role)
Human resource management cluster	Managing group process [b] (skill) Use of socialized power (skill, social role)	Accurate self-assessment (skill) Positive regard[c] (skill)
Directing subordinates cluster		Developing others (skill, social role) Spontaneity (skill) Use of unilateral power (skill, social role)
Focus on others cluster	Perceptual objectivity (skill) Self-control[d] (trait) Stamina and adaptability (trait)	
Specialized Knowledge		Specialized knowledge (social role)

[a]Items in parentheses indicate levels of competency for which empirical support was found.
[b]Supported as a competency at middle and executive level management jobs only.
[c]Supported as a competency at middle level management jobs only.
[d]Supported as a competency at entry level management jobs only.

ory; self-control, at the skill level; and stamina and adaptability, at the skill level.

The competencies and threshold competencies were found to relate to each other at the skill level in a manner that yielded five clusters. These clusters were: the goal and action management cluster, which included efficiency orientation, proactivity, diagnostic use of concepts, and concern with impact; the leadership cluster, which included self-confidence, use of oral presentations, logical thought, and conceptualization; the human resource management cluster, which included use of socialized power, managing group process, accurate self-assessment, and positive regard; the directing subordinates cluster, which included developing others, use of unilateral power, and spontaneity; and the focus on others cluster, which included perceptual objectivity, self-control, stamina and adaptability, and concern with close relationships. The relationships within each cluster and between the clusters were thought to represent primary and secondary relationships, respectively, among the competencies. Although not at the skill level, the sixth cluster, specialized knowledge, is also an integral part of the model.

Differences were found in the degree to which one aspect of the environment in which managers operate demanded, required, or stimulated these competencies, in terms of whether the organizations were located in the public or the private sectors. Differences were also found in the degree to which one aspect of the managers' jobs demanded, required, or stimulated these competencies, in terms of entry, middle, or executive level management jobs.

Analysis of the combined effect of the set of competencies at the skill level was conducted to determine the degree of accuracy they would show in predicting the performance group (i.e., poor, average, or superior performers) of the managers. The results indicated that the competencies correctly classified 51 percent of the managers, as compared to a random prediction that would have correctly classified only 33 percent of them.

A word of caution is in order regarding the summary and potential application of the findings from this study. First, the study was an initial attempt to determine what a generic competency model of management should include. A precise determination of causality would require additional research through longitudinal studies, as well as replication in other sets of organizations. Since the selection of organizations and jobs included in the study was not random, generalizing from these findings beyond a certain point may not be appropriate. The major risk in excessive generalization from this sample is that the particular organizations and jobs examined may not fully represent the entire populations from which they came. Second, exploration of findings within managerial level and function was not segregated by sector. Therefore, to the extent that sector differences occur, some findings regarding level and function may have been diminished in their importance by the aggregate sample. Third, development of a comprehensive model of management would require that a similar effort be completed regarding additional job and environment variables not examined in this study.

A GENERIC MODEL OF MANAGEMENT

Although job and environmental demands were not empirically examined in this study, with the exception of the sector and managerial level factors, it would be difficult to conclude a discussion of the findings without hypothesizing, or proposing, how an integrated generic model of management might appear. In Chapter 2, a framework was presented to explain the relationships of three basic components affecting competent managerial behavior. These were: (1) job demands; (2) organizational environment demands; and (3) competencies of a person. This framework represents the basic hypothesis that competent performance of a management job will be maximized when there is a maximum "fit" or consistency among these three components. In Chapter 10, results were presented that suggested an integrated competency model for managers. This model resulted in six clusters of competencies. At this point, it would be appropriate to explore how these clusters of competencies may be related to the job and organizational demands that the manager experiences.

Linking Competencies and Job Demands

Since this study is based on examination of people in management jobs, it would probably be easier to understand a generic model of management built around the demands, or requirements, of management jobs, rather than using competencies or the enviroment as the point of reference.

The demands, or requirements, made on a person in a management job can be considered functional requirements of the particular job, situational demands, or specific demands emerging from day-to-day events on the job. Although it would be difficult to propose a framework for the varying day-to-day demands of a management job, the functional requirements of management jobs can be described in terms of five basic functions, which are: (1) planning; (2) organizing; (3) controlling;

(4) motivating; and (5) coordinating. Each one of these functions can be further examined in terms of the various activities, or tasks, which constitute the function.

In performing the planning function, the manager is determining the goals and plans for the organization and communicating them to others. The type of planning may vary from management job to management job. An executive may be responsible for determining the strategic direction of the organization. He or she would be determining how the organization will respond to the marketplace and competitive environment in the years ahead. An executive may also be responsible for determining overall organizational performance goals, such as increase in earnings per share or return on assets. An entry level manager may be responsible for determining the performance goals of individual contributors (i.e., salespeople, bookkeepers, engineers, production workers) and work units. These goals may appear in terms of the amount of product produced (i.e., number of units off the production line, amount of sales), human resources needed to produce certain amounts of the product (i.e., 10 person hours per unit), or physical resources used (i.e., 1 foot of wire and 6 ounces of dielectric per dozen resistors produced).

Although the specific types of goals and plans for which the manager is responsible may vary, every manager has some degree of responsibility for establishing goals and developing plans for achieving these goals. For some managers, the overall goal may be handed to them and they must establish the activity plan to achieve it. It is the competencies in the goal and action management cluster that will enable a manager to perform these tasks effectively, regardless of whether he or she is determining the goals and plans or working with others to develop them.

The degree to which the manager must communicate the goals and plans and the rationale for the goals and plans to his or her subordinates will also vary from job to job. When this is required of the manager, it is the competencies in the leadership cluster that will enable him or her to communicate this to others most effectively. Through the use of these competencies, the manager is communicating to others in the organization the direction of the organization's efforts and basic expectations as to the level of organizational performance.

In performing the organizing function, the manager is determining what human and other resources are needed and how they should be structured to accomplish the plan and achieve the goals. In addition, he or she is establishing standards of performance for individuals and groups. This will vary from determining the design of the organization (i.e., the organization structure) to the design of specific jobs (i.e., who is expected to do what) to the day-to-day decisions of how to reallocate or reorganize resources to solve problems. Not all managers will have the same opportunity or impact on many of these organizing tasks. Since all managers must be prepared to explain the organization of people, other resources, and activities to their subordinates, all managers should at least understand the basis for the organization of resources. Often, it is this understanding that is the basis for day-to-day decisions that the manager must make regarding the use of resources in addressing priorities and changes in priorities.

It is the competencies in the goal and action management cluster that enable the manager to determine effectively what resources are needed, how they should be structured, and what the standards of performance should be. These competencies are needed whether the manager is performing these tasks himself or herself or working with others to perform these tasks. It is the competencies in the leadership cluster that enable a manager to determine how the resources should be structured or organized, what the standards of performance should be, and communicate the rationale for the organization of resources to others. It is the competencies in the human resource management cluster that enable a manager to communicate the rationale and importance for the particular organization of resources to his or her subordinates as well as to other groups in the organization.

In performing the controlling function, a manager is monitoring the performance of individuals and groups, providing feedback on their performance, and rewarding and disciplining them based on their performance. Every manager has some degree of responsibility for monitoring performance of others or an organizational unit, providing feedback to others, and taking appropriate actions (i.e., rewarding or disciplining others).

It is the competencies in the goal and action management cluster that enable a manager to effectively perform all of these tasks. Without these competencies, the manager cannot provide the *context* within which others' performance is being monitored, nor provide a basis for the rewards given nor disciplinary actions taken. It is the competencies in the directing subordinates cluster and the human resource management cluster that enable a manager to effectively provide performance feedback to others and dispense rewards and punishments.

As with the other functions, the way in which the tasks in the controlling function are performed will vary at different levels of management. For example, it is expected that at executive levels, managers will perform the monitoring and feedback tasks more through the use of management information systems than through personal interactions. As the methods of performing these tasks vary, so will the competencies needed by the manager to perform them. At the executive level, where personal performance monitoring and feedback is probably less frequent and possibly less relevant, the competencies in the directing subordinates cluster would be less relevant.

In performing the motivating function, a manager must build commitment, identity, pride, and spirit in the organization. He or she must also stimulate an interest in work and develop capability in his or her subordinates. Building the commitment, identity, and pride of others is a responsibility for the executive, which is focused on the organization as a whole. For the middle level manager, the focus is more on the work group, or groups, reporting to him or her rather than on the organization as a whole. It is the competencies in the human resource management cluster and the leadership cluster that enable a manager to effectively perform these tasks. It is the competencies in the directing subordinates cluster that enable a manager to develop his or her subordinates' capability.

In performing the coordinating function, a manager must stimulate cooperation among departments, divisions, and other work groups. He or she must also negotiate resolution of conflicts or differences that emerge. It is the competencies in the human resource management cluster and the focus on others cluster that enable a manager to effectively perform these tasks.

As part of this function, managers are often expected to "represent" the organization and its products to various groups within the organization, but also to groups external to the organization (i.e., the community, the financial community, professional associations, government agencies, consumers, etc.). This responsibility is particularly important to managers at executive levels. It is the competencies in the leadership cluster that enable a manager to effectively represent the organization and its products to others.

These relationships are summarized in Table 12-2. Certain activities, such as communicating and decision making, are essential tasks involved in the performance of each of the five basic functions of management. The competencies within a particular cluster will vary in their importance and relevance to effective performance of the tasks according to both the centrality of the function to the manager's job and the level of management job.

Links to the Organizational Environment

To complete the proposed integrated model of management, as outlined in Figure 2-1, links between the job demands, competencies, and aspects of the organizational environment must be established. Although a list

TABLE 12-2   The Relationship Between Management Functions and Competency Clusters

Function	Tasks	Relevant Competency Clusters
Planning	1. Determining the goals of the organization 2. Establishing plans of action for achieving those goals 3. Determining how the plan should be accomplished	Competencies in the goal and action management cluster
	4. Communicating this to others	Competencies in the leadership cluster
Organizing	1. Determining what people and resources are needed to accomplish the plan	Competencies in the goal and action management cluster
	2. Determining how these people and resources should be structured to do it 3. Establishing the standards of performance	Competencies in the leadership cluster
	4. Communicating this to others	Competencies in the human resource management cluster
Controlling	1. Monitoring performance of individuals and groups	Competencies in the goal and action management cluster
	2. Providing feedback to individuals and groups 3. Rewarding or disciplining based on performance	Competencies in the directing subordinates cluster and human resource management cluster
Motivating	1. Building commitment, identity, pride, and spirit in the organization 2. Stimulating an interest in work	Competencies in the human resource management cluster and the leadership cluster
	3. Developing capability in subordinates	Competencies in the directing subordinates cluster
Coordinating	1. Stimulating cooperation among department, divisions, and other work groups 2. Negotiating resolution of conflicts and differences	Competencies in the human resource management cluster and the focus on others cluster
	3. Representing the organization to outside groups	Competencies in the leadership cluster

of these links cannot be comprehensive nor exhaustive without a great deal more study, it is possible to identify certain elements of the organizational environment that appear primarily related to each of the basic managerial functions and the corresponding competencies. It should be noted that when people think about the organizational environment, they usually consider aspects of the environment in which the organization exists (i.e., the marketplace, culture, industry). These are aspects of the environment *external* to the organization. In a model of management rather than a model of organizations, the external environment should be addressed through elements in the organization's *internal* environment. These are the environmental demands over which managers have the most control. For example, the strategic condition of the industry of which an organization is a part and its position in the industry should be reflected in the organization's strategic plan. The comparability of the wages and benefits offered by an organization and their competitors, or other organizations, should be reflected in the organization's compensation and benefits system. Throughout this section, therefore, organizational environment or environment will refer to the *internal* organizational environment.

There are two elements in the organizational environment that appear most related to the performance of the planning function: (1) the strategic planning process; and (2) the business planning process. The strategic planning process requires assessment of the competitive position of the organization, anticipated changes in the marketplace and environment external to the organization (i.e., changes in technology or consumer preferences), and the relative capability of the organization to respond to those changes. The business planning process includes the articulation of specific goals and objectives and can be considered the identification of the tactics associated with the overall strategy chosen. Business planning processes include operational planning (i.e., day-to-day or week-to-week establishment of goals and planning of activities).

There is an additional aspect of the organizational environment linked to the planning function that is the organizational climate, or organizational culture. This was not listed above because it is not really a separate element in the organizational environment but reflects the way in which people in the organization perceive and react to the elements listed above. Aspects of the organizational climate should be considered indicators of how the people in the organization are responding to elements in the internal environment related to each of the managerial functions. With respect to the planning function, clarity and standards are particularly important aspects of the climate. The clarity aspect of climate refers to the degree to which people know what is expected of them (i.e., performance goals) and why it is expected of them (i.e., the rationale for those goals and how they correspond to the corporate objectives) (Klemp, 1975). The standards aspect of climate refers to the degree to which challenging but attainable goals (i.e., performance expectations) are established and the degree of emphasis placed on continually improving performance (Klemp, 1975).

A manager's ability to effectively address these elements in the organizational environment through performance of the planning function will be a result of: (1) the planning tasks which are part of his or her job; and (2) the degree to which he or she possesses the corresponding competencies in the goal and action management cluster and the leadership cluster.

There are seven elements in the organizational environment that appear most related to the performance of the organizing function: (1) organization design; (2) job design; (3) the personnel planning process; (4) the selection and promotion system; (5) the succession planning and career pathing system; (6) the job evaluation system; and (7) the financial resource allocation process. The organization design (i.e., organization structure) should reflect appropriate flow of goods and information from one organizational unit to another, and the transformation of raw materials from suppliers to the products made available to customers. The design of jobs addresses the issues of whether the set of demands, which constitute each job is meaningful to the job occupant, can be performed by a person, and correspond to the organization design.

The personnel planning process, formerly called the manpower planning process, is essential in determining the number and type of human resources needed to work toward the organization's goals. The selection and promotion system addresses the appropriate placement of personnel into jobs. The succession planning and career pathing system addresses the efficient placement of people into jobs in response to current needs and in anticipation of future needs. The job evaluation system provides the organization with a vehicle for assessing the value of the performance of each job to the accomplishment of its objectives (i.e., the relative value of the contribution from people performing each of the jobs). The job evaluation system is most often used for establishing salary scales.

The financial resource allocation process includes allocating the financial and other resources to accomplish the organization's goals. This element is closely linked to the strategic and business planning processes, especially in addressing the formation and use of capital, cash flow, debt management, and similar considerations.

Another aspect of the environment linked to the organizing function is the organizational climate, in particular, the responsibility, clarity, and standards aspects of climate. The responsibility aspect of climate refers to the degree and appropriateness of the delegation of decision-making authority to various jobs in the organization and the degree of risk taking encouraged (Klemp, 1975).

A manager's ability to effectively address these elements of the organizational environment through performance of the organizing function will be a result of: (1) the organizing tasks which are part of his or her job; and (2) the degree to which he or she possesses the competencies in the goal and action management cluster, the human resource management cluster, and the leadership cluster.

There are four elements in the organizational environment that appear most related to the performance of the controlling function: (1) the product and business unit performance review process; (2) the individual performance review process; (3) the management information system; and (4) the compensation and benefits system. The product and business unit performance review process and the individual performance review process provide management with an assessment of the performance of products, business units, and individuals toward the corporate objectives. They also provide managers and individual contributors with information as to how their own performance is contributing to corporate performance. Through these review processes and the management information system, managers are able to monitor and supervise others and the flow of work.

The compensation and benefits system is associated with performance of the controlling function as a system of rewards and punishments. This would work effectively only if the operation of the compensation and benefits system was directly related to job performance. To the extent that it is related to seniority, tenure, favoritism, or other forms of nonperformance-based discrimination, the compensation and benefits system would not be associated with effective performance of the controlling function.

An additional aspect of the organizational environment linked to the controlling function is the organizational climate, in particular the rewards, clarity, and conformity aspects of the climate. The rewards aspect of the climate refers to the degree to which people feel that effective performance is recognized in an equitable manner and that rewards are used more often than punishments and threats (Klemp, 1975). The conformity aspect of climate refers to the amount of rules and regulations that are thought to be unnecessary and the degree to which people are told how to perform their jobs (Klemp, 1975).

A manager's ability to effectively address these elements in the organizational environment through performance of the controlling function will be a result of: (1) the controlling tasks which are part of his or her job; and (2) the degree to which he or she possesses the competencies in the goal and action management cluster, the human resource management cluster, and the directing subordinates cluster.

There are four elements in the organizational environment that appear most related to the performance of the motivating function: (1) the training and development system; (2) the compensation and benefits system; (3) the career planning process; and (4) the management information system. The training and development system includes developmental assessment of people's ability, mentoring or guidance, and training programs. All of these activities are oriented toward helping people improve their abilities. The compensation and benefits system is associated with the motivating function to the extent that it operates as an incentive system. The career planning process helps individuals make personal decisions about developmental activities and job changes in the context of long-term personal objectives and organizational needs. The management information system can be an element of the organizational environment related to the motivating function if it provides subordinates with performance information directly (i.e., not requiring the personal interpretation of the manager). Of course, the management information system would only be effective in this context if individuals had clear and meaningful performance goals.

An additional aspect of the organizational environment associated with performance of the motivating function is the organizational climate, in particular the team spirit and rewards aspects of climate. The team spirit aspect of climate refers to the degree to which people feel proud to belong to the organization and they have a sense of relationships being warm, friendly, or trusting (Klemp, 1975).

A manager's ability to effectively address these elements in the organizational environment through performance of the motivating function will be a result of: (1) the motivating tasks which are part of his or her job; and (2) the degree to which he or she possesses competencies in the human resource management cluster, the leadership cluster, and the directing subordinates cluster.

There are three elements in the organizational environment that appear most related to the performance of the coordinating function: (1) the public relations program; (2) the grievance procedure; and (3) the cross-functional and interdepartmental coordinating process. An appropriate grievance procedure can help to establish a framework and setting for resolution of conflicts, whether the conflicts are based on an interpersonal difficulty, a problem with an organizational system or policy, or among organizational units. The cross-functional and interdepartmental coordinating process may be formal or informal. This process is often established on the basis of interpersonal relationships. The process may be supported by existence of "integrating" jobs, task forces, and other similar vehicles. The process is an important element in the potential of the organization to facilitate cooperation, collaboration, and smooth functioning. The public relations program addresses the representational task in the coordinating function. Aspects of this element may be focused on internal representation, often called internal communications programs. It is usually focused on representing the organization and its products to the world outside of the organization.

An additional aspect of the organizational environment associated with the coordinating function is the organizational climate, in particular, the team spirit and clarity aspects of the climate.

A manager's ability to effectively address these elements in the organizational environment through performance of the coordinating function will be a result of: (1) the coordinating tasks which are part of his or her job; and (2) the degree to which he or she possesses the competencies in the human resource management cluster, the focus on others cluster, and the leadership cluster.

The linkages between competencies, job demands as presented by managerial functions, and the internal organizational environment are summarized in Table 12-3.

IMPLICATIONS FOR INCREASING MANAGEMENT COMPETENCE

The findings from this study, and the frameworks offered, suggest a number of options to people concerned about increasing the level of competence of people in management jobs and stimulating competent managerial performance in organizations. The implications vary from broad issues in systems diagnosis to specific issues as to the design of components in the human resource management system.

Management Systems Diagnosis

The integrated model of management proposed in the preceding section offers guidance in determining what aspect of an organization needs attention in solving problems. The specific types of problems that could be addressed have to do with the human resources of the organization.

TABLE 12-3 Elements of an Integrated Model of Management

Competency Clusters	Functions	Elements in the Organizational Environment
Goal and action management cluster Leadership cluster	Planning	Strategic planning process Business planning process Related climate: clarity, standards
Goal and action management cluster Leadership cluster Human resource management cluster	Organizing	Organization design Job design Personnel planning process Selection and promotion system Succession planning and career pathing systems Job evaluation system Financial resource allocation process Related climate: responsibility, clarity, standards
Goal and action management cluster Directing subordinates cluster Human resource management cluster	Controlling	Product and business unit performance review process Individual performance review process Compensation and benefits system Management information system Related climate: rewards, clarity, conformity
Human resource management cluster Leadership cluster Directing subordinates cluster	Motivating	Training and development system Compensation and benefits system Career planning process Management information system Related climate: team spirit, rewards
Human resource management cluster Focus on others cluster Leadership cluster	Coordinating	Public relations program Grievance procedures Crossfunctional and interdepartmental coordinating processes Climate: team spirit, clarity

Although organizations may have other types of problems, they are beyond the scope of this study.

If an organization is performing effectively, in terms of its various performance measures and indicators, a periodic assessment of the soundness of its human resource system is useful. It can help to confirm the effectiveness and appropriateness of current policies, practices, systems, and programs. This type of assessment may take the form of a human resource system audit. Members of an organization could take the model proposed in Table 12-3 and systematically assess the status and responsiveness of the elements in its organizational environment to organizational needs. In addition, an assessment can be made as to the performance of its managers in terms of the five basic functions of management (i.e., the management job demands). The organization can also assess the degree of managerial competence possessed by its management personnel. Through such an audit, each of the three components in the overall model can be assessed and the degree of "fit" of the three components can be determined.

The emphasis on *systematic* assessment cannot be exaggerated. Because of the commonly held perception that human resource systems and issues are "soft" and difficult to quantify, managers often settle for assessment methods and techniques that do not satisfy the level of rigor and soundness that they apply to assessment methods used in other aspects of organizational functioning, such as financial measurement, product quality measurement, and so forth. Although the field still has a long way to go, managers need not settle for this "soft" approach. Ongoing developments in the organizational and behavioral sciences make it possible for managers to use rigorous and sound assessment methods and techniques. The users of this technology should be cautious and use the same level of thoroughness in choosing these methods as they use in choosing methods for market research, product testing, financial performance analysis, and capital investment analysis.

Beyond a confirmation of current policies, practices, systems, and programs, a periodic assessment of the human resource system can help managers prepare for future needs. This is particularly important when an organization is contemplating a change in strategy, implementing a change in product technology, or offering new products to the marketplace.

Most often the perceived need for such an assessment, or audit, emerges from recognition of a performance problem. This may appear as a loss of market share, high costs associated with turnover of personnel, a drop in earnings, failure of a new product to meet its performance expectations, difficulty in finding enough personnel for a rapidly growing company, or litigation. In this situation, the organization is most vulnerable to inappropriate diagnosis of the problems in the human resource system. Due to the pressure to identify the problem and take action to solve it, managers can easily fall prey to the confusion of symptoms and problems or choosing a problem for which they understand available solutions.

Using the model proposed in Table 12-3, guidance can be offered to the manager attempting such a diagnosis. The manager must first determine the domains in which the problem or problems exist. The domain refers to the aspects of organizational functioning that are involved. The domain of the problem may be clear. For example, an industrial products company had lost 20 percent of its middle level managers in a year. Knowing that the industry average had been 12 percent, and realizing that there was no dramatic change in the organization's external condition (i.e., it did not have a product failure, or the emergence of a new competitor), the managers focused on this problem. Termination interviews and follow-up conversations with several managers three months after they left were conducted. They discovered that the organization had not kept up with several competitors in incentive programs. The compensation and benefits system was not functioning adequately.

Unfortunately, identifying the domain of concern is not always as easy. Often, the domain is prematurely diagnosed because of a "pet" theory, peeve, or value of top management. Executives who do not believe that people can be trained or developed to perform jobs effectively will identify the human problem as a selection or promotion problem. You might hear them say, "If we could just get the right people, this inefficiency would stop." Or they might say, "Fire the lot of them. Let's give some of the young ones a chance. Some new blood, that's what we need!"

In situations in which the domain of the problem is unclear or highly complex, or certain executives are prone to postulate their "pet peeve," a simpler but more general approach should be taken. Assessment of the organizational climate may be a useful beginning for such an analysis. Merely administering surveys or having group catharsis sessions will not provide the needed information. Surveys and other forms of information collection are helpful only if they are part of a procedure where the people involved wrestle with the interpretation of the data. Specific, concrete examples of situations in which something is not working adequately or causing difficulties is essential. This makes the interpretation of the data *real*, and avoids the possibility of a "data-dump" with no understanding of the information.

For example, through a climate survey process a consumer products company discovered that middle management personnel felt that standards were substantially lower than they should have been. Several of the executives were shocked when they heard the middle level managers contend that mediocrity was being accepted in performance. The executives knew that the company had been reaching its objectives consistently. Managers in the marketing, research and development, and manufacturing departments explained that they could be doing even better (i.e., there were lost opportunities). After probing several specific incidents, which occurred over the prior three months, it was determined that the strategic plan was not understood by middle level managers and even a number of the executives. The business plans for the current year were comprehensive and well intergrated with the strategic plan, but no one was paying attention to them. The plans were not functioning as guides for the managers in day-to-day decision making. The problem in this organization was uncovered after several days of meetings with various groups in the company. The product, business unit, and individual performance review processes were not functioning adequately. At the business unit level, several businesses were kept, despite their lack of attainment of performance objectives. This resulted in managers questioning the credibility of the strategic plan and deciding to shelve it. At the product level, several innovations had failed in one of the business groups. Research and development funds were continually being allocated to these products and new marketing campaigns were being developed. Managers within this group interpreted this information to mean that the business plan for those products was not to be taken seriously. The products were to be given a chance, no matter what the plan stipulated as the bench-marks for continuing investment in them. At the individual level, effort was being rewarded through salary increases, not accomplishment of results.

What had started as a climate survey process to "take stock of where we are" uncovered a major problem in the internal organizational environment. The company was able to define the problem domain and began to explore various alternative methods for addressing the problem with their product, business unit, and individual performance review process. As this company found, the source of the problems may be either: (1) the implementation and use of an existing system or process that is adequately designed; or (2) the inadequate or inappropriate design of that element in the organizational environment (i.e., a problem at the organization design level). The company discovered that at the product and business unit levels, the problem was implementation of the system that they had. The strategic and business planning process provided the framework and mechanism for these reviews. They were not being conducted properly and the results were not being addressed. At the individual performance review level, the company found that the system was not designed properly. The system allowed individuals to receive favorable reviews for demonstrated efforts toward objectives, but did not hold people accountable for results in terms of goal attainment.

Unfortunately, such an assessment may not go far enough to establish whether the malfunction of this element of the organizational environment is a problem or merely a symptom of another problem. The problem may be found in the assessment of the performance of the management job. Are the managers performing the basic functions and tasks that are part of the demands of their jobs? If a number of the elements in the organizational environment related to one particular managerial function are malfunctioning, then that particular function needs to be examined. If the difficulty appears endemic to performance of a number of managerial functions, then there may be a complex set of problems occurring. In either case, the problem may be found in: (1) the implementation and practice of the managerial functions where the jobs have been designed appropriately; or (2) the management jobs are not designed to respond to the organization's needs (i.e., a problem at the job design level).

In the example discussed, an observation had been made by one of the executives that some of his peers did not understand that they were supposed to take action concerning products and businesses based on the performance reviews at these levels. He claimed that several of the executives "couldn't tell if they were alive with a stethoscope." The corporate vice president of personnel reviewed the performance of three particular executives through documents available. He did not want to arouse fears or suspicions until he had a chance to examine the data.

The corporate vice president concluded that none of these three executives were performing the controlling function of their jobs completely. They were not providing feedback, nor taking action when the information was negative. They would let the information emerge in other forms, and their boss, the president, could take action if he wanted. As long as events proceeded smoothly and positive results were obtained, they performed the controlling function of their jobs admirably. The corporate vice president of personnel decided that he would have to confront the president with this information. He felt that there was nothing wrong with the implementation and use of the business unit and product performance review processes, but that these three particular executives were not performing an important aspect of their jobs.

Again, the inadequate or inappropriate performance of basic managerial functions may be an indication of a more fundamental problem than the design of the jobs or implementation of the existing design of the jobs. The problem may be that people who are in the jobs are not using the corresponding competencies that enable them to perform the managerial functions. This may be the result of a problem in: (1) the selection or promotion system, which means that people with the needed competencies are not being placed into the jobs; (2) the training and development system, in that people being placed in the jobs are not prepared adequately; or (3) the design of the management jobs or elements in the organizational environment are not utilizing the talent available in the managers (i.e., the managers have the needed competencies but the use of the competencies is not being stimulated, demanded, or supported). In the first case, the problem may be that the selection and promotion criteria are not adequate. In the second case, there may be a problem in the competency development of managerial personnel. In the third case, the problem is probably an underutilization of managerial talent available within the organization.

In the example being discussed, the problem was difficult to see. The president of the company argued with the corporate vice president of personnel about his assessment of the three executives. The president felt that they were all loyal, competent managers who had been committed to the company for many years. After several hours, the president finally agreed that each of the three executives had made some poor decisions regarding certain products and businesses in the past two years. He added, "Their history of performance with this company, and exceptional accomplishments in their current jobs during the prior five years gives them a basis for making a few mistakes." The corporate vice president of personnel suggested that his information did not mean that they should be fired, but that the competitive pressure in their businesses had increased tremendously in the past four years and that they had not grown along with their jobs in this one aspect. He recommended some training programs.

The criteria for promoting someone into one of these three jobs had changed in the past four years. Without recognition of this change in the competencies needed by executives in these jobs over this period, the company had not taken steps to help the executives grow and develop, nor to change the people in the jobs. Even if the three executives took early retirement or left for other companies, without altering the selection criteria, the president might find himself with the same problem next year.

In assessing the human resource system through such an "audit trail," there may be one or more of four basic types of problems uncovered. One type of problem is that *adequately designed organizational systems, procedures, processes, or programs are not being utilized.* A second type of problem may be that the *elements in the internal organizational environment or management jobs are not designed appropriately.* Another type of problem may be that the *placement of personnel (i.e., selection and promotion) is not being conducted with appropriate criteria.* The fourth type of problem may be that the *development of personnel is not being adequately addressed* (i.e., the quantity of activity is not adequate, the types of activities are not appropriate, or the objectives and criteria for design of the development activities are inappropriate). Each one of these problems may also be symptoms of one of the other types of problems. That is, in terms of the model of management proposed in Figure 2-1 and Table 12-3, the individual competencies, the management job demands, and the internal organizational environment may not be consistent.

An Integrated Human Resources System

Attempts to address any of the types of problems mentioned above may only be temporarily effective or merely remove the problem from sight if they are not conducted as part of an integrated human resource system. Although some companies, government institutions, and other organizations are making advances toward this objective, most still suffer from fractionated, piecemeal, or ad hoc components and, therefore, lack an integrated human resource system (Kotter & Boyatzis, 1979).

The lack of a model or paradigm on which to base such a system inhibits progress. The management model proposed and the concept of competence, specifically job competency, can be used as the basis for developing and operating an integrated human resource system. It will not be easy. A great deal more research, development, and testing will be needed before all of the specifications for such a system can be determined. The following sections of this chapter attempt to describe what a number of the components in such a system may require. They are presented as possibilities, not definitive answers.

An overall context of the discussion of specific topics is human resource system planning. A human resource system or human resource development plan should become a part of the strategic and business plans generated by organizations. The plan would encourage recognition of the importance of the human resources, or assets, of the organization, and would provide a process in which to examine the adequacy of the organization's systems, policies, procedures, and programs. It would help organizations to determine the desired and expected return on human assets. It would also aid organizations in preparing for changes in human resources available in the future (i.e., changes in work force values, number of people available, preparation of the work force prior to entering the organization, etc.) in the same way that organizations prepare for changes in product technology and market demand.

Development of Competency Models

Prior to application within a human resource system, the competencies needed must be identified and empirically determined. Because the competencies are related to effective performance of a particular job within a specific organizational environment, models must be developed and tested on many, and eventually all, of the jobs and job families (i.e., sets of jobs with similar job demands) within an organization. Identification of tasks and functions (i.e., job demands) is needed but is not sufficient. The problems mentioned in Chapter 2 as to identification and definition of competencies must be carefully considered.

Research designs must incorporate methods that allow for the inductive identification of competencies and not merely test a priori models. The validated competencies in a model must also be related to the functional and task demands of jobs and to aspects of the organizational environment to be of the most utility. The methods must include a number of operant techniques to avoid method-bound or culturally-specific results. The results must be cross-validated if applications to certain human resource systems are desired, such as selection, promotion, or performance appraisal systems, to conform to legal and ethical guidelines.

Job Design

Management jobs can be designed to allow managers to utilize the competencies they have (Hackman & Oldham, 1980). Of course, to change the functions and tasks involved in a management job, those that currently exist must be identified and clarified. For example, effective entry level managers demonstrated more use of socialized power than did their less effective peers. It was suggested that this aided them in coordinating their activities with other entry level managers. To utilize this competency more effectively, such coordination activities could be made a part of the entry level manager's job. Similarly, effective middle level managers demonstrated more of the competencies in the leadership cluster than did their less effective peers. Certain middle level management jobs could be designed so as to require these managers to represent the organization to outside groups and to other divisions within the organization. Such changes would utilize these competencies of the effective middle level managers and have the effect of reducing some of the work load of executive level managers. It would also communicate, through job requirements, to managers in middle level jobs that they should have or develop these competencies. Although these are overly simplistic options, by examining those competencies that effective managers demonstrated but were not particularly demanded by management jobs at their level, guidelines for such redesign could be determined.

Selection and Promotion Systems

The most critical implication of the findings and model for selection and promotion systems is that there *are* competencies that are directly related to effectiveness in management jobs. Assessment of these competencies can be incorporated into selection systems, but probably requires different assessment technology than many organizations are using. Testing job applicants for specialized knowledge or assessing their ability to perform job functions does not provide an opportunity to assess competencies (Klemp, 1980). Even assessment centers, as they are often designed, currently do not assess competencies as much as they assess performance of job functions (Williamson & Schaalman, 1980). By tapping generic characteristics, rather than specific manifestations of them (i.e., specific behaviors), new groups of people in the work force can be identified who have the capability to perform management jobs effectively. A person who has developed and demonstrated these competencies, but who for various reasons has not had the opportunity to do so in a job directly related to an opening, may be overlooked during a typical screening process but would be identified through an approach based on these competencies.

Promotion procedures can be developed to assess a person's possession and demonstration of the competencies. Again, such procedures would require an assessment technology somewhat different from that currently used in most organizations. Some organizations have designed their assessment centers and selection techniques to assess competencies by methods such as coding of semistructured interviews, simulations, and operant tests (Williamson & Schaalman, 1980; Boyatzis & Williamson, 1980). Basing such systems on competencies would require that organizations be prepared to replace seniority-based systems with competency-based systems. Such systems would highlight the "competencies" that people need to perform certain management jobs, and would avoid the often costly mistake of promoting the most effective individual contributor into a management job (e.g., promoting the best salesperson to sales manager). When such procedures fail, it is probably because the competencies that enabled the person to be effective as an individual contributor are not the same competencies needed to perform effectively as a manager.

The particular findings in this study merely highlight the potential for these applications. They do not provide enough information for the development or implementation of selection or promotion systems. To develop and implement such systems and procedures, an organization would have to conduct studies to validate competencies against performance in their organization and in specific jobs or job families. This step is necessary to conform to legal and professionally accepted practices, but also to identify those characteristics specific to the organization and the particular jobs that are not part of a generic model of management.

Performance Appraisal

Ideally, a performance appraisal process should include two components: (1) assessment of recent performance; and (2) assessment of recent development and identification of future development needs. The assessment of recent performance, which can be considered the performance assessment component, is the determination as to whether the individual has met output objectives or task accomplishment objectives. The assessment of development, which can be considered the competency assessment component, is the documentation and recognition of competencies that the individual has demonstrated in the recent performance period and identification of competencies that should be addressed during the next performance period. To conduct the latter component of the performance appraisal, the competencies related to effective performance in the job would have to be identified. In addition, methods for documenting the demonstration of the competencies would have to be developed. These may take the form of behaviorally-anchored scales or a review of specific incidents or events that occurred during the performance period. With such methods, both the manager and the person being reviewed can state their perceptions and test the accuracy of these perceptions against the other's perceptions.

Succession Planning and Career Pathing

The findings and model have implications for succession planning and the development of a career pathing system. In such a system, people can be offered a variety of options that would facilitate development of the competencies needed to perform effectively in current and future jobs. Instead of leaving the development of the generic characteristics to chance, a career pathing system in an organization can facilitate and recognize the development of such characteristics. It will also help to ensure that the organization has a sufficient number of qualified people for their management jobs. For example, if an organization knows that certain people would like to hold executive management positions a number of years in the future, the organization can assist them in preparing for the promotions, and for becoming effective in the jobs once obtained, by a sequence of middle level management jobs. These jobs can be chosen so that these people could develop the generic characteristics that are known to be needed for effective performance of executive management jobs. It is evident from the discussion in Chapter 11 that organizations without such a career pathing system are incorporating a threat to productivity and efficiency into their organization by not helping managers who receive promotions across levels to develop needed competencies.

Information on the specific competencies needed to effectively perform various jobs in a particular organization should be gathered before a comprehensive and thorough career pathing system can be developed. For example, certain individual contributor jobs may prepare a person for a management job through the development of particular generic characteristics. To obtain the full set of generic characteristics needed for a specific management job, the person may have to rotate through several different individual contributor jobs, and possibly certain lower level management jobs.

Career Planning

The findings and model have implications for the individual's counterpart (i.e., career planning) to the succession planning and career pathing system which primarily addresses the organization's needs. Through the same type of framework and assessment methods used in the selection, promotion, or performance appraisal systems, the individual can determine what type of job for which he or she is best prepared in terms of competencies. The individual would be able to identify a sequence of jobs in an organization that would satisfy future needs. These jobs could be identified in terms of development of competencies needed for the subsequent jobs. A career planning process based on competencies would also help the individual to identify developmental activities, which would be the most efficient and appropriate preparation for the desired career progression.

Training

One option an organization has available is to provide special training programs for its managers. The findings and model have implications for the choice of training programs and the design of the training. To be effective in competency development, the training must involve far more than teaching participants about the functions of management.

Evidence indicates that these and other generic characteristics can be developed through specific training and education programs (McClelland, 1978; McClelland & Winter, 1979; Winter, McClelland, & Stewart, in press; Miron & McClelland, 1979; Boyatzis, 1976; McClelland & Burnham, 1976). There are a variety of ways to design such training and education programs. To maximize the probability that training will result in the development of competencies, there are six stages of adult competency development that should be incorporated in the training design (McClelland, 1978; Spencer, 1979; McClelland, 1965; Knowles, 1970; Kolb & Fry, 1975; Kolb & Boyatzis, 1970). The six stages, called the Competency Acquisition Process (Spencer, 1979), are:

1. Recognition of the competency.
2. Understanding of the competency and how it relates to managerial effectiveness.
3. Self-assessment or instrumented feedback on the competency.
4. Experimentation with demonstrating the competency, or demonstrating it at a higher level of effectiveness.
5. Practice using the competency.
6. Application of the competency in job situations and in the context of other characteristics.

People must learn to recognize the competency and understand how it relates to performance. Material covered in activities in these stages provides people with specificity as to which competencies and behaviors are being addressed. The competencies demonstrated by superior-performing managers become the actual training or educational objectives. The various assessment methods used in the competency research studies provide specific, behavioral descriptions of how superior-performing managers think and act. They also provide case study material of people using the competencies in specific situations and events which occur on the job. People are not left wondering what relevance the training or education program has following these first two stages.

Once the image of how a superior-performing manager should think and act has been developed through the first two stages (i.e., an image of the ideal), people can determine where they stand on each competency through the use of self-assessment or assessment instruments specifically chosen to measure the competency (McClelland & Boyatzis, 1980). Without this third stage, people are left wondering whether they have the competency or to what degree they possess the competency.

The integration of the information on how superior-performing managers think and act (i.e., the ideal) and how the potential manager stands on these competencies (i.e., the real) forms the beginning of a process of self-directed change, which has been shown to result effectively in behavioral change (Kolb & Boyatzis, 1970). It is through the realization of personal discrepancies between the ideal and the real on such competencies that people can perceive and feel a need for change.

The fourth stage is experimentation, allowing people to try new behaviors. During this stage, people explore how the generic characteristic may be developed. In some situations, this means experimenting with ways of thinking and acting that are different from those used previously. In other situations, this means expanding the repertoire of ways of thinking and acting related to the competency.

During the fifth and sixth stages of the process, practice and application, people refine and continue to develop ways of thinking and acting that relate to the competency. They engage in activities in which they must apply these competencies to specific situations and problems encountered in their jobs. Without the last two stages, people may not be prepared to utilize the new or different competencies in real settings.

Training or education programs designed to develop competencies in managers must utilize methods of experiential learning and self-directed change as part of an adult education experience (Kolb, 1971; Kolb & Boyatzis, 1970; Knowles, 1970). Missing any of the stages will result in only partial development of the competency. An example of such a training course designed to increase the competencies of entry level managers appears in Appendix C.

Often training that is directed at "teaching people about the job" involves transmitting a great deal of specialized knowledge to the job incumbent. Programs designed to teach someone about their job are really attempting to develop a person's social-role level of the competencies needed for the job. They should be designed to provide for integration of the information into the social-role level of the person's competencies. Therefore, whether the training objectives are to improve a person's competencies, or to help them understand the responsibilities and demands of their job, experiential learning will be more effective than mere communication of facts and concepts.

An individual who wants to develop managerial competencies may choose to attend a formal educational program. A number of colleges and universities have begun to utilize competencies as guides to and objectives for their educational programs (Winter, McClelland, & Stewart, in press). The relevance of liberal arts education to developing some of the competencies related to managerial effectiveness has been shown (Winter, 1979). Specifically in regard to business programs, both undergraduate and graduate, the American Assembly for Collegiate Schools of Business has begun a multiyear project to determine the feasibility and effectiveness of using output standards (i.e., demonstrated capability on generic characteristics related to business and management) as the basis for accreditation of business programs (Laidlaw & Zoffer, 1979; "A Plan to Rate B-schools," 1979). The use of such output standards or generic characteristics to assess the value added to a person by attending a college or university business program would help to establish the relevance and effectiveness of such programs in preparing people for jobs in business, including jobs in management.

Other educational opportunities have begun to emerge for individuals. The American Management Associations have developed a Masters in Management program specifically aimed toward providing just such an opportunity. This new program has been designed to provide people in management jobs with a practical and comprehensive system to develop managerial competence which is more accessible than are other approaches (Evarts, 1979; Hayes, 1979), and has been designed to incorporate the six stages of adult competency development into the entire program. By basing the program on generic characteristics that have been related to managerial performance, competencies will be addressed that otherwise may not be in a graduate degree program.

Graduation from the program will require that a person demonstrate various generic characteristics during special assessment activities and in actual job settings. Early in the program, people will go through a week of assessment activities on various generic characteristics, including specialized knowledge and skills. Following the assessment experience, people will engage in a week of feedback, guidance, and counseling to establish a specific competency learning plan. The competency development learning plan will include options for self-study or for attending courses at universities, training programs, or special training programs offered by the American Management Associations to develop the various competencies. Once people have attended these programs or feel that they have developed the competencies that they did not demonstrate during the initial assessment experience, they will go through an additional assessment experience to document possession of the competencies.

Once people have demonstrated that they possess the various competencies, they will then be asked to demonstrate them in actual job situations. As a part of the program, people may engage in specific projects in their jobs to develop, as well as demonstrate, the competencies. Evidence will have to be obtained from these experiences in the actual job settings to document and validate that the person has demonstrated the competencies. Upon entry into the program, some people may be able to provide evidence that documents the demonstration of some of the competencies that they possess through situations in recent management jobs.

The findings and model suggest a framework for evaluating the effectiveness of an organization's training programs. Increased demonstration of competencies and subsequent improvement in performance can be the criteria for evaluating the cost and benefits of training programs.

Other Developmental Activities

The findings and model have implications for two other types of developmental activities: (1) developmental assessment; and (2) mentoring or guidance. Developmental assessment of competencies can help individuals and their managers choose appropriate training programs that the individual may attend. It may also help to provide bench marks for the individual in terms of his or her career plan, or for the organization in terms of the timing of promotion decisions. It can provide recognition of competencies developed and, therefore, contribute to the competency assessment component of the performance appraisal process.

The concept of competence and results from job competency studies can provide the framework for the oldest management development practice used, providing guidance for subordinates. Although this has been termed many things over the years (i.e., apprenticeship, mentoring, coaching, etc.), the competency framework can help managers increase the effectiveness of their day-to-day advising of subordinates as to development and performance improvement.

Compensation and Benefits

The findings and model have implications for assessing the utility of the compensation and benefits system. Does the dispensation of compensation and benefits correspond to the demonstration of needed competencies? Does the system provide incentives for performance improvement and competency development? For example, in one company that had many retail branches, the regional sales managers were being constrained by the company car policy. The regional manager job included a requirement that the regional manager periodically assess the operation of the branches and provide the branch managers with feedback and recommendations for improvements. The company car policy provided automobiles for the branch managers but not for regional managers, nor were the regional managers reimbursed for their use of personal cars. It was not surprising that the periodic reviews were often held at the regional manager's office. This not only constrained the regional managers from seeing the branches in operation, but also limited the type of performance feedback and recommendations that they could provide to the branch managers. The regional managers would only see information provided by the company's management information system and the information brought to them by the branch managers. After changing the car policy and providing the regional managers with cars, corporate management noted a substantial increase in the demonstration of competencies in the human resource management cluster and goal and action management cluster by the regional managers. Sales performance of a number of the branches also increased.

Bob Jamison, the president of a division of another company had two performance objectives that provided somewhat conflicting demands as to competencies and performance. His salary review and tenure in the job was based on market share obtained each year. His bonus, which represented a significant proportion of his compensation, was based on earnings for the year. Unfortunately, the business and type of product was such that an increase in market share in one year was often associated with decreased earnings in that year. Competitive pressure was strong so prices could not be raised without a loss of market share. If Bob utilized primarily competencies in the leadership cluster, he could increase market share but would probably not increase earnings and not receive a sizable bonus, if any. If Bob primarily utilized the competencies in the goal and action management cluster, he could increase earnings and get a sizable bonus but would probably not increase market share that year and not receive a salary increase, and possibly lose his job. If the performance measures had been revised to represent some balance between the two, and the compensation system altered accordingly, he would have been encouraged to utilize his competencies in both clusters. Unfortunately, Bob never got the chance.

Other Human Resource System Components

There are a number of components of an integrated human resource system that are not directly affected but may be indirectly affected by the findings and the model. Although a personnel planning process would not be directly altered through application of these findings or concepts, an organization's ability to identify, hire, and keep personnel with the desired competencies would result in more efficient use of human resources. This may reduce the number of people needed, or make human resources available for work on other activities.

Although a job evaluation system must be based on the relative contribution of a person in each job to the organization's overall performance, understanding the competencies needed to perform each job effectively may help in establishing comparability to wages paid by other organizations for people performing similar work. Also the development of a selection and promotion system based on competencies would contribute information to the job evaluation system as to the relative ease of obtaining and retaining people with the needed competencies.

The findings and model can even make a contribution to the effectiveness of a grievance procedure. Through the use of the model, an organization can make appropriate diagnoses as to what may be causing or stimulating the grievances, and determine what steps should be taken to address the grievance and preclude its occurrence, if possible, in the future.

CONCLUDING COMMENT

If you are part of the scientific management tradition, you may view competencies as the specifications for the human machinery desired to provide maximum organizational efficiency and effectiveness. If you are part of the humanistic management tradition, you may view competencies as the key that unlocks the door to individuals in realizing their maximum potential, developing ethical organizational systems, and providing maximum growth opportunities for personnel. If you are one of the people who work in organizations and/or one of the people who studies, thinks about, and tries to help organizations utilize their human resources effectively, the findings and model should provide a needed relief from the eclectic cynicism or parochial optimism concerning management that many of us have developed.

Management has been the focus of a great deal of study and commentary over the years. Some people profess to understand management through study. Others feel that it can only be understood through being a manager. What is a competent manager? Only years of systematic research may provide a comprehensive answer to that question, if it can be answered. In the meantime, people *can* improve their model of management and thereby improve their return on human capital and possibly assist in developing human capital. With increasingly accurate and appropriate models of management, managers can help their organizations effectively use their human resources.

References

A plan to rate B-schools by testing students. *Business Week*, November 19, 1979, 171–174.

Anderberg, M. R. *Cluster analysis for applications.* New York: Academic Press, 1973.

Appley, L. A. *A management concept.* New York: American Management Associations, 1969.

Argyris, C. *Interpersonal competence and organizational effectiveness.* Homewood, IL: Irwin-Dorsey, 1962.

Argyris, C., & Schon, D.A. *Theory in practice: Increasing professional effectiveness.* San Francisco: Jossey-Bass, 1974.

Atkinson, J.W. (Ed.). *Motives in fantasy, action and society.* Princeton, NJ: Van Nostrand, 1958.

Atkinson, J.W., & Feather, N.T. (Eds.). *A theory of achievement motivation.* New York: John Wiley & Sons, 1966.

Baldwin, A.L. The role of an ability construct in a theory of behavior. In D. C. McClelland et al. (Eds.), *Talent and society.* Princeton, NJ: Van Nostrand, 1958.

Bales, R. F. *Personality and interpersonal behavior.* New York: Holt, Rinehart, & Winston, 1970.

Barnard, C. I. *The functions of the executive.* Cambridge: Harvard University Press, 1938.

Bass B. M., Burger, P. C., Doktor, R., & Barrett, G. V. *Assessment of managers: An international comparison.* New York: The Free Press, 1979.

Berlew, D.E. Leadership and organizational excitement. In D. A. Kolb, I. M. Rubin, & J. M. McIntyre (Eds.), *Organizational psychology: A book of readings* (2nd ed.). Englewood Cliffs, NJ: Prentice-Hall, 1974

Blake, R. R., & Mouton, J. A. *The managerial grid.* Houston: Gulf Publishing, 1964.

Bower, J. L. Effective public management. *Harvard Business Review*, 1977, **55**(2), 131–140.

Boyatzis, R. E. Building efficacy: The effective use of managerial power. *Industrial Management Review*, 1969, **11**(1), 65–76.

Boyatzis, R. E. Affiliation motivation: A review and a new perspective. In D. C. McClelland & R. S. Steele (Eds.), *Human motivation: A book of readings.* Morristown, NJ: General Learning Press, 1973.

Boyatzis, R. E. The need for close relationships and the manager's job. In D. A. Kolb, I.M. Rubin, & J. M. McIntyre (Eds.), *Organizational psychology: A book of readings* (2nd ed.). Englewood Cliffs, NJ: Prentice-Hall, 1974.

Boyatzis, R. E. Power motivation training: A new treatment modality. In F. Seixas & S. Eggleston (Eds.), *Work in progress on alcoholism: Annals of the New York Academy of Sciences,* 1976, **273**, 525–532.

Boyatzis, R. E. *Managing motivation for maximum productivity* Paper presented at the Annual Convention of the American Psychological Association, New York, September 1979.

Boyatzis, R. E., & Williamson, S. A. *Designing, selecting, and using assessment methods in human resource development.* Paper presented at the National American Society of Training and Development Convention, Anaheim, CA, April 1980.

Bray, D. W., Campbell, R. J., & Grant, D. L. *Formative years in business: A long term AT&T study of managerial lives.* New York: John Wiley & Sons, 1974.

Breiger, R. L., Boorman, S. A., & S. Arabie, P. An algorithm for clustering relational data, with applications to social network analysis and comparison with multidimensional scaling. *Journal of Mathematical Psychology,* 1975, **12**, 328–383.

Bruner, J. Cognitive growth: I and II. In J. Bruner, R. Oliver, & P. Greenfield (Eds.), *Studies in cognitive growth.* New York: John Wiley & Sons, 1966.

Brush, D. H., & Manners, G. E. *The nature of the managerial role* (Early Identification of Managerial Talent Research Report 3-79). Troy, NY: Rensselaer Polytechnic Institute, 1979.

Campbell, J. P., Dunnette, M. D., Lawler, E. E., III, & Weick, K. E., Jr. *Managerial behavior, performance, and effectiveness.* New York: McGraw-Hill, 1970.

Dalziel, M. Confidential report to an industrial organization. Boston: McBer and Company, 1979.

DeCharms, R. *Personal causation.* New York: Academic Press, 1968.

Drucker, P. *The practice of management.* New York: Harper & Row, 1954.

Drucker, P.F. *Management: Tasks, responsibilities, practices.* New York: Harper & Row, 1973.

Erikson, E. *Childhood and society.* New York: W. W. Norton, 1963.

Evarts, H.F. *The AMA manager competency model.* Annual Conference of the Society for the Advancement of Management, Newport Beach, CA, May 1979.

Flanagan, J.C. The critical incident technique. *Psychological Bulletin,* 1954, **51**(4), 327–358.

Freud, S. *The complete introductory lectures on psychoanalysis.* New York: W. W. Norton, 1966, original date 1933.

Ginzberg, E., & Vojta, G. J. The service sector of the U.S. economy. *Scientific American,* 1981, **244**(3), 48–55.

Greenberg, H. M., & Greenberg, J. Job matching for better sales performance. *Harvard Business Review,* 1980, **58** (5), 128–133.

Hackman, J. R., & Oldham, G. R. *Work redesign.* Reading, MA: Addison-Wesley, 1980.

Hall, R. L. *Predicting bomber crew performance the aircraft commander's role.* San Antonio, TX: Lackland Air Force Base, Crew Research Laboratory, 1956.

Hayes, J. L. A new look at managerial competence: The AMA model of worthy performance. *Management Review,* 1979, **68**(11), 2–3.

Heckhausen, H. *The anatomy of achievement motivation.* New York: Academic Press, 1967.

Hersey, P., & Blanchard, K. H. *Management of organizational behavior: Utilizing human resources.* Englewood Cliffs, NJ: Prentice-Hall, 1969.

Hodgson, R. C., Levinson, D. J., & Zaleznick, A. *The executive role constellation.* Boston: Graduate School of Business Administration, Harvard University, 1965.

Hood, P. D., et al. *Crew member agreement on RB-47 crew operating procedure.* San Antonio, TX: Lackland Air Force Base Crew Research Laboratory, 1957.

Howard, A. *Management practices study.* In preparation.

Kagan, J. X., & Lesser, G. S. (Eds.). *Contemporary issues in thematic apperceptive methods.* Springfield, IL: Charles C. Thomas Publishers, 1961.

Kane, J. S., & Lawler, E. E., III. Methods of peer assessment. *Psychological Bulletin,* 1978, **85**, 555–586.

Kincaid, M., & Becklean, K. *The organizational audit.* Cambridge, MA: Entretech, 1968.

Klemp, G. O., Jr. *Technical manual for the organization climate survey questionnaire.* Boston: McBer and Company, 1975.

Klemp, G. O., Jr. Three factors of success. In D. W. Vermilye (Ed.), *Relating work and education: Current issues in higher education 1977.* San Francisco: Jossey-Bass Publishers, 1977.

Klemp, G. O., Jr. *Job competence assessment.* Boston: McBer and Company, 1978.

Klemp, G. O., Jr. On the identification, measurement, and integration of competence. In M. Keeton & P. Pottinger (Eds.), *Competence: The concept, its measurability and implications for licensing, certification, and education.* San Francisco: Jossey-Bass Publishers, 1979.

Klemp, G. O., Jr. (Ed.). *The assessment of occupational competence.* Report to the National Institute of Education, Washington, DC, 1980.

Klemp, G. O., Jr., & Spencer, L. M., Jr. *Job competence assessment.* Reading, MA: Addison-Wesley, in press.

Knowles, M. S. *The modern practice of adult education: Androgogy versus pedagogy.* New York: Association Press, 1970.

Kohlberg, L. Stage and sequence: The cognitive-development approach to socialization. In D. Goslin (Ed.), *Handbook of socialization theory and research.* New York: Rand-McNally, 1969.

Kolb, D. A. *Individual learning styles and the learning process* (working Paper #535-71). Cambridge, MA: Sloan School of Management, Massachusetts Institute of Technology, 1971.

Kolb, D. A. *Learning style inventory* (technical manual). Boston: McBer and Company, 1976.

Kolb, D. A., & Boyatzis, R. E. Goal-setting and self-directed behavior change. *Human Relations,* 1970, **23**(5), 439–457.

Kolb, D. A., & Fry, R. Toward an applied theory of experimental learning. In C. Cooper (Ed.), *Theories of group processes.* London: John Wiley & Sons, 1975.

Kotter, J. P. *Power in management.* New York: AMACOM, 1979.

Kotter, J. P. *The general manager.* New York: The Free Press, 1982.

Kotter, J. P., & Boyatzis, R. E. *Human resource management: The challenge of the 1980s.* Unpublished paper, 1979.

Kuhn, T. S. *The structure of scientific revolutions.* Chicago: Univeristy of Chicago Press, 1962.

Laidlaw, W., & Zoffer, J. Personal communication, October 1979.

Lawrence, P., & Lorsch, J. *Organization and environment.* Boston: Graduate School of Business Administration, Harvard University, 1967.

Levinson, D., et al. *The seasons of a man's life.* New York: Alfred A. Knopf, 1978.

Levinson, H. Management by whose objectives? *Harvard Business Review,* 1970, **48**(4), 125–134.

Levinson, H. Criteria for choosing chief executives. *Harvard Business Review,* 1980, **58**(4), 113–120.

Lewin, A. Y., & Zwany, A. *Peer nominations: A model, literature critique, and a paradigm for research.* Springfield, VA: National Technical Information Service, 1976.

Litwin, G., & Stringer, R. *Motivation and organization climate.* Cambridge: Harvard University Press, 1968.

Maccoby, M. *The gamesman.* New York: Simon and Schuster, 1976.

McClelland, D. C. *Personality.* New York: Holt, Rinehart & Winston, 1951.

McClelland, D. C. Measuring motivation. In J. W. Atkinson (Ed.), *Motives in fantasy, action, and society.* Princeton, NJ: Van Nostrand, 1958.

McClelland, D. C. *The achieving society.* Princeton, NJ: Van Nostrand, 1961.

McClelland, D. C. Toward a theory of motive acquisition. *American Psychologist,* 1965, **20**(2), 321–333.

McClelland, D. C. Achievement motivation can be developed. *Harvard Business Review,* 1965, **43**(6), 6–24, 178.

McClelland, D. C. *Assessing human motivation.* New York: General Learning Press, 1971.

McClelland, D. C. Testing for competence rather than for "intelligence." *American Psychologist,* 1973, **28**(1), 1–40.

McClelland, D. C. *Power: The inner experience.* New York: Irvington Publishers, Inc., 1975.

McClelland, D. C. *A guide to job competency assessment.* Boston: McBer and Company, 1976.

McClelland, D. C. Managing motivation to expand human freedom. *American Psychologist,* 1978, **33**(3), 201–210.

McClelland, D. C. *Is personality consistent?* Paper presented at the Special Symposium Honoring Henry A. Murray. Ann Arbor, MI: University of Michigan, May 1979.

McClelland, D. C., Atkinson, J. W., Clark, R. A., & Lowell, E. L. *The achievement motive.* New York: Appleton-Century Crofts, 1953.

McClelland, D. C., Baldwin, A. L., Bronfenbrenner, U., & Strodtbeck, F. L. *Talent and society.* Princeton, NJ: Van Nostrand, 1958.

McClelland, D. C., & Boyatzis, R. E. New directions for counselors from the competency assessment movement. *Journal of Personnel and Guidance,* 1980, pp. 368–372.

McClelland, D. C., & Burnham, D. H. Power is the great motivator. *Harvard Business Review,* 1976, **54**(2), 100–111.

McClelland, D. C., Davis, W. N., Kalin, R., & Wanner, E. *The drinking man: Alcohol and human motivation.* New York: The Free Press, 1972

McClelland, D. C., & Winter, D. G. *Motivating economic achievement*. New York: The Free Press, 1969.

McGrath, J. E., & Altman, J. *Small group research: A synthesis and critique of the field*. New York: Holt, Rinehart & Winston, 1966.

McGregor, D. *The human side of enterprise*. New York: McGraw-Hill, 1960.

Mintzberg, H. *The nature of managerial work*. New York: Harper & Row, 1973.

Miron, D., & McClelland, D. C. The impact of achievement motivation training on small business. *California Management Review*, 1979, **21**(4), 13–28.

Morrison, A. M. The boss as pitchman. *Fortune*, August 25, 1980, 66–73.

Murray, H. *Explorations in personality*. New York: John Wiley & Sons, 1938.

Murstein, B. I. *Theory and research in projective techniques*. New York: John Wiley & Sons, 1963.

Overall, J. E., & Klett, C. J. *Applied multivariate analysis*. New York: McGraw-Hill, 1972.

Pettigrew, T. F. Social evaluation theory: Convergences and applications. In D. Levine (Ed.), *Nebraska symposium on motivation: 1967*. Lincoln: University of Nebraska Press, 1967.

Primoff, E. *How to prepare and conduct job element examinations*. Washington, DC: U.S. Civil Service Commission, 1973.

Putting excellence into management. *Business Week,*, Week, July 21, 1980, 196–205.

Rotter, J. B. Generalized expectancies for internal versus external control of reinforcement. *Psychological Monographs*, 1966, **80.**

Schoenfeldt, L. F. *Some possible applications for knowledge of the manager's role*. Paper presented at the American Psychological Association Annual Convention, New York, September 1979.

Sheehy, G. *Passages*. New York: Dutton, 1976.

Skinner, B. F. *Science and human behavior*. New York: The Free Press, 1953.

Spencer, L. M., Jr. *Identifying, measuring, and training soft skill competencies which predict performance in professional managerial, and human service jobs*. Paper presented at the Soft Skill Analysis Symposium, Department of the Army Training Development Institute, Fort Monroe, VA, August 1979.

Spencer, L. M., Jr., Klemp, G. O., Jr. & Cullen, B. J. *Work environment questionnaires and Army unit effectiveness and satisfaction measures*. Report to the Army Research Institute, Washington, DC, 1978.

Stewart, A. J. *Scoring manual for stages of psychological adaptation to the environment*. Unpublished paper, Boston University, 1977.

Stewart, A. J., & Winter, D. G. Self-definition and social definition in women. *Journal of Personality*, 1974, **42**(2), 238–259.

Stogdill, R. M. *Handbook of leadership*. New York: The Free Press, 1974.

Taguiri, R., & Litwin, G. H. *Organizational climate: Explorations of a concept*. Boston: Graduate School of Business Administration, Harvard University, 1968.

Tomkins, S. S. *The thematic apperception test: The theory and technique of interpretation*. New York: Grune & Stratton, 1947.

White, R. W. Sense of interpersonal competence: Two case studies and some reflections on origins. In R. W. White (Ed.), *The study of lives: Essays in honor of Henry A. Murray.* New York: Atherton Press, 1963.

Williams, S. B., & Leavitt, J. J. Group opinion as a predictor of military leadership. *Journal of Consulting Psychology,* 1947, **11**, 228–291.

Williamson, S. A., & Schaalman, M. L. Assessment centers: Theory, practice, and implications for education. In G. O. Klemp, Jr., (Ed.), *The assessment of occupational competence.* Report to the National Institute of Education, Washington, DC, 1980.

Winter, D. G. *The power motive.* New York: The Free Press, 1973.

Winter, D. G. Business leadership and the liberal arts. *New Jersey Bell Journal,* 1978–79 **1**(3), 41–47.

Winter, D. G. *An introduction to LMET theory and research.* Report to the U.S. Department of the Navy, Bureau of Personnel, August 1979.

Winter, D. G. *Correcting projective test scores for the effect of significant correlation with length of protocol* (technical note). Boston: McBer and Company, 1979.

Winter, D. G., & McClelland, D. C. Thematic analysis: An empirically derived measure of the effects of liberal arts education. *Journal of Educational Psychology,* 1978, **70**(1), 8–16.

Winter, D. G., McClelland, D. C., & Stewart, A. J. *Competence in college: Evaluating the liberal university.* San Francisco: Jossey-Bass Publishers, in press.

Winter, D. G., & Stewart, A. J. Power motive reliability as a function of retest instructions. *Journal of Consulting and Clinical Psychology,* 1977, **45**(3), 436–440.

Zaleznick, A. *Human dilemmas of leadership.* New York: Harper & Row, 1966.

Tables of Means, Sample Sizes, and Statistical Significance Levels for Analyses Discussed in the Text

TABLE A–1 Mean Skill Level for the Entire Interview Sample ($N = 253$)[a]

	Performance Groups			Significance Level of T-Tests		
	Poor $N=63$	Average $N=91$	Superior $N=99$	P vs. A	P vs. S	A vs. S
Accurate self-assessment[d]	.175	.231	.303	n.s.	.035	n.s.
Conceptualization[b, d]	.143	.231	.354	n.s.	.006	.077
Concern with close relationships	.206	.242	.172	n.s.	n.s.	n.s.
Concern with impact[b, d]	.984	1.09	1.444	n.s.	.001	.009
Developing others[b, e]	.286	.769	.485	.0001	.027	.017
Diagnostic use of concepts[b, d]	.476	1.12	1.263	.0001	.0001	n.s.
Efficiency orientation[b, d]	.730	1.132	1.263	.013	.002	n.s.
Logical thought	.254	.440	.434	.033	.039	n.s.
Managing group process[b, d]	.302	.506	.657	.027	.0005	.099
Perceptual objectivity[b, d, e]	.206	.121	.323	.088	.067	.001
Positive regard	.143	.198	.273	n.s.	.062	n.s.
Proactivity[b, d]	.905	1.033	1.414	n.s.	.001	.008
Self-confidence[b, d]	.111	.264	.364	.007	.0001	.069
Self-control	.127	.088	.364	n.s.	n.s.	n.s.
Spontaneity[c, d]	0	.110	.141	.004	.001	n.s.
Stamina and adaptability	.159	.165	.101	n.s.	n.s.	n.s.
Use of oral presentations[b, d]	.048	.143	.273	.037	.0001	.033
Use of socialized power[b, d]	.286	.604	.899	.003	.0001	.019
Use of unilateral power[b, e]	.397	.747	.475	.003	n.s.	.018

[a]Significance levels for performance group comparisons were determined on the basis of one-tailed tests of significance using a correction for unequal sample sizes and an estimate of separate variance in the t-tests.
[b]Statistically significant F test.
[c]Near significant F test.
[d]Significant or near significant linear trend.
[e]Significant or near significant nonlinear trend.

TABLE A–2   Mean Skill Level Comparison of Sector Samples ($N = 253$)[a]

	Public $N=154$	Sector Groups Public (Average and Superior Groups Only) $N=91$	Private $N=99$	Significance Level of T-Tests[b]
Accurate Self-Assessment	.208	.231	.303	n.s.
Conceptualization	.182	.209	.374	.054
Concern with close relationships	.253	.286	.131	.036
Concern with impact	1.065	1.121	1.414	.054
Developing others	.435	.539	.697	n.s.
Diagnostic use of concepts	.669	.802	1.556	.0001
Efficiency orientation	.909	1.033	1.354	.051
Logical thought	.338	.396	.475	n.s.
Managing group process	.403	.473	.687	.066
Perceptual objectivity	.201	.198	.253	n.s.
Positive regard	.169	.187	.283	n.s.
Proactivity	.968	1.011	1.434	.008
Self-confidence	.247	.341	.293	n.s.
Self-control	.117	.110	.121	n.s.
Spontaneity	.058	.099	.111	n.s.
Stamina and adaptability	.162	.165	.131	n.s.
Use of oral presentations	.104	.143	.273	.063
Use of socialized power	.558	.747	.768	n.s.
Use of unilateral power	.513	.593	.616	n.s.

[a]Significance levels for sector, managerial level, and function comparisons were determined on the basis of two-tailed tests of significance using a correction for unequal sample sizes and an estimate of separate variance in the t-tests.
[b]T-tests were conducted on the limited public sector sample (average and superior performance groups only) versus the private sector sample to insure comparability.

TABLE A-3   Mean Skill Level for the Public Sector Sample (N = 154)[a]

	Performance Groups			Significance Level of T-Tests		
	Poor N=63	Average N=52	Superior N=39	P vs. A	P vs. S	A vs. S
Accurate self-assessment	.175	.192	.282	n.s.	n.s.	n.s.
Conceptualization	.143	.192	.231	n.s.	n.s.	n.s.
Concern with close relationships	.206	.269	.308	n.s.	n.s.	n.s.
Concern with impact	.984	1.019	1.256	n.s.	.086	n.s.
Developing others	.286	.769	.231	.0005	n.s.	.0001
Diagnostic use of concepts	.476	.712	.923	.068	.004	n.s.
Efficiency orientation	.730	1.077	.974	.058	n.s.	n.s.
Logical thought	.254	.481	.282	.036	n.s.	.069
Managing group process	.302	.442	.513	n.s.	.037	n.s.
Perceptual objectivity	.206	.154	.256	n.s.	n.s.	n.s.
Positive regard	.143	.173	.205	n.s.	n.s.	n.s.
Proactivity	.905	.712	1.41	n.s.	.0053	.0005
Self-confidence	.111	.269	.436	.017	.0001	.053
Self-control	.127	.096	.128	n.s.	n.s.	n.s.
Spontaneity	0	.096	.103	.029	.051	n.s.
Stamina and adaptability	.159	.173	.154	n.s.	n.s.	n.s.
Use of oral presentations	.048	.058	.256	n.s.	.004	.007
Use of socialized power	.286	.673	.846	.005	.002	n.s.
Use of unilateral power	.397	.635	.539	.031	n.s.	n.s.

[a]Significance levels for performance group comparisons were determined on the basis of one-tailed tests of significance using a correction for unequal sample sizes and an estimate of separate variance in the t-tests.

TABLE A-4   Mean Skill Level for the Private Sector Sample ($N=99$)[a]

	Performance Groups		Significance Level of T-Tests
	Average $N=39$	Superior $N=60$	
			A vs. S
Accurate self-assessment	.282	.317	n.s.
Conceptualization	.282	.433	n.s.
Concern with close relationships	.205	.083	.063
Concern with impact	1.180	1.567	.031
Developing others	.769	.650	n.s.
Diagnostic use of concepts	1.667	1.483	n.s.
Efficiency orientation	1.205	1.45	n.s.
Logical thought	.385	.5333	n.s.
Managing group process	.590	.750	n.s.
Perceptual objectivity	.077	.367	.0005
Positive regard	.231	.317	n.s.
Proactivity	1.462	1.417	n.s.
Self-confidence	.256	.317	n.s.
Self-control	.077	.150	n.s.
Spontaneity	.128	.100	n.s.
Stamina and adaptability	.154	.117	n.s.
Use of oral presentations	.256	.283	n.s.
Use of socialized power	.513	.933	.013
Use of unilateral power	.897	.433	.019

[a]Significance levels for performance group comparisons were determined on the basis of one-tailed tests of significance using a correction for unequal sample sizes and an estimate of separate variance in the t-tests.

TABLE A-5 Mean Skill Level Comparison of Managerial Level Samples
(N = 253)[a]

	Level Groups			Significance Level of T-Tests		
	Entry $N=36$	Middle $N=142$	Exec-utive $N=75$	Entry vs. Middle	Entry vs. Exec.	Middle vs. Exec.
Accurate self-assessment	.278	.247	.227	n.s.	n.s.	n.s.
Conceptualization	.194	.247	.307	n.s.	n.s.	n.s.
Concern with close relationships	.250	.183	.227	n.s.	n.s.	n.s.
Concern with impact	1.028	1.190	1.307	n.s.	.078	n.s.
Developing others	1.111	.493	.347	.001	.0001	.064
Diagnostic use of concepts	1.361	.923	1.027	.025	.069	n.s.
Efficiency orientation	1.278	1.099	.960	n.s.	.071	n.s.
Logical thought	.361	.444	.307	n.s.	n.s.	.083
Managing group process	.444	.500	.573	n.s.	n.s.	n.s.
Perceptual objectivity	.139	.225	.253	n.s.	.083	n.s.
Positive regard	.194	.268	.120	n.s.	n.s.	.012
Proactivity	1.194	1.099	1.227	n.s.	n.s.	n.s.
Self-confidence	.222	.218	.373	n.s.	.049	.016
Self-control	.194	.141	.040	n.s.	.032	.006
Spontaneity	.111	.099	.027	n.s.	n.s.	.019
Stamina and adaptability	.083	.183	.120	.044	n.s.	n.s.
Use of oral presentations	.139	.190	.147	n.s.	n.s.	n.s.
Use of socialized power	.500	.634	.720	n.s.	n.s.	n.s.
Use of unilateral power	.806	.556	.427	n.s.	.038	n.s.

[a]Significance levels for sector, managerial level, and function comparisons were determined on the basis of two-tailed tests of significance using a correction for unequal sample sizes and an estimate of separate variance in the t-tests.

TABLE A-6 Mean Skill Level for the Entry Management Sample ($N = 36$)[a]

	Performance Groups			Significance Level of T-Tests		
	Poor $N=6$	Average $N=26$	Superior $N=4$	P vs. A	P vs. S	A vs. S
Accurate self-assessment	0	.346	.250	.0005	n.s.	n.s.
Conceptualization	.167	.231	0	n.s.	n.s.	.016
Concern with close relationships	.333	.231	.250	n.s.	n.s.	n.s.
Concern with impact	.667	1.039	1.500	n.s.	n.s.	n.s.
Developing others	.833	1.192	1.000	n.s.	n.s.	n.s.
Diagnostic use of concepts	.667	1.615	.750	.062	n.s.	.088
Efficiency orientation	1.167	1.231	1.750	n.s.	n.s.	n.s.
Logical thought	.333	.385	.250	n.s.	n.s.	n.s.
Managing group process	.333	.539	0	n.s.	.088	.0005
Perceptual objectivity	.167	.115	.250	n.s.	n.s.	n.s.
Positive regard	.167	.231	0	n.s.	n.s.	.016
Proactivity	.500	1.423	.750	.027	n.s.	.045
Self-confidence	.167	.231	.250	n.s.	n.s.	n.s.
Self-control	.333	.115	.500	n.s.	n.s.	n.s.
Spontaneity	0	.077	.500	.080	n.s.	n.s.
Stamina and adaptability	0	.077	.250	.080	n.s.	n.s.
Use of oral presentations	.167	.154	0	n.s.	n.s.	n.s.
Use of socialized power	0	.539	1.000	.0005	n.s.	n.s.
Use of unilateral power	.500	.692	2.000	n.s.	.065	.072

[a]Significance levels for performance group comparisons were determined on the basis of one-tailed tests of significance using a correction for unequal sample sizes and an estimate of separate variance in the t-tests.

TABLE A-7 Mean Skill Level for the Middle Management Sample $(N = 142)^a$

	Performance Groups			Significance Level of T-Tests		
	Poor $N=38$	Average $N=50$	Superior $N=54$	P vs. A	P vs. S	A vs. S
Accurate self-assessment	.158	.160	.389	n.s.	.006	.006
Conceptualization	.158	.220	.333	n.s.	.071	n.s.
Concern with close relationships	.237	.160	.167	n.s.	n.s.	n.s.
Concern with impact	.921	1.060	1.500	n.s.	.003	.023
Developing others	.263	.580	.574	.021	.016	n.s.
Diagnostic use of concepts	.395	.880	1.333	.011	.0001	.032
Efficiency orientation	.737	1.18	1.278	.039	.015	n.s.
Logical thought	.263	.540	.482	.024	.049	n.s.
Managing group process	.237	.380	.796	n.s.	.0001	.005
Perceptual objectivity	.184	.100	.370	n.s.	.032	.001
Positive regard	.184	.200	.389	n.s.	.062	.045
Proactivity	.947	.820	1.463	n.s.	.012	.001
Self-confidence	.105	.200	.315	n.s.	.005	.091
Self-control	.132	.060	.222	n.s.	n.s.	.019
Spontaneity	0	.140	.130	.016	.003	n.s.
Stamina and adaptability	.237	.200	.130	n.s.	n.s.	n.s.
Use of oral presentations	.026	.140	.352	.023	.0001	.017
Use of socialized power	.211	.580	.982	.004	.0001	.013
Use of unilateral power	.316	.840	.463	.001	n.s.	.018

^{a}Significance levels for performance group comparisons were determined on the basis of one-tailed tests of significance using a correction for unequal sample sizes and an estimate of separate variance in the t-tests.

TABLE A-8 Mean Skill Level for the Executive Management Sample $(N=75)^a$

	Performance Groups			Significance Level of T-Tests		
	Poor $N=19$	Average $N=15$	Superior $N=41$	P vs. A	P vs. S	A vs. S
Accurate self-assessment	.263	.267	.195	n.s.	n.s.	n.s.
Conceptualization	.105	.267	.415	n.s.	.007	n.s.
Concern with close relationships	.105	.533	.171	.050	n.s.	.082
Concern with impact	1.211	1.267	1.366	n.s.	n.s.	n.s.
Developing others	.158	.667	.317	.027	.093	.087
Diagnostic use of concepts	.579	1.067	1.220	.065	.002	n.s.
Efficiency orientation	.579	.800	1.195	n.s.	.013	.098
Logical thought	.211	.200	.390	n.s.	n.s.	n.s.
Managing group process	.421	.867	.537	.081	n.s.	n.s.
Perceptual objectivity	.263	.200	.268	n.s.	n.s.	n.s.
Positive regard	.053	.133	.146	n.s.	n.s.	n.s.
Proactivity	.947	1.067	1.415	n.s.	.041	n.s.
Self-confidence	.105	.533	.439	.005	.001	n.s.
Self-control	.053	.133	0	n.s.	n.s.	.082
Spontaneity	0	.067	.024	n.s.	n.s.	n.s.
Stamina and adaptability	.053	.200	.122	n.s.	n.s.	n.s.
Use of oral presentations	.054	.133	.195	n.s.	.044	n.s.
Use of socialized power	.526	.800	.781	n.s.	n.s.	n.s.
Use of unilateral power	.526	.533	.342	n.s.	n.s.	n.s.

aSignificance levels for performance group comparisons were determined on the basis of one-tailed tests of significance using a correction for unequal sample sizes and an estimate of separate variance in the t-tests.

TABLE A-9 Mean Skill Level Comparison of Function Samples ($N=253$)[a]

	Function Groups			Significance Level of T-Tests		
	Market- ing $N=54$	Manu- fac- turing $N=143$	Per- sonnel $N=38$	Mktg. vs. Mfg.	Mktg. vs. Pers.	Mfg. vs. Pers.
Accurate self-assessment	.389	.196	.132	.009	.003	n.s.
Conceptualization	.352	.182	.342	.041	n.s.	.085
Concern with close relationships	.093	.280	.158	.003	n.s.	.059
Concern with impact	1.315	1.077	1.500	.055	n.s.	.038
Developing others	.574	.601	.342	n.s.	.083	.039
Diagnostic use of concepts	1.093	.853	1.553	.063	.037	.003
Efficiency orientation	1.241	.979	1.421	.080	n.s.	.023
Logical thought	.407	.364	.553	n.s.	n.s.	.065
Managing group process	.593	.462	.684	n.s.	n.s.	.083
Perceptual objectivity	.241	.189	.342	n.s.	n.s.	.054
Positive regard	.259	.189	.316	n.s.	n.s.	n.s.
Proactivity	1.259	1.063	1.421	n.s.	n.s.	.047
Self-confidence	.333	.238	.316	.100	n.s.	n.s.
Self-control	.074	.112	.211	n.s.	.065	n.s.
Spontaneity	.056	.063	.184	n.s.	.058	.063
Stamina and adaptability	.185	.133	.132	n.s.	n.s.	n.s.
Use of oral presentations	.148	.126	.447	n.s.	.009	.004
Use of socialized power	.704	.587	.947	n.s.	n.s.	.037
Use of unilateral power	.222	.608	.842	.0001	.002	n.s.

[a]Significance levels for sector, managerial level, and function comparisons were determined on the basis of two-tailed tests of significance using a correction for unequal sample sizes and an estimate of separate variance in the t-tests.

TABLE A-10   Mean Skill Level for the Manufacturing Sample ($N=143$)[a]

	Performance Groups			Significance Level of T-Tests		
	Poor $N=52$	Average $N=57$	Superior $N=34$	P vs. A	P vs. S	A vs. S
Accurate self-assessment	.154	.228	.206	n.s.	n.s.	n.s.
Conceptualization	.115	.228	.206	.101	n.s.	n.s.
Concern with close relationships	.231	.298	.324	n.s.	n.s.	n.s.
Concern with impact	.981	.965	1.412	n.s.	.032	.029
Developing others	.327	.965	.412	.0005	n.s.	.001
Diagnostic use of concepts	.462	1.140	.971	.0005	.005	n.s.
Efficiency orientation	.769	1.000	1.265	n.s.	.036	n.s.
Logical thought	.308	.439	.324	n.s.	n.s.	n.s.
Managing group process	.327	.561	.500	.042	n.s.	n.s.
Perceptual objectivity	.213	.123	.265	n.s.	n.s.	.077
Positive regard	.154	.175	.265	n.s.	n.s.	n.s.
Proactivity	.942	.965	1.412	n.s.	.018	.026
Self-confidence	.135	.263	.353	.047	.014	n.s.
Self-control	.135	.088	.118	n.s.	n.s.	n.s.
Spontaneity	0	.105	.088	.017	.092	n.s.
Stamina and adaptability	.173	.088	.147	.087	n.s.	n.s.
Use of oral presentations	.058	.123	.235	n.s.	.017	n.s.
Use of socialized power	.269	.667	.941	.004	.002	n.s.
Use of unilateral power	.404	.754	.677	.008	.065	n.s.

[a]Significance levels for performance group comparisons were determined on the basis of one-tailed tests of significance using a correction for unequal sample sizes and an estimate of separate variance in the t-tests.

TABLE A-11 Mean Motive, Trait, or Self-Image Levels for the Entire Test Sample[a,b]

	Performance Groups			Significance Level of T-Tests		
	Poor	Average	Superior	P vs. A	P vs. S	A vs. S
Activity Inhibition	2.367	2.067	2.702	n.s.	n.s.	.008
N	90	252	141			
Learning style: abstract conceptualization	16.125	15.787	15.118	n.s.	n.s.	n.s.
N	16	61	17			
Learning style: active experimentation	16.250	16.787	17.235	n.s.	n.s.	n.s.
N	16	61	17			
Learning style: concrete experience	15.125	15.361	15.412	n.s.	n.s.	n.s.
N	16	61	17			
Learning style: reflective observation	13.750	13.820	14.176	n.s.	n.s.	n.s.
N	16	61	17			
n Achievement	50	48	51	n.s.	n.s.	.002
N	71	200	119			
n Affiliation	51	48	48	.016	.025	n.s.
N	90	243	134			
n Power	51	48	50	.005	n.s.	.011
N	90	243	134			
Self-Definition	50	44	50	.006	n.s.	.001
N	31	21	34			
Stage I	4.889	4.169	4.353	.023	.085	n.s.
N	45	207	102			
Stage II	1.867	1.459	1.784	.027	n.s.	.021
N	45	207	102			

TABLE A-11 *(Continued)*

	Performance Groups			Significance Level of T-Tests		
	Poor	Average	Superior	P vs. A	P vs. S	A vs. S
Stage III	1.089	.845	1.235	n.s.	n.s.	.004
N	45	207	102			
Stage IV	1.956	1.633	1.814	n.s.	n.s.	n.s.
N	45	207	102			

[a]Significance levels for perfromance group comparisons were determined on the basis of one-tailed tests of significance using a correction for unequal sample sizes and an estimate of separate variance in the t-tests.

[b]The means and the t-tests on n Achievement, n Affiliation, n Power, and Self-Definition were based on the scores after adjusting for length of protocol. Significance levels reflect these t-tests.

TABLE A-12 Mean Motive, Trait, or Self-Image Level Comparison of Sector Samples[a,b]

	Sector Groups		Significance Level of T-Tests
	Public	Private	
Activity Inhibition	1.428	2.716	.001
N	276	349	
Learning style: abstract conceptualization	15.723	15.771	n.s.
N	59	35	
Learning style: active experimentation	17.169	16.114	.032
N	59	35	
Learning style: concrete experience	15.339	15.314	n.s.
N	59	35	
Learning style: reflective observation	13.797	14.000	n.s.
N	59	35	

	Sector Groups		Significance Level of T-Tests
	Public	Private	
n Achievement	53	49	.001
N	184	348	
n Affiliation	53	48	.001
N	260	348	
n Power	52	48	.001
N	261	348	
Self-Definition	50	47	.041
N	183	35	
Stage I	1.800	4.448	.001
N	15	348	
Stage II	1.533	1.626	n.s.
N	15	348	
Stage III	.267	1.014	.001
N	15	348	
Stage IV	3.067	1.655	.021
N	15	348	

[a]Significance levels for sector, managerial level, and function comparisons were determined on the basis of two-tailed tests of significance using a correction for unequal sample sizes and estimate of separate variance in the t-tests.

[b]The means and the t-tests on n Achievement, n Affiliation, n Power, and Self-Definition were based on the scores after adjusting for length of protocol. Significance levels reflect these *t-tests*.

TABLE A-13   Mean Motive, Trait, or Self-Image Levels for the Public Sector Sample[a,b]

	Performance Groups			Significance Level of T-Tests		
	Poor	Average	Superior	P vs. A	P vs. S	A vs. S
Activity Inhibition	1.511	1.204	1.477	n.s.	n.s.	n.s.
N	45	54	44			
Learning style: abstract conceptualization	16.182	15.667	15.000	n.s.	n.s.	n.s.
N	11	42	6			
Learning style: active experimentation	16.818	17.119	18.167	n.s.	n.s.	n.s.
N	11	42	6			
Learning style: concrete experience	14.182	15.548	16.000	.065	.087	n.s.
N	11	42	6			
Learning style: reflective observation	13.818	13.762	14.000	n.s.	n.s.	n.s.
N	11	42	6			
n Achievement	52	46	55	.017	.079	.006
N	26	2	23			
n Affiliation	53	54	51	n.s.	n.s.	n.s.
N	45	45	38			
n Power	52	48	53	.023	n.s.	.043
N	45	45	38			
Self-Definition	49	41	50	.079	n.s.	.063
N	26	2	23			

[a]Significance levels for performance group comparisons were determined on the basis of one-tailed tests of significance using a correction for unequal sample sizes and an estimate of separate variance in the t-tests.

[b]The means and the t-tests on n Achievement, n Affiliation, n Power, and Self-Definition were based on the scores after adjusting for length of protocol. Significance levels reflect these t-tests.

TABLE A-14   Mean Motive, Trait, or Self-Image Levels for the Private Sector Sample [a, b]

	Performance Groups			Significance Level of T-Tests		
	Poor	Average	Superior	P vs. A	P vs. S	A vs. S
Activity Inhibition	3.222	2.303	3.258	.009	n.s.	.001
N	45	198	97			
Learning style: abstract conceptualization	16.000	16.053	15.182	n.s.	n.s.	n.s.
N	5	19	11			
Learning style: active experimentation	15.000	16.053	16.727	n.s.	.104	n.s.
N	5	19	11			
Learning style: concrete experience	17.200	14.947	15.091	.025	.054	n.s.
N	5	19	11			
Learning style: reflective observation	13.600	13.947	14.273	n.s.	n.s.	n.s.
N	5	19	11			
n Achievement	49	48	51	n.s.	n.s.	.023
N	45	198	96			
n Affiliation	49	47	47	.060	.088	n.s.
N	45	198	96			
n Power	49	47	49	n.s.	n.s.	.075
N	45	198	96			
Self-Definition	53	44	51	.018	n.s.	.005
N	5	19	11			
Stage I	4.889	4.263	4.542	.042	n.s.	n.s.
N	45	198	96			
Stage II	1.867	1.444	1.823	.024	n.s.	.012
N	45	198	96			

	Performance Groups			Significance Level of T-Tests		
	Poor	Average	Superior	P vs. A	P vs. S	A vs. S
Stage III	1.089	.869	1.302	n.s.	n.s.	.002
N	45	198	96			
Stage IV	1.956	1.515	1.844	.076	n.s.	.058
N	45	198	96			

[a]Significance levels for performance group comparisons were determined on the basis of one-tailed tests of significance using a correction for unequal sample sizes and an estimate of separate variance in the t-tests.

[b]The means and the t-tests on n Achievement, n Affiliation, n Power, and Self-Definition were based on the scores after adjusting for length of protocol. Significance levels reflect these t-tests.

TABLE A-15 Mean Motive and Trait Level Comparison of Managerial Level Groups[a, b]

	Level Groups			Significance Level of T-Tests		
	Entry	Middle	Execu-tive	Entry vs. Middle	Entry vs. Exec.	Middle vs. Exec.
Activity Inhibition	2.522	1.599	1.455	.001	.001	n.s.
N	387	137	101			
n Achievement	49	52	55	.001	.001	.045
N	364	122	46			
n Affiliation	49	51	51	.083	.039	n.s.
N	386	121	101			
n Power	49	52	53	.002	.002	n.s.
N	386	122	101			
Self-Definition	50	49	52	n.s.	n.s.	n.s.
N	51	121	46			
Stage I	4.537	3.100		.001		
N	313	50				
Stage II	1.562	2.000		.017		
N	313	50				
Stage III	1.058	.520		.001		
N	313	50				
Stage IV	1.326	4.140		.001		
N	313	50				

[a]Significance levels for sector, managerial level, and function comparisons were determined on the basis of two-tailed tests of significance using a correction for unequal sample sizes and an estimate of separate variance in the t-tests.
[b]The means and the t-tests on n Achievement, n Affiliation, n Power, and Self-Definition were based on the scores after adjusting for length of protocol. Significance levels reflect these t-tests.

TABLE A-16 Mean Motive and Trait Levels for the Entry Management Sample [a,b]

	Performance Groups			Significance Level of T-Tests		
	Poor	Average	Superior	P vs. A	P vs. S	A vs. S
Activity Inhibition	2.500	2.346	3.261	n.s.	.078	.002
N	60	188	92			
n Achievement	49	47	51	n.s.	n.s.	.009
N	47	181	89			
n Affiliation	52	48	48	.002	.004	n.s.
N	60	188	91			
n Power	51	47	49	.006	n.s.	.056
N	60	188	91			
Self-Definition	50	41	48	n.s.	n.s.	n.s.
N	7	2	4			
Stage I	4.925	4.352	4.659	.075	n.s.	n.s.
N	40	179	85			
Stage II	1.775	1.385	1.753	.04	n.s.	.018
N	40	179	85			
Stage III	1.225	.866	1.412	.041	n.s.	.001
N	40	179	85			
Stage IV	1.525	1.151	1.612	.071	n.s.	.008
N	40	179	85			

[a]Significance levels for performance group comparisons were determined on the basis of one-tailed tests of significance using a correction for unequal sample sizes and an estimate of separate variance in the t-tests.

[b]The means and the t-tests on n Achievement, n Affiliation, n Power, and Self-Definition were based on the scores after adjusting for length of protocol. Significance levels reflect these t-tests.

TABLE A-17 Mean Motive, Trait, or Self-Image Levels for the Middle Management Sample [a,b]

	Performance Groups			Significance Level of T-Tests		
	Poor	Average	Superior	P vs. A	P vs. S	A vs. S
Activity Inhibition	2.278	1.357	1.769	.059	n.s.	n.s.
N	18	28	26			
Learning style: abstract conceptualization	16.125	15.787	15.118	n.s.	n.s.	n.s.
N	16	61	17			
Learning style: active experimentation	16.250	16.787	17.235	n.s.	n.s.	n.s.
N	16	61	17			
Learning style: concrete experience	15.125	15.361	15.412	n.s.	n.s.	n.s.
N	16	61	17			
Learning style: reflective observation	13.750	13.820	14.176	n.s.	n.s.	n.s.
N	16	61	71			
n Achievement	53	55	54	n.s.	n.s.	n.s.
N	18	19	20			
n Affiliation	50	48	49	n.s.	n.s.	n.s.
N	18	19	20			
n Power	48	50	50	n.s.	n.s.	n.s.
N	18	19	20			
Self-Definition	50	44	52	.017	n.s.	.001
N	18	19	20			
Stage I	4.600	3.000	2.824	.020	.023	n.s.
N	5	28	17			
Stage II	2.600	1.929	1.941	n.s.	n.s.	n.s.
N	5	28	17			

TABLE A-17 (Continued)

	Performance Groups			Significance Level of T-Tests		
	Poor	Average	Superior	P vs. A	P vs. S	A vs. S
Stage III	0.0	.714	.353	.011	.021	.061
N	5	28	17			
Stage IV	5.400	4.714	2.824	.090	.001	.002
N	5	28	17			

[a]Significance levels for performance group comparisons were determined on the basis of one-tailed tests of significance using a correction for unequal sample sizes and an estimate of separate variance in the t-tests.

[b]The means and the t-tests on n Achievement, n Affiliation, n Power, and Self-Definition were based on the scores after adjusting for length of protocol. Significance levels reflect these t-tests.

TABLE A-18 Mean Motive and Trait Levels for the Executive Management Sample[a,b]

	Performance Groups			Significance Level of T-Tests		
	Poor	Average	Superior	P vs. A	P vs. S	A vs. S
Activity Inhibition	1.833	1.167	1.522	.072	n.s.	n.s.
N	12	36	23			
n Achievement	49		54		.039	
N	6		10			
n Affiliation	47	53	51	.039	.089	n.s.
N	12	36	23			
n Power	53	49	55	n.s.	n.s.	.035
N	12	36	23			
Self-Definition	47		48		n.s.	
N	6		10			

[a]Significance levels for performance group comparisons were determined on the basis of one-tailed tests of significance using a correction for unequal sample sizes and an estimate of separate variance in the t-tests.

[b]The means and the t-tests on n Achievement, n Affiliation, n Power, and Self-Definition were based on the scores after adjusting for length of protocol. Significance levels reflect these t-tests.

TABLE A-19 Mean Motive and Trait Level Comparison of Function Samples[a,b]

	Function Groups			Significance Level of T-Tests		
	Market-ing	Manu-fac-turing	Finance	Mktg. vs. Mfg.	Mktg. vs. Fin.	Mfg. vs. Fin.
Activity Inhibition	2.267	1.842	2.972	n.s.	n,s,	.014
N	101	405	36			
n Achievement	51	50	50	n.s.	n.s.	n.s.
N	85	328	36			
n Affiliation	48	51	45	.005	n.s.	.001
N	85	404	36			
n Power	48	51	45	.011	.034	.001
N	85	405	36			
Self-Definition	47	50		.041		
N	35	183				
Stage I	3.842	4.413	4.861	.027	.003	n.s.
N	101	143	36			
Stage II	1.842	1.524	1.417	.055	.095	n.s.
N	101	143	36			
Stage III	.851	.909	1.250	n.s.	.092	n.s.
N	101	143	36			
Stage IV	2.762	1.280	1.333	.001	.001	n.s.
N	101	143	36			

[a]Significance levels for sector, managerial level, and function comparisons were determined on the basis of two-tailed tests of significance using a correction for unequal sample sizes and an estimate of separate variance in the t-tests.

[b]The means and the t-tests on n Achievement, n Affiliaction, n Power, and Self-Definition were based on the scores after adjusting for length of protocol. Significance levels reflect these t-tests.

TABLE A-20 **Mean Motive, Trait, or Self-Image Levels for the Marketing Sample[a,b]**

	Performance Groups			Significance Level of T-Tests		
	Poor	Average	Superior	P vs. A	P vs. S	A vs. S
Activity Inhibition	.600	2.180	2.657	.047	n.s.	n.s.
N	5	61	35			
Learning style: abstract conceptualization	16.125	15.787	15.118	n.s.	n.s.	n.s.
N	16	61	17			
Learning style: active experimentation	16.250	16.787	17.235	n.s.	n.s.	n.s.
N	16	61	17			
Learning style: concrete experience	15.125	15.361	15.412	n.s.	n.s.	n.s.
N	16	61	17			
Learning style: reflective observation	13.750	13.820	14.176	n.s.	n.s.	n.s.
N	16	61	17			
n Achievement	49	47	51	.003	.030	n.s.
N	5	52	28			
n Affiliation	47	48	47	n.s.	n.s.	n.s.
N	5	52	28			
n Power	44	49	47	.043	n.s.	n.s.
N	5	52	28			
Self-Definition	53	44	51	.018	n.s.	.005
N	5	19	11			
Stage I	4.600	3.738	3.914	n.s.	n.s.	n.s.
N	5	61	35			
Stage II	2.600	1.770	1.857	n.s.	n.s.	n.s.
N	5	61	35			

	Performance Groups			Significance Level of *T*-Tests		
	Poor	Average	Superior	*P* vs. *A*	*P* vs. *S*	*A* vs. *S*
Stage III	0.0	.918	.857	.002	.003	n.s.
N	5	61	35			
Stage IV	5.400	2.770	2.371	.001	.001	n.s.
N	5	61	35			

[a]Significance levels for performance group comparisons were determined on the basis of one-tailed tests of significance using a correction for unequal sample sizes and an estimate of separate variance in the *t*-tests.

[b]The means and the *t*-tests on *n* Achievement, *n* Affiliation, *n* Power, and Self-Definiton were based on scores after adjusting for length of protocol. Significance levels reflect these *t*-tests.

TABLE A-21   Mean Motive and Trait Levels for the Manufacturing Sample[a,b]

	Performance Groups			Significance Level of *T*-Tests		
	Poor	Average	Superior	*P* vs. *A*	*P* vs. *S*	*A* vs. *S*
Activity Inhibition	1.511	2.026	2.329	.057	.023	n.s.
N	45	154	73			
n Achievement	52	46	53	.001	n.s.	.001
N	26	111	58			
n Affiliation	53	49	50	.027	.092	n.s.
N	45	154	73			
n Power	52	47	52	.002	n.s.	.002
N	45	154	73			
Self-Definition	49	41	50	.079	n.s.	.063
N	26	2	23			

[a]Significance levels for performance group comparisons were determined on the basis of one-tailed tests of significance using a correction for unequal sample sizes and an estimate of separate variance in the *t*-tests.

[b]The means and the *t*-tests on *n* Achievement, *n* Affiliation, *n* Power, and Self-Definition were based on the scores after adjusting for length of protocol. Significance levels reflect these *t*-tests.

APPENDIX B

Tables Describing the Distribution of the Samples Used in the Study

TABLE B-1   Job Performance or Criterion Measure Sample

	Number of People In:	
Criterion Measure	Test and Measure Subsample	Behavioral Event Interview Subsample
Total sample	756	253
Supervisor rating	242	79
Supervisor nomination	203	174
Work output measure	370	
Both supervisor nomination and work output measure	59	

TABLE B-2   The Job Element Analysis Sample

Classification	Number of People	Number of Organizational Samples
Total sample	345	7
Sector		
Private	103	4
Public	242	3
Managerial level		
Entry	23	1
Middle	174	4
Executive	148	3
Function		
Marketing or public relations	44	1
Manufacturing or operations	110	2
Personnel	36	2
Other	155	2

TABLE B-3   The Behavioral Event Interview Sample

Classification	Number of People	Number of Organizational Samples
Total sample	253	10
Sector		
Private	99	8
Public	154	2
Managerial level		
Entry	36	3
Middle	142	7
Executive	75	3
Function		
Marketing or public relations	54	5
Manufacturing or operations	143	5
Personnel	38	4
Other	18	2

TABLE B-4   The Test and Measure Sample

Classification	Number of People	Number of People with Criterion Data	Number of Organizational Samples
Total sample	1503	756	8
Sector			
Private	372	363	4
Public	1131	393	4
Managerial level			
Entry	569	341	3
Middle	727	343	7
Executive	207	72	2
Function			
Marketing or public relations	283	283	4
Manufacturing or operations	1101	365	5
Finance or budget and procurement	36	36	2
Other	83		2

APPENDIX C

Objectives and Outline of a Competency-Based Training Course

The course described in this appendix is entitled *The Competent First-Level Manager*. It was designed and developed by the staff of McBer and Company. It is the proprietary material of McBer and Company and is used here with their permission as an illustration of a competency-based training course designed for new or incumbent entry-level managers.

OVERVIEW

The Competent First-Level Manager covers the following topics:

The relationship of competencies to productivity, efficiency, and other measures of effectiveness

The impact on performance effectiveness of the interaction of the manager's competencies, the job demands, and the organizational environment

How the first-level manager can improve his or her performance, through:

Goal setting

Planning

Efficient use of time, people, and resources

Initiating action and overcoming obstacles

Using frameworks to solve problems

How the first-level manager can help his or her subordinates to improve their performance, by:

Providing meaningful feedback

Providing necessary assistance and resources

Giving clear directions

How the first-level manager can influence the organizational environment to improve his or her performance, through:

Acquiring a realistic view of his or her own strengths and weaknesses

Building coalitions and networks

Focusing on organizational needs

Planning for continued professional development, by:

Establishing goals and action plans

Evaluating the risk associated with goals

TABLE C-1 Program Map[a]

	MONDAY	TUESDAY	WEDNESDAY	THURSDAY	FRIDAY	ON THE JOB
MORNING	INTRODUCTION TO COMPETENCY-BASED TRAINING (1) → YOU AND YOUR ORGANIZATION (2) → Lunch	MORE: GETTING YOUR OWN JOB DONE BETTER (4,5,6) → Lunch	MORE: GETTING YOUR OWN JOB DONE BETTER (8,10) → Lunch	MORE: GETTING YOUR SUBORDINATES TO DO THEIR JOBS BETTER (15,16) → Lunch	INTEGRATING ALL EIGHT COMPETENCIES (20,21) → Lunch	IMPLEMENTING WHAT YOU LEARNED IN THE PROGRAM
AFTERNOON	GETTING YOUR OWN JOB DONE BETTER (3) → (2)	(7,8)	GETTING YOUR SUBORDINATES TO DO THEIR JOBS BETTER (11,12,13)	INFLUENCING THE ENVIRONMENT TO GET YOUR JOB DONE BETTER (17,18)	(21) → PLANNING FOR CONTINUED PROFESSIONAL DEVELOPMENT → (22,23,24)	
EVENING		STUDY GROUP (9)	STUDY GROUP (14)	STUDY GROUP (19)		

[a] Numbers in parentheses refer to session numbers found on the annotated list of sessions attached.

296

ANNOTATED OUTLINE

Session	Title	Brief Description
1	Introduction to the course	Clarifying objectives and methods of the course; developing a learning contract
2	The manager, the job, and the organization	Lecture on the model relating job demands, organizational environment demands, individual competencies, and specific behavior to effective job performance; self-assessment exercise and discussion as to the functions and tasks of management required in their jobs; self assessment exercise and discussion as to the impact of various organizational environment elements on their effectiveness as a manager
3	Market expansion exercise	Simulation exercise providing self-assessment to participants on the three relevant competencies from the goal and action management cluster (efficiency orientation; proactivity; and diagnostic use of concepts)
4	Preview of day two	Preview of the schedule for the day
5	Introduction to the first three competencies	Participants describe several recent incidents or events in which they felt that they were effective; lecture and discussion of the three competencies in the goal and action management cluster; case analyses of effective and ineffective managers in terms of these three competencies
6	Goal setting and setting a 12-hour goal	Practice setting a goal for the next 12-hour period, emphasizing the efficiency orientation competency

Session	Title	Brief Description
7	Optimizing your resources	A film, lecture, discussion, and self-assessment exercise on time management and delegation, emphasizing the efficiency orientation and diagnostic use of concepts competencies
8	Integration exercise: Practac Fan Co.	Business simulation exercise requiring participants to practice using the three competencies in the goal and action management cluster
9	Study groups 1	Assessment as to whether each of the participants demonstrated the competencies in the goal and action management cluster in their own incidents and events described earlier
10	Review of goal and preview of day three	Assessment of each participant's effectiveness in reaching his or her 12-hour goal (additional assessment on efficiency orientation); preview of the schedule of the day
11	Introduction to the next two competencies	Lecture and discussion on the two competencies from the directing subordinates cluster, developing others and use of unilateral power; film and case analysis
12	Unilateral directives	Additional case analyses of effective and ineffective managers
13	Improving subordinates performance	Role play of manager subordinate with performance problems provides self-assessment on these two competencies
14	Study Groups 2	Assessment as to whether each of the participants demonstrated the competencies in the directing subordinates cluster in their own in-

Session	Title	Brief Description
		cidents and events described earlier
15	Review of evening assignment and preview of day four	Review of the assessment of the incidents and preview of the schedule for the day
16	Practice and application of these two competencies	Role plays of performance review situations in which the faculty participate and provide participants with opportunities to practice the two competencies in the directing subordinates cluster
17	The final three competencies	Lecture, discussion, and case analysis regarding self-control, accurate self-assessment, and the use of socialized power competencies
18	Review of the eight competencies	Creating and describing a managerial incident in which a first-level manager used all eight of the competencies
19	Study groups 3	Assessment as to whether each of the participants demonstrated the additional three competencies in their own incidents and events described earlier
20	Review of the evening assignment and preview of day five	Review of the assesssment of the competencies demonstrated and preview of the schedule of the day
21	Integration and application exercise: Zupples, Inc.	Business simulation in which participants practice all eight of the competencies
22	Planning for continued professional development	Using the competencies to establish a plan for continued development and use of the competencies on the job
23	The competencies of a middle-level manager	Lecture and discussion of the competencies used by the effective middle-level managers
24	Course summary	

Index